Directors/Directing

Insightful, in-depth and evocative, this is a collection of conversations with nine of the most innovative theatre directors of our time in Europe and North America:

- Eugenio Barba
- Lev Dodin
- Declan Donnellan
- Elizabeth LeCompte
- Robert Lepage
- Simon McBurney
- Katie Mitchell
- Peter Sellars
- Max Stafford-Clark

All these directors have developed their own, highly individual theatre language across a wide range of practices from opera, dance, epic spectacle or hybrid and multi-media performances, to verbatim theatre or small-scale interventionist theatre, and have been influential, nationally and internationally, in a variety of ways. The length, depth and scope of the discussions distinguishes this collection from others, each director providing a fascinating insight into his/her particular working processes. The book reveals the complex world of directors and their creative relationships with actors, in rehearsal and performance, and with playwrights. Each conversation is framed by an introduction to the work of the director, a detailed chronology of productions and an indicative bibliography to inspire further reading and research.

MARIA SHEVTSOVA is Professor of Drama and Theatre Arts and Director of Graduate Studies at Goldsmiths, University of London.

CHRISTOPHER INNES is Professor of English at York University, Ontario, and holds the Canada Research Chair in Performance and Culture.

Directors/Directing
Conversations on Theatre

Maria Shevtsova

and

Christopher Innes

CAMBRIDGE
UNIVERSITY PRESS

CAMBRIDGE UNIVERSITY PRESS

Cambridge, New York, Melbourne, Madrid, Cape Town, Singapore, São Paulo, Delhi

Cambridge University Press
The Edinburgh Building, Cambridge CB2 8RU, UK

Published in the United States of America by Cambridge University Press, New York

www.cambridge.org
Information on this title: www.cambridge.org/9780521731669

© Maria Shevtsova and Christopher Innes 2009

First published 2009

Printed in the United Kingdom at the University Press, Cambridge

A catalogue record for this publication is available from the British Library

Library of Congress Cataloguing in Publication data
Directors/directing : conversations on theatre / Maria Shevtsova, Christopher Innes.
 p. cm.
 Includes bibliographical references and index.
 ISBN 978-0-521-88843-1 (hardback)
 1. Theater–Production and direction–History–20th century. 2. Theater–Production and direction–History–21st century. 3. Theatrical producers and directors–Interviews. I. Shevtsova, Maria. II. Innes, C. D. III. Title.
 PN2053.D573 2009
 792.02'33–dc22   2008052566

ISBN 978-0-521-88843-1 hardback
ISBN 978-0-521-73166-9 paperback

Contents

Illustrations

Acknowledgements

We warmly thank all the directors – Eugenio Barba, Lev Dodin, Declan Donnellan, Elizabeth LeCompte, Robert Lepage, Simon McBurney, Katie Mitchell, Peter Sellars, Max Stafford-Clark – for finding the time and energy in their incredibly busy lives to have with us the conversations published in this book. Chasing them was not always easy, but they always responded to our pursuit with generosity and humour, giving us insights into the wellsprings of their creativity. In every case they devoted hours to talking with us and followed up by answering our queries in a process that spanned months. We are greatly indebted to them.

We are also indebted to the following people for their invaluable help: Julia Varley and Rina Skeel of Odin Teatret; Dina Dodina and Anna Ogibina of the Maly Drama Theatre-Théâtre de l'Europe of St Petersburg, and Aleksandr Chepurov of the St Petersburg Academy of Theatre Arts; Nick Ormerod and Jacqui Honess-Martin of Cheek by Jowl; Cynthia Hedstrom, Katie Valk and Clay Hapaz of The Wooster Group; Eve-Alexandra St Laurent of Ex Machina; Marieke Sander and Chip Horne of Theatre de Complicite; Alena Melichar for providing the photo by her late husband, Ivan Kyncl, of *Iphigenia at Aulis*, directed by Katie Mitchell; John Bradfield from Out of Joint; Julia Carnahan for her help with arranging the interview with Peter Sellars, and for providing the photos of his production. Thank you Sherine Dahy, Anna Porubcansky, Annabel Rutherford, Rachel Shapiro and Sasha Shevtsova.

We wish to thank all the photographers for granting permission to publish their work: figure 1 courtesy of Torgeir Wethal © Odin Teatret;

Acknowledgements

figure 2 courtesy of Viktor Vasiliyev; figure 3 courtesy of Keith Pattison; figure 4 courtesy of Paula Court © Paula Court; figure 5 courtesy of Eric Mahoudeau; figure 6 courtesy of Sebastian Hoppe; figure 7 courtesy of Alena Melichar; figure 8 courtesy of Kevin Higa; figure 9 courtesy of John Haynes.

Introduction

The conversations in this book are with directors who have significantly marked the Western theatre of the late twentieth and early twenty-first centuries. The majority of them represent a middle generation flanked on the upper side by Peter Brook, Giorgio Strehler and Yury Lyubimov, one of the few Russian directors well established in the 1960s and 1970s whose fame crossed the borders of the Soviet Union before its collapse in 1991. Lev Dodin, who speaks here, has had far greater influence internationally with the Maly Drama Theatre of St Petersburg than his older predecessor from Moscow, thereby reminding the world that the tradition in which he has his roots – that of Stanislavsky, Meyerhold and Vakhtangov – still provides points of reference for the middle generation, as several of the directors observe from their respective, widely different, perspectives. Peter Sellars, for instance, who is renowned for his avant-garde innovations, notably looks towards Meyerhold. But Jerzy Grotowski is also a major touchstone. Although younger than Brook, his impact on Brook, let alone on his own generation, is such that he appears to be out of his time, influential sooner than a chronological view might have expected. Thus it is that Eugenio Barba, who serves in this volume as a bridge to an earlier generation, acknowledges Grotowski as one of the 'masters' (Barba's term) who helped to shape his practice, and this despite a mere three-year age difference between them.

Another bridge to the older 'upper side' is Max Stafford-Clark, a director whose commitment to text-based theatre and whose role in the development of new theatre writing define his particular qualities, linking him to a mode of theatre-making that is far from falling into oblivion, as Katie Mitchell and Declan Donnellan show, while affirming their own highly corporeal approach to 'text'. At the same time, Stafford-Clark's focus on nurturing playwrights for his work on the stage distinguishes him from a polymath like Robert Lepage, who writes, directs and performs his own scripts – a strong tendency of the middle generation, as Simon McBurney also demonstrates. In this respect, both he and Lepage not only anticipate but also provide a model for the next generation of theatre practitioners aspiring to multi-generic and cross-over production. Barba and Stafford-Clark, exemplary bridges, began their directing careers within a year of each other, with Barba founding Odin Teatret in 1964 and Stafford-Clark starting his work with the Edinburgh Traverse Theatre in 1965; and each is still very much an active force in the contemporary theatre, suggesting a continuum between a decade that saw the proliferation of many types of performance and the performance of today, much of it framed, as it must be, by the otherwise inventive culture of the first decade of the twenty-first century. Dodin and Elizabeth LeCompte, both slightly younger and born in 1944, began their directing careers in 1967 and 1970 respectively (LeCompte as Assistant Director to Richard Schechner), while Sellars, Donnellan, Lepage and McBurney all started their professional directing careers within a year of each other: Sellars directing his first pieces outside university in 1980, Donnellan directing his first play with Cheek by Jowl in 1981, Lepage joining Théâtre Repère in 1982 and McBurney co-founding Theatre de Complicite in 1983.

All these directors, European – including British – and North American, have developed their unique approach together with a clearly identifiable style; and all have established a coherent and distinct *oeuvre*. They have also established an international reputation, yet are still at the cutting edge; and they are now having a major influence, affecting a whole range of newer practitioners in ways they are not always conscious of both at home and abroad, well beyond their geographic frontiers which they cross and recross as they reconfigure the artistic dimensions of their work. In addition, this is the first generation where women have reached world-class rank, and it is only regrettable that Ariane Mnouchkine, a major pioneer, was so

thoroughly tied up by her most recent production *Les Ephémères*
(2006) with the Théâtre du Soleil, the elections in France of 2007, in
which she campaigned vigorously for the Socialist candidate Ségolène
Royal, and her company's subsequent, all-consuming touring abroad
that she was finally unable to find the time for the kind of in-depth
conversation necessary for this volume. The complications of logistics,
of being in the same place at the same time, made it similarly
extremely difficult and, ultimately, impossible to have an appropriate
interview with Anne Bogart, an emergent compelling voice at the
younger end of the spectrum that we have identified as the middle
generation of powerful directors. We wish to thank Mnouchkine and
Bogart again for their tireless efforts and good will in attempting to
meet the demands of our project.

In their diversity, directors we have interviewed represent the
major innovations of our time; and they all, either implicitly or
sometimes explicitly, raise theoretical questions about the nature and
status of contemporary performance, since all are in some way challenging the principles of their earlier work or extending it past the
expected boundaries. The conversation with each director is framed by
an introduction giving biographical data and insight into some of his/
her major productions, and by a chronology of selected productions as
well as an indicative bibliography.

The conversations in this volume were all conducted between
the end of 2004 and mid-2007, a relatively long timescale required by
the need to fit in with the busy schedules of these directors, several of
whom regularly tour internationally, and by the detailed editing process. After an extended discussion with each director – sometimes
conducted over several sessions, sometimes accompanied by attending
rehearsals, and in one case extended through performing a role in the
current performance – the transcripts were edited, passed on to the
director for comment, corrections and checking of facts. In some cases
texts were re-edited; and all have been given final approval by our
interlocutors.

A network of links between these directors emerged, both
personal and thematic. Barba's development of Third Theatre and
theatre anthropology indicates alternative, non-mainstream as well as

non-avant-garde modes of directing and raises the issue of how far the definition of 'directing' can be stretched. His use of Asian performance forms links him to Peter Sellars, despite the great difference in their approach. Cross-cultural interplay, albeit in divers ways, links Barba, Sellars, Lepage and, increasingly, McBurney. A second grouping centres around devised, physically based acting and directing, with LeCompte, McBurney and Dodin; and the fact that LeCompte and Dodin have several points in common in their directorial approach comes as a surprise, given the great difference between their cultural legacies, their perception as to what constitutes play, and their performance results. Even so, the connecting links between them are real enough, and reveal a good deal about the processes of performance-making. McBurney's stress on physical expression (having studied with Jacques Lecoq in Paris, following his involvement with the Footlights at Cambridge University) leads him to an exploration of comic modes. Lepage uses the body to explore narrative modes, also frequently in a comic vein. Sellars and LeCompte owe much to their North American context: LeCompte to the modern and postmodern dance and visual arts scene of New York, Sellars to the vibrant multicultural environment of Los Angeles, onto which he has grafted his critical politics, European experience and 360-degree view of the world, which make him a director with a truly global vision and commitment. Dodin's emphasis on the moving body is imbued with the comprehensive training to be found in Russia, thus complicating the picture of the relationship between the director and the actor, which is a principle of collaboration respected by all the directors cited in this paragraph.

Although these directors have taken 'physical theatre' to new levels, as a form it is of course not new. The importance of Lecoq to him also links McBurney to two of the older generation of directors not represented in this volume – Mnouchkine, whose 'transgression of cultures' (our terminology) in the pursuit of the art of directing and acting is physically based, and Andre Serban, whose recovery of *commedia dell'arte* represents another form of physical theatre – while Mnouchkine and Lepage share a strong appreciation of each other's work. Similarly, Lepage, throughout his career, has been in continual contact as well as competition with Robert Wilson, and shares his exploration of new media in performance with Peter Stein, who was working with new mechanisms in the 1970s: each of them directors who, like Brook or Grotowski, can be seen as *éminences grises* behind much contemporary directing in Europe. McBurney, for instance, admired Stein greatly while studying in Paris.

Devising is key to Barba, Lepage, McBurney and Dodin, their explorations having become, today, a model for the younger generation still in search of its own 'language'. Devising also links Elizabeth LeCompte to this grouping, while her experimentation with multimedia specifically parallels Lepage. However, LeCompte's emphasis on deconstructing texts is very much her hallmark. Her iconoclasm can be likened to that of Sellars, whose breaking of shibboleths, both social and theatrical, is a markedly sharp response to the contemporary world. By contrast, Stafford-Clark, Mitchell and Donnellan are strongly text-based and author-centred directors with very powerful and individual theatrical practices. Stafford-Clark has been instrumental in inventing a particular kind of verbatim theatre, which is highly political. Mitchell, although anchored in texts, finds ways to subvert canonical images and expectations of them, and she works from a scientific, neurological perspective, while claiming her theatre heritage in Polish and Russian theatre rather than from the British stage. In this she is as unusual a British director as Donnellan, who runs both a British company and a Russian one, the one working in English and the other in Russian. Donnellan brings his Russian experience (which includes *The Winter's Tale* in 1997 with Dodin's company) to his direction of British actors, thereby also extending conceptions of direction in Britain.

In addition to Donnellan's links with Dodin, there are also numerous personal connections that are revealed through these conversations, as one might expect. It turns out that as well as admiring LeCompte, Sellars worked in collaboration with The Wooster Group, in addition to training with LaMaMa. Similarly, a number of these directors – from Mitchell, Donnellan and McBurney to Lepage and even the autonomous Stafford-Clark – have produced work on the same stage, specifically, the Royal National Theatre (NT) in London.

Sellars, Lepage and Dodin are regularly invited to show their productions at London's Barbican Centre, the latter having become a primary focus for internationally acclaimed work, especially in the first decade of the twenty-first century. The MC93 Bobigny plays a similarly high-profile curating role in Paris, enlarging the perception of audiences in France of what contemporary theatre can be and do.

Donnellan, who is personally close to Brook (as indeed is Dodin), is welcomed by Brook's theatre the Bouffes du Nord in Paris, as well as by the Odéon-Théâtre de l'Europe, which had promoted Stein and Strehler in the 1970s. Strehler had a five-year tenure of the latter theatre from 1983 for showcasing adventurous and challenging work, as well as work not yet fully discovered, setting an example for those to follow him. Core productions of Dodin's Maly Drama Theatre, for instance, were presented at the Odéon-Théâtre de l'Europe's 1994 Russian Season under the direction of Lluis Pasqual, opening out this ensemble company's achievements to spectators travelling to the event from the four corners of the globe. Thus it is that the programming of the Barbican and the Parisian venues named was beneficial to the dissemination of innovative theatre from which home theatres could also draw inspiration. Together with sites not here named – the Centre Beaubourg, for example, which offers a more intimate space suitable for The Wooster Group – they have channelled the energies of directors, performers and spectators alike, running the risk, perhaps, of homogenising work, yet failing to do so precisely because each artistic idiom, as developed by the directors we have selected, is strong and rich enough to maintain its singular identity.

There are also other forms of connection that emerge. For instance, Lepage and McBurney both speak about their work with music, in particular their recent collaborations with one specific group of musicians, the Emerson Quartet. Lepage, Sellars and Dodin are opera directors of renown, ranging, for Lepage, from adaptations of Brecht (*The Threepenny Opera/The Busker's Opera*, 2004) to the development of a new opera (Loren Maazel's *1984* at The Royal Opera House, Covent Garden, in London, 2005) and modern classics (Schoenberg's *Erwartung*, 1992, or Stravinsky's *The Rake's Progress*, 2007). Mitchell, apart from directing opera, including *The Sacrifice*

(2007) by contemporary composer James MacMillan (and she has fewer opera productions to date than her colleagues), has also staged the oratorio *Jephtha* by Handel (2003) and Bach's *St Matthew Passion* (2007). In fact it is not surprising, given the precedents set as regards opera by Brook, Strehler and Lyubimov and then Stein and Wilson, how many of these contemporary directors have moved easily from straight drama to opera. The main exceptions are those who have theatre companies of their own, such as LeCompte or Stafford-Clark, or Barba, or McBurney, although of course Lepage and Dodin also have their own companies, while even McBurney has involved not only string quartets, but also played against a full orchestra performing a Shostakovich symphony. Donnellan adds a new musical dimension by working on ballet at the Bolshoi in Moscow.

Possibly the reason is, as Sellars puts it, that only opera has the resources that allow for a long enough rehearsal time to develop interesting new performance work – particularly when (as he customarily does) the production is developed through a consortium of opera companies spanning Europe and the United States, which means being able to work with the same group of singers and dancers throughout (as with *Doctor Atomic*, 2005, which started out in Los Angeles, moved to Vienna and Brussels, then back to Chicago). The same luxury of time and resources is also available through companies that attract government or philanthropic funding, in a way that a single director on his or her own cannot. This is also an explanation why so many of the directors selected for inclusion in this volume run their own, long-standing theatre companies, or, like Dodin, head up a major state company. These all have the time to experiment and, in working with the same group of actors over a period, have the option of developing devised, strongly physically embodied theatre or, like Stafford-Clark, of developing new work by young playwrights.

MARIA SHEVTSOVA
CHRISTOPHER INNES

Eugenio Barba (b. 1936)

Born in Gallipoli in the heel of Italy, Eugenio Barba fled the military academy destined for him by his family to Norway, where he became a seaman. A UNESCO scholarship took him to Poland where, at Opole, he spent three years with Jerzy Grotowski as both his apprentice and assistant, subsequently disseminating information about Grotowski's work internationally with an integrity and efficacy that have been frequently overlooked by his admirers. Refused re-entry into Poland after his travels abroad, which included India and his discovery of Kathakali, Barba returned to Oslo to find that, as a foreigner, he had no chance whatsoever of directing in the established theatres of this city. Barba's solution to the problem of how to continue as a theatre practitioner was to found Odin Teatret in 1964 with young people who had not been accepted by the National Theatre School – 'rejects', as he ironically defines them and himself (*New Theatre Quarterly* (2007) 23: 2, 100). His was to be an alternative practice outside the confines of institutional regulations and demands.

In 1966, invited by the town council of Holstebro in Denmark, Barba settled in this out of the way rural spot with three of the original four actors of Odin, building living spaces, working spaces and a library in the farmhouse offered to him for his purposes. This complex was named the Nordisk Teaterlaboritorium (NTL) to signal Barba's goal of researching the art of the actor, and it was here that he set up supporting publishing ventures and film-making faciles and where he edited a journal; the seventh issue in 1968 was composed of the essays by Grotowski to be published almost immediately in English as *Towards a Poor Theatre*. The Odin was, and still is, the epicentre of the various activities of the NTL, all of which have promoted the group's interests across the globe. Barba's own writings have sustained Odin's fame and longevity – one of the longest-existing groups in Western theatre (albeit with some changes in its composition over the decades), rivalled only by Ariane Mnouchkine's Théâtre du Soleil, followed by The Wooster Group in the United States.

Formed in the spirit of utopian communities, the Odin evolved from the principles that Barba had inherited from Grotowski: improvisation-based practice, intensely personal internal experience made flesh, and the idea that performance was not only a craft but a way of life and, first and foremost, a matter of research in laboratory conditions. This was Odin's model in the first ten years of its existence as its members, all autodidacts, trained behind closed doors. The Grotowskian legacy, together with Barba's experience of negotiating different cultures and languages, his sense of being an outsider (to which he refers freely in his books and articles) and his thirst for intellectual research, much of which took a pedagogical turn, has certainly shaped his and the Odin's numerous projects. Apart from the productions that eventually came out of the actors' immersion in training, these projects include the encounters started at Holstebro during the 1970s with renowned practitioners – Jacques Lecoq, Etienne Decroux, Jean-Louis Barrault, Dario Fo, among them – and with such scholars as the anthropologists Clifford Geertz and Kirsten Hastrup and theatre specialists Ferdinando Taviani and Nicola Savarese. Barba's aim was to interconnect workshops, demonstrations, round-table discussions and conferences so that making theatre and thinking about it or conceptualising it could be part and parcel of each other. The academic side of practice, then, was not filtered out into a parallel area but integrated with practice as such.

The 1970s also saw the beginnings of Barba's life-long commitment to barters, the Third Theatre and the International School for Theatre Anthropology (ISTA). As is well known, the barters are an exchange of performances between the Odin and groups from different cultures, whether they are from remote communities (the Yanomani in Amazonian Venezuela, 1976), in suburban Montevideo (1987) or farming groups gathering in a local school during *Festuge*, a festival

9

week in Holstebro (2004). These barters, based on cultural 'goods', involve songs, dances, acrobatics, Odin exercises and other informal, usually daily-life cultural pieces and are essentially about making human contact rather than promoting art. They are the precursors of Third Theatre, which might be best described as a networking operation between small, unofficial and even off-track theatre groups. The latter, in Barba's view, are disconnected from mainstream theatre but are just as removed from the various avant-gardes in train that, despite their apparent non-conformism, are actually legitimated by the social structures and values in place. Third Theatre, as he defines it,

> lives on the fringes, often outside or on the outskirts of the centres and capitals of culture. It is a theatre created by people who define themselves as actors, directors, theatre workers, although they have seldom undergone a traditional theatrical education and therefore are not recognized as professionals.
>
> But they are not amateurs. Their entire day is filled with theatrical experience. Sometimes by what they call training, or by the preparation of performances for which they must fight to find an audience
>
> (*Beyond the Floating Islands*, 1986, p. 193).

This is, of course, a fairly accurate description of the Odin itself, and of relevance to Barba's account is the fact that Odin's daily 'theatrical experience' is made up of hours of training targeting the particular skills of the individuals in the group. Take Iben Nagel Rasmussen, for instance, who joined Odin in 1966 and has defined her performance identity through her elliptical narratives and her vocal and musical abilities, especially in playing the flute and drums. Or there is Julia Varley, who joined in 1976 and has become an expert storyteller, stiltwalker and otherwise adept street-theatre performer. The Odin has also maintained its own 'tradition' during these past decades by welcoming new apprentices who are supervised by an older actor but are expected to seek their own path. In other words, the group's community ethos is not meant to infringe upon self-regulated self-development, any more than Barba's overview of work-in-progress is meant to control that work. Nevertheless, this libertarian approach is embedded in a paradox in so far as Barba, a paragon of discipline, has always engaged with the actors' training process, especially during the Odin's earlier years; and he has always asserted his directorial role when it came to pulling together the performance bits and sequences created individually by the actors into a production to be presented to audiences. Similarly, the utopian principle of the Odin community, while giving free rein to the talents of individuals – Rasmussen, for example, runs her own performance group outside the Odin precincts – also anticipates that these individuals will subsume their ego under the social principle, which is the principle of togetherness that defines them as a performance group in the first place.

Increasingly, over the years, more than Grotowski and perhaps still more than any living director other than Mnouchkine, Barba has sought the principles or 'laws' of performance – 'laws' that are immutable, irrespective of time, place and culture, like the underlying geological layers of the earth – a metaphor he frequently uses – or like the 'deep structures' (Noam Chomsky), recurrent 'units' (Claude Lévi-Strauss) or 'archaeology' (Michel Foucault) familiar from the Structuralist thought of the 1970s. This search led him to found The International School of Theatre Anthropology (ISTA), where not only performers and academics meet, but where Eastern and Western performers share their embodied knowledge, opening possibilities for Barba to pinpoint similar principles of intention, preparation and execution behind disparate performance origins and styles. Thus, among the illustrious performers whom he has invited and from whom he has drawn a great deal is Sanjukta Panigrahi, the re-creator of the Odissi 'tradition' and the woman who herself sought the principles of one form (and not across forms, like Barba) that had been lost to view for centuries. In the European theatre, apart from the living practitioners from whom he has learned, Barba's touchstones have been Stanislavsky, Meyerhold and Vakhtangov for their ceaseless search for the wellsprings of their art. His research into the elements of performance that Barba believes are common to cultures culminated in his highly influential book with Nicola Savarese, *A Dictionary of Theatre Anthropology: The Secret Art of the Performer*, in 1991.

The interchange between East and West fostered by Barba has had fruitful consequences both for the research of the Odin actors and Barba's hopes for a reinvented theatre where the principles of performance can transcend cultural differences and merge Eastern and Western particularities to found a Eurasian theatre, one of the main subjects of conversation in the interview to follow. The journey from the early hieratic and ritualistic *Ferai* (1969) based on chanting (complex vocal scores using body resonators to the full were to become the norm of subsequent works) has been a variegated one. It has included the incantatory and myth-based *Kaosmos* (1993), which, like most Odin productions, is constructed from the personal associations of the Odin actors, the puppet and fairy-tale, intimate *Andersen's Dream* (2005) and the large-scale, sumptuous (rich costumes, masks, headdress) and spectacular 'Eurasian' *Ur-Hamlet* (2006), discussed by Barba in some detail in the interview. All of it has been guided by interrelated and consistently revisited and reconfirmed goals.

Maria Shevtsova: *It may be difficult to speak of you as a director, given the way Odin Teatret works. Odin actors are self-directed and largely self-trained. Yet, when we look at the programmes of productions, we see your name as the director of the* mise en scène. *How do you see the role of director? More importantly, how do you **do** this role?*

Eugenio Barba: There is a difference between a theatre company and a group. In established theatre companies the director is at the top of the hierarchy. In a group, there is no hierarchy; there is competence – what each individual member knows. Actors remain with me not because they have signed a contract, but because they feel that I'm still able to give them something. They stay at the Odin because they feel that their colleagues, artistically speaking, still inspire them. The moment one feels that someone is not trying to go beyond their limits, accepting the level attained and not generating new sparks of life, that person has become a burden. Our nervous system is attracted by what is alive, not what is inert. There is nothing worse than working together with people who are creatively 'lifeless'.

Eugenio Barba (b. 1936)

My role as a director is to remain 'alive' and make my group react to the manifestations of this 'life'. This life consists in being unpredictable, astonishing, challenging, heading towards a bizarre or even dull aim, changing the demands, assigning new and unprecedented tasks. All this provokes reactions in my actors, and their sparks nourish our common working dynamics. Concretely, when I begin a production, I have first to startle myself. I must have a point of departure – certain stories, space solutions or technical problems – that I don't know how to handle, that confuses me and makes me feel insecure. It is an ambiguous process. On the one hand, I know, 'We have fought so many battles, this battle will also be won.' But on the other hand, I state, 'Now we will walk across the ocean.' And my actors think, 'But we can't walk on water.' Yet they try, go into the water, are submerged by it and use all their cleverness to face the consequences of this totally uncontrollable situation. This is the way I go forward, and my actors know it.

It is an agonising process for the actors, as it is for me, because it demands an excess of work in an atmosphere of uncertainty. They have to improvise or compose one scene after another without knowing whether these will be used. At times I give them tasks and themes; at others I ask them to prepare one hour of material – rhythmic or structured sequences of actions, scenes, songs or texts that they have to collect. All this heterogeneous material provides the compost in which the seeds of the new production grow. But it's up to the actors to research, invent and structure what they have found. They can come with an hour, an hour and a half of material, and I might select only five minutes of it. Perhaps I'll just take a few minutes of what they had been preparing for one year, even two years. In the case of *Andersen's Dream* (2005), they worked for two-and-a-half years, and had hours of material. I picked up just a few minutes from each actor. It is a great privilege to have actors who still, at an advanced age, accept these sorts of demands. But a director cannot expect actors to behave in this way. You have to educate them to think and act like this.

You said in an earlier conversation I had with you [New Theatre Quarterly *(2007) 23: 2, 99–114*] *that it is important for us to escape from our culture. Could you please elaborate on this because I would probably argue against you that we cannot do this, nor is it necessary to do it.*

In the context of our conversation I was talking about diversity, and how people argue that ethnic minorities in Britain, as everywhere, try to build a common 'identity' by emphasising their cultural patrimony and characteristics. Diversity, by itself, is not a value. It is a given circumstance that may be lived with affliction or pride. It may be a chosen or supposed segregation. It may precede integration. Normally, foreign bodies that we call 'different' generate indifference, and we place them at the margins of our mind and society. If we consider them to be threatening, they generate hostility. When they no longer scare us, when we feel they are innocuous and no longer strange, we turn them into museum objects or performance, whereby they acquire the fascination of the exotic.

Diversity becomes fertile only if it is disquieting, when it is a point of arrival, an arduous conquest. When we are young, we see ourselves as a small blank spot in a world that we feel we don't belong to. When we get older, it is this feeling of 'not belonging' that, at times, helps us to live in the world. In theatre, we know how much this 'not belonging' is worth, this diversity that arouses respect.

Disquieting diversity is synonymous with independence. It is the consequence of a personal need, an individual quest that incites you to free yourself from the conditioning of your own culture. It is a mental de-familiarisation and estrangement from the categories within which you have grown in order to gain an intellectual, technical, emotional autonomy of your own. I say 'freeing from conditioning', and by this I mean from the prejudices, ways of judging, expectations and patterns of behaviours that any culture distils in a wide and subtle range of expressions. Growing within a culture develops in us reflexes about what is good and bad, beautiful and ugly, decent and indecent. The variety of these reflexes is coloured by a moral mind-set imbibed through the family and social environment in which we were raised.

Of course, you cannot free yourself totally from what you have absorbed since childhood, from the body technique and conventions of

your milieu, from the multiple encrustations of many years of incul-
turation. You are a result of the language you spoke with your parents
and grandparents, the types of relationships you had established in
your community, how you were treated as a child, your spirit of
acceptance or rebellion as an adolescent, your family's economic
situation and religious beliefs, the historical events that you lived
through – all these are factors which determine your uniqueness. Here
lies the crucial point: our identity is biographical–historical, yet we
have a tendency to let our specific biography coincide with a generalised, if complex, concept of culture or nation.

We always have problems of adjustment. For instance, being a
homosexual in a society where this is repressed creates tensions and
conflicts with the dominant values of this society. Spontaneously you
feel the need to live according to other norms and behaviours. This is
what I mean by 'escaping' from your culture. On the other hand, you
can come back to certain aspects in your culture and feel that your
childhood is given back to you: the taste of particular foods, the shape
and colours of a landscape, the intonation of the language which your
mother spoke, your dialect's melody. When I speak of escaping from
one's own culture, I am referring to a personal need, not to a condition
that should be met by everyone. When I was eighteen, leaving the
narrow-minded rural universe of southern Italy and emigrating to Oslo
was a cultural shock. Sexual habits and the familiarity between university teachers and students, the behaviour of sailors and their offi-
cers on a merchant ship, or the lack of distance between the owner and
the workers in the workshop where I had a job as a welder – all this
confused my view of politics, people and myself.

In addition, there were poets and authors whom I had never
dreamed could write the way they did. I was fascinated, for example,
by Knut Hamsun and his world of freedom-loving anarchists. Nor-
wegian society stigmatised him for his pro-Nazi feelings during World
War II. In my eyes he embodied the split I felt. He was a writer capable
of depicting human nature and exalting nature in his novels. On the
other hand, he capitulated his desire for transcendence to a hideous
ideology. Then I discovered religions and philosophies – Buddhism,
Hinduism, Jainism and the various schools of yoga, which blew like a

15

hurricane through my head. Then, of course, there were my years with Grotowski, which we have also discussed [New Theatre Quarterly, 2007]. My old horizons cracked and through the fissures I could see a galaxy of planets, exhaling energy – an array of intoxicating ferments, unimaginable prospects.

This feeling of illumination still resounds within me as if I had inherited the whole earth, all of its landscapes and cultures, its manifold past and radiant future. But accepting a legacy means embodying it and allowing it to metamorphose. Age made me understand that theatre craft may be a self-exploration and involves taking a stand. This attitude is always accompanied by the resurrection of the past according to our intimate temperature. For me, this past is not cloaked only in one culture and nation. All pasts co-exist simultaneously.

This clarifies the issue to some extent, but when you recognised the difference of Indian culture, you recognised that it had value as a culture. I think that the way we live in our culture affects our body – its very structure and how we sit and move. I'm not sure that the body is purely biological. I think it is also 'cultured'. I would have thought that there are very important aspects of a person's culture that are rich and life-affirmative, that can give great breadth and depth to his/her development as a human being. You've clarified the issue in so far as you only mean the negative aspects of a culture when you speak of the need to 'escape from culture'. By 'culture' here you mean prejudices, bigotry, deep social constraints, don't you?

Not necessarily. One can live in a family, environment and country which are 'open minded' and, yet, the simple fact that an individual and a culture define themselves by stressing their achievements and norms in opposition to the 'other' sets off specific mental and physical reflexes. How can we be aware of these reflexes and not just submit blindly to them? 'To escape' has to do with this process and with self-insight. In other words, to 'escape' does not mean simply to widen the horizons of one's culture, but to obliterate them and let one's personal needs, longings, superstitions, beliefs and norms strike roots in an 'unquantifiable region' which belongs only to you and cannot be represented by a generalised 'North American', 'Indian', 'Kenyan' culture.

Eugenio Barba (b. 1936)

It is a culture where your body and mind can be open to aesthetic stimuli, sexual experiences, healing procedures or juridical solutions without being prejudiced too much by the baggage you carry from your place of origin. Living in this 'unquantifiable region' permits me, slowly, to absorb the features of diversity and appreciate its worth in others.

Take my family of origin in South Italy, part of it devout Catholics and others anti-religious and freemasons. To which culture should I belong? What characterises a living culture is the antagonistic tensions that manage to co-exist and mingle through organic evolution and abrupt changes, thus avoiding stagnation.

Do you see your work in the theatre as a way of pushing back the barriers and going out into the wider zones of other cultures? Perhaps this is not even 'other cultures', but certain areas that might feed back into what we, performers and spectators, become as human beings?

We witness situations where we forget all about culture and history, and we become just vulnerable, astonished children. We see a mother rejecting her baby, an old man whipping a dog, a dog attacking a child, a person agonising and dying. In the face of such situations we don't think in terms of cultural values or habits; we feel an impulse within us; our 'human animality' reacts. In a performance, the scenes that touch the spectator in his/her 'human animality' and reach the intimate zones of his/her biography and historical experience have nothing to do with a generalised concept of culture. It is a murky individual reaction. I speak from experience as a director who regularly presents his performances to spectators of various nations, social environments and religious beliefs.

I began my career with an intuition, which, today, has become a conscious attitude: theatre is a paradoxical space. It follows ambiguous, subversive and amoral rules, norms and conducts, but its results are accepted under the alibi of art. Theatre is both a mental dimension and a material craft; it may be a commercial enterprise, a spiritual path, a scientific laboratory, a didactic and educational tool, nationalistic brain-washing, ludic entertainment and rigorous self-discipline. It is a social network since you have to intertwine your doing with the doings of other people carefully. At the same time, it is a galaxy that you navigate, uttering the most intimate sides of your solipsism.

Above all, theatre may become a no-man's-land, independent of the prevailing norms in both the theatre and society. This no-man's-land, this no-place and utopia is a paradoxical space, an enclave of dissidence. It has to interact with society, but is built with norms, objectives, technical devices and production processes that are driven by individual needs and not by aesthetic rules, ideologies or fashions.

For me, theatre is, above all, an environment in which a sort of elementary justice is possible. Justice is connected to the fact that everybody, irrespective of competence, intelligence and natural aptitudes is treated alike and offered the same opportunities. As an immigrant, who experienced injustice and discrimination (but also endless generosity and openness from people who didn't know me), I first thought that I would strive for justice through politics, through the communist ideology. I did not go far. So, for me, theatre became the paradoxical space where elementary justice could be a daily norm. But this is *my* solution. Each one of us has to find the solution for his or her very particular needs by building an environment which, through the craft's objective demands, lets his/her diversity grow and be conquered.

From my point of view, what is individual is always social because the individual always lives with others, and the struggle for values, or the defence of values, or the growth of one's own personal values, needs and so on, is always contingent upon this interrelationship. Interrelationship is a social principle. I wonder whether you don't tend to separate the individual from society? You place a great deal of emphasis on the individual as such, but what about the way in which social interrelationships shape and develop individuals? After all, a personal biography is a social biography.

You are right. As an individual, I am part of a social organism, but I also have a private dimension that determines my attitude towards society. When I stress the role of individuals in history, it is to contest the comfortable justification that, if you are anonymous and have no power, talent or competence, you cannot influence anything. This is wrong because, in our anonymity and smallness, we are masters of our humble actions. Of course, we have to pay a price and cannot expect immediate results. An obvious example is the mothers of the Plaza de Mayo in Argentina whose sons and daughters were taken by the military dictatorship and disappeared. The mothers, with white scarves on their heads, started walking around the Plaza de Mayo every Wednesday. People shook their heads. Nobody believed they could achieve anything by just repeatedly going around the same square. With the years, they became an unbearable accusation against the military dictatorship. When we think, 'Who was fighting in Argentina?' we think of the guerrillas, of the montoneros. But, I would also like to include the particular heroism of these anonymous women who knew that the result would not be immediate. Like modern Antigones, they fought the power of the city through a self-effacing coherent action.

Do you see the Odin's barters in South America, in countries of great political oppression like Argentina and Venezuela, as a kind of guerrilla politics? It seems to me that much of the Latin American small theatre groups – 'Third Theatre' groups, we could call them, using your vocabulary – can be seen as a form of guerrilla theatre in the way in which Che Guevara was a guerrilla fighter. Are the Odin's barters a form of guerrilla theatre?

I would say that any barter has a subversive value, even those we do today in peaceful Holsterbro. What does barter subvert? It subverts norms, routines. A bunch of foreigners arrives as a theatre group and does not behave according to normal expectations. What are normal expectations? That our theatre will play a performance and those interested can see it by buying a ticket. The barter subverts this relationship. It says, 'We won't do anything if you don't do something, too.' Since people are always busy and absorbed in their daily activities, I have to find individuals who are motivated to carry out such an event. It could be a priest, who wants to gather together his/her congregation in a non-religious situation, or a teacher, who wishes to assemble both pupils and parents, or a cultural club aiming to attract new members. When I arrive, I never present the group as a political one. I portray Odin Teatret in simple and naïve terms: actors interested in songs and dances.

Julian Beck said that theatre was a Trojan horse, and this is the most pertinent definition of a barter. We introduce ourselves as a harmless group of people who like dances and songs. Nothing dangerous, and people gather around us ready to participate. If our hosts went from door to door saying 'a political group wants to make a cultural exchange', many people would react with indifference. But if a local activist came to your door and said, 'I have some foreigners who are interested in our local songs and dances, would you please come and join us?' they would have no objections. When a barter takes place, you open up the multiple sociocultural layers and facets of the neighbourhood.

Well, what do you think of activist groups like the Living Theatre?

I have a huge respect and admiration for the Living Theatre, and they have been a source of inspiration and stimulation for me. Their provocative strategy, however, is far from mine. Provocation makes me close up. I remember our intense arguments when I first met them in Holstebro in 1975 and we discussed our views and practices. My actors were angry with me because they thought I was aggressive and impolite. But Julian Beck and Judith Malina were big-hearted and forgave my impatience. It was always a pleasure to meet them later in different parts of Europe – and in Holstebro, where Malina and Hannon Reznikov participated in Odin Teatret's thirtieth anniversary in 1994.

It has been a privilege and satisfaction to welcome to Holstebro the people I dreamed of meeting. I organised seminars as a part of our 'laboratory' activity and invited the Living Theatre in collaboration with the Venice Biennale and the Sigma Festival in Bordeaux (1975). They came with *The Money Tower* (1974) and *Seven Meditations on Political Sado-Masochism* (1973). After Denmark, they settled in Italy, which has always been open to alternative theatre. It was interesting to see how the European countries reacted to the new theatre wave that appeared during the 1960s. In England, critics like Martin Esslin or Kenneth Tynan supported the new playwrights while, in France, critics like Bernard Dort and the other editors of *Théâtre Populaire* stressed the ideological aspects, especially those who had seen Brecht's Berliner Ensemble.

Eugenio Barba (b. 1936)

Critics in Italy were more affected by the reality of a totally new performance, both in their own country and abroad – Carmelo Bene, the Living Theatre, Grotowski and Odin Teatret. These critics were very active, but not only in the press. They supported young artists and planned meetings and gatherings. Take Franco Quadri, who organised Odin Teatret's first tour to Milan and paid out of his own pocket. The Italian critic's personal involvement contributed to the blossoming of theatre groups and nurtured their strategy for doing not only per-formances, but also other activities such as seminars, courses, guest performances and small festivals. It was a model of organic theatre – to use [Antonio] Gramsci's terminology – that promoted a grass-roots cultural policy in the regions as well as interaction with similar groups at home and abroad. This was a remarkable feature of part of the Third Theatre in Italy in the 1970s.

Well, the Odin Teatret has organised workshops and seminars for theatre professionals at Holstebro for the past forty years. In a sense, you have almost operated like cultural facilitators, haven't you? Perhaps 'facilitator' is not the right word. Perhaps the idea is that of weaving a thread between theatre people.

I felt as a duty that a citizen of my town should not be encap-sulated in only one vision of theatre. Theatre is manifold. Therefore, as soon as we moved to Holstebro in 1966, we began to invite those artists we wanted to see, aware of how much we could learn from them: Otomar Krejca, who was working in Prague, Luca Ronconi and Dario Fo, who had never been abroad, Joseph Chaikin, Jean-Louis Barrault and Madeline Renaud, when they were kicked out of the Odéon in Paris. [This happened in the wake of the events of May '68 when protesting students and allied activists occupied the Odéon of which Barrault was the director. Barrault conceded to the insurgents and was sacked accordingly by André Malraux, Minister of Culture.] Then, of course, there were the Asian theatres, which I didn't know at all, and which I brought to the Odin from the early 1970s: many forms of Javanese, Balinese, Japanese, Chinese and Indian dance/theatre.

This activity had a double aim. On the one hand, it allowed me to increase my knowledge at a time when it was difficult for me to travel, and their presence greatly widened my horizons. On the other hand, it helped our spectators to become familiar with other styles and conventions, thus letting them become aware that our 'strange' performances were part of the manifold universe of theatrical expression. Odin Teatret was just part of an old tradition and of a new contemporary process taking place everywhere. We helped our spectators not to remain caught in only one idea of theatre.

Thirdly – also very important – we implemented a policy through the theatre, which the cultural authorities were not doing. You would expect the funding authorities and the larger theatres to invite foreign artists and performances, but this was not the case. So *we* started this practice of exchange, of opening up to the diverse so as to scrutinise what different theatres had in common under their specific stylistic layers.

When you say 'your spectators', do you mean, first of all, the spectators of Holstebro? Who are your spectators?

I could roughly divide our spectators into at least four main groups. The first is the Holstebro population. For many of them, especially the children, Odin Teatret is their first theatre experience. The second group is made up of theatre-interested people who have heard about us and come to see us. The third group is made up of loyal spectators who feel they really need our theatre. I call them our 'abnormal' spectators; they are both in Holstebro and elsewhere, and come to the same performance four, five, up to ten times. The fourth group of spectators is very particular: some, like my father, are dead, some are alive, but come very seldom. Their presence, even through absence, is essential to me.

I was always aware that a theatre cannot depend on the press, that information about its activity must go in a subterranean way because the spread of information from person to person *does* exist and is a decisive factor in keeping interest in a performance alive. Our English tour in November 2005 is a good example of this. It was organised by Organic Theatre, a small group in Exeter, and although we played in several towns, there was not a single notice or review in the newspapers. Nevertheless, we played to full houses. But this sort of information depends on artistic credibility, which we built through harsh conditions when, at the beginning, we had only a handful of spectators; and, by 'beginning', I mean for several years. We had very few spectators in Holstebro, and it was normal for us to play for ten or twenty spectators; it happened that we only had one person.

I am going to bring up that terrible word 'intercultural', which has been used to describe the Odin's work. You talked about bringing Asian theatre to the Odin. Well, 'Asian' is a big term, but let's use it for the moment. You brought, for example, Kanze from the Noh theatre, Sardono, I Made Djimat and I Made Bandem from Bali and Sanjukta Panigrahi, the leading Odissi dancer from India, along with other performers from Asia. Do you think 'intercultural' is relevant to the Odin Teatret? What does 'intercultural' mean for you?

The reason why 'intercultural' has become an issue today is because people do not know the history of the theatre. European theatre was always based on an intracultural theme, an intracultural substance.

You're saying 'intra', and 'intra' is different from 'inter'.

'Intra' means different cultures together within the same society.

That's right.

So, it has to do with diversity. When you meet another theatrical culture, tradition or scenic style, you can look at them through the eyes of a geographer or a geologist. If your attitude is that of a geographer, you think in categories of borders. You will say, 'Here is Poland, and here is Russia. Here is Bulgaria, and here is Romania.' Then you will add, 'This is what the Romanian landscape looks like and this is the Bulgarian one', and you start pointing out the differences. But as a geologist, you look deeper, into the subterranean layers, which do not respect borders. When you watch the theatre as a geographer, you will notice the differences. I look at it as a geologist, trying to find shared layers.

Today, in Europe, we are able to see Asian theatre more frequently. In fact, when you use the term 'intercultural', you are talking about a process of syncretism, of intermingling and fusion between Asian classical forms and Western modern forms. For instance, no one speaks much about 'intercultural' dance or film. The term is applied only to theatre. Yet dance has been inspired by other artistic disciplines, by sculpture and painting, for instance. How much inspiration

23

has European painting absorbed from other cultures? I consider 'interculturalism' an academic concern, which inspires the writing of books. A scholar may comment on a Kathakali performance of Shakespeare in hundreds of pages in order to enhance an academic career. The 'inter' and the 'intra' have always belonged to our profession. All theatre histories mention Meyerhold's fascination with the circus and the *balagan*, the Russian popular theatre form, and the fact that Brecht was inspired by Karl Valentin and his cabaret style. These are typical examples of intracultural contact.

So, do you think that debates around 'intercultural' theatre and its 'intercultural' borrowings are a false problem?

For me it is, and I base this assertion on my personal experience. In a group like Odin Teatret, which has people from different nations and cultures, each actor's personal creative universe is nourished not by a generalised 'cultural identity', but by his/her unique biographical–historical identity. In addition, they all have to submit to Odin's theatrical convention. Everywhere in the world an actor, when performing, may choose only between two conventions: a formalised and a non-formalised one. If you work according to a formalised convention – also called stylisation – you have to submit to its rules. Take classical ballet. You can be from Japan, Argentina or Namibia, but if you want to be a ballet dancer, you have to learn to stand on your pointes and do arabesques and pirouettes. If you work according to a non-formalised convention, the director decides what sort of expressive patterns you have to follow. Of course, if you have a director who is rather clever, he/she will exploit the traditional formalised patterns known by his/her actor. But, once again, creative power depends on individuals. You can take an Argentinian, a Botswanian and an Inuit, and very poor theatre can come out of their endeavours. The fact that they are from different cultures is not a guarantee of inventiveness or originality.

So, 'interculturalism' is a false problem, but 'intraculturalism' is not?

Both interculturalism and intraculturalism are false problems, although they are essential factors within a theatre artist's personal dynamics of observing, studying, learning and personalising foreign

24

technical results and practices that are inspiring and seem efficient. This inspiration can take many forms. Let me give a personal example. When I went to India in 1963, I saw this astonishing theatre form, which was Kathakali, in the open air, with people sleeping, or drinking tea bought from sellers moving around during the performance. The length – one whole night – was almost agonising for me. The mythological story didn't interest me much. I was bewildered by what the actors were doing; I had never seen anybody behaving like this on a stage. A recurrent thought kept crossing my mind: 'Why are these actors captivating my attention?' This bizarre question remained with me for many years and, in the end, gave birth to theatre anthropology.

When Odin Teatret went to Latin America, discussions were always about cultural identity and what it meant. They would say: 'You are a European theatre. You have your own identity and we want to build a theatre with our Bolivian or Colombian identity.' I always asked myself what this 'European identity' consisted of and how it manifested itself. And did my Latin American friends wish to have the identity of the upper class or of the indigenous population who, at times, didn't even speak the 'national' language?

It was a big issue in those years, wasn't it, and I mean 'big'. Terra Nostra (1975) by Carlos Fuentes, for instance, was incredibly important in Latin America because he really probed these questions deeply.

Yes, there was a lot of talk about it, and there still is. They said, 'You want to impose your norms.' For them, Odin Teatret was a sort of imperialism, and they were deeply politically committed. I understood them: I felt a similar urge, even if I expressed it in a very different way.

Their reactions made me think that, when I read Stanislavsky or Vakhtangov, I get something from them, although I am aware that what they are saying is strictly connected with their own time and society, cultural conditions, personal aspirations and difficulties. Nevertheless, I feel there is a core of objective knowledge in their writings, and I can use this to enhance my professional skills. I had a similar thought when seeing Kathakali actors in Kerala, who said a lot to me even though I didn't understand what they were doing.

So I started thinking about a 'professional identity', which was rooted in specific technical values or, rather, laws or principles, that are the foundation for any performer facing a spectator in an organised performance situation. There is no doubt that this way of thinking sprang from my encounters with Kathakali and my Latin American friends who wanted to discover what made them unique and different from me and my theatre.

This is how, in 1979, I began ISTA, The International School of Theatre Anthropology. ISTA is an itinerant environment dedicated to comparative studies of the principles of the performer's technique. It gathers in different places every two or three years, attracting scholars, dancers, actors and directors both from traditional theatre and from Third Theatre groups who wish to observe the practical self-questioning of master performers from Japan, India, China, Bali and the Afro-Brazilian tradition, or of artists like Grotowski, Dario Fo, Clive Barker, Tom Leabhart, Richard Schechner, Santiago Garcia or Flora Lauten.

ISTA taught me to see. Today, when I watch a performer, I see three distinct aspects blending together: the personality of the performer, the genre or the style of the performance and, finally, a living anatomy, a biology of the theatre that we would call 'presence'. A performer's anxiety, anywhere in the world, is *how* to keep the attention of the spectator alive. Which resources or options can help? I started looking for them through a patient, comparative study in a variety of performance styles and uncovered a few constant technical principles: the alteration of daily balance, simultaneous opposing tensions and the subscore or flow of inner actions – what Stanislavsky called the 'subtext'. These principles mark out the field of theatre anthropology.

Is theatre anthropology an attempt to identify principles of working with the body in performance that are common to all cultures? Would that be a correct way of defining it?

Yes, the performing 'body–mind' because you cannot speak about the body alone. It is not just a question of technical devices, but of psychosomatic involvement. Therefore, the subscore is very important. It shows the deep personal motivation that is often obscure and difficult to formulate in a sensible way. This motivation makes a performer's action alive, vibrating, burning. What I discovered, through the many sessions of ISTA, was that we could detect the principles I was talking about just now in any performer of any performance genre beneath the cultural or stylistic patterns and shapes being made. These are the geological layers I was also talking about. When we see a performer, especially one whose style comes from afar, his/her aesthetic and stylistic aspects are taken into consideration above all else. I would call it the 'surface'. *Surface* has nothing to do with *superficiality*. In an artistic product, the surface is the perceptible formal dimension which is the culmination of the creative process. It is a point of arrival, which becomes a bridge for a live relationship with spectators.

Creative processes, however, have points of departure. These are quite different from the points of arrival. The points of departure do not coincide with what our eyes perceive, or with form, style and aesthetics. What the skin reveals is totally different from the blood, nerves, muscles, organs and bones which the skin hides and beautifies.

Is this what you mean by 'pre-expressive', a term you often use in your writings?

Pre-expressive is the road you take to achieve an expressive result that captivates the spectator. All the preparatory process is pre-expressive. Say we are two characters in a play and I want to drink a glass of wine with you. Through the way I lift the bottle and where I look when pouring the wine in the glass, I can indicate that I want to know you – or do the opposite. I offer you the glass, and my body goes away from you. It suggests to the spectators that I don't want any intimacy with you. So there are many ways an actor can work on this single action. It is pre-expressive because it is still not established for presentation to the spectator.

So the 'pre-expressive' is, in fact, all the working process.

It *is* all this process and it does not involve the presence of the spectator. It applies only to the performer and his/her director until the moment, during the rehearsals, when they start taking into consideration the effect of their composition on the spectator.

And the 'expressive' is when it becomes scenic, so to speak.

Exactly. Of course, if you go to see a rehearsal, actors seem expressive to you. You see their behaviour as a *spectator*. You judge automatically: this works or does not. But the actors are not thinking

Fig 1 *Ur-Hamlet* (2006). Directed by Eugenio Barba. Photograph by Torgeir Wethal

of your presence. They are rehearsing, trying to refine their actions' associative density, rhythm and musicality so as to achieve a satisfactory artistic result which will be fixed in the performance structure at a later stage.

This leads us to your most recent work Ur-Hamlet, *which was performed in August 2006 in the Kronborg courtyard at Elsinore, allegedly (incorrectly) Hamlet's castle. What was your first reaction when you were asked to do it for the Hamlet Summer Festival?*

I wanted this performance to be an homage to the autonomous and transcendent reality that is the theatre. I longed to recreate the equivalent of an aristocratic Renaissance performance and, so, wanted the presence of the most ancient and valuable theatre traditions in existence: a full Balinese Gambuh ensemble and Noh actors. The thirty-three Gambuh performers and musicians were to recreate, with their suggestive recitative style and hypnotic music, the refined environment in which uncle and nephew struggle for power. About forty actors of different nationalities were to materialise the threat coming from the plebeians – the foreigners who infiltrate and disturb Hamlet's noble abode.

The one hundred or so performers on stage did not share a common language, either among themselves or with the spectators. Hamlet was Afro-Brazilian, his mother, an Italian Odin actress, and his uncle, a Balinese dancer. It was impossible, therefore, to unravel a stage story through the text. The performance had to communicate through sensory and specifically theatrical factors: a dramaturgy based on allusions, associations and images, all rich in contrasts; tragedy, vulgarity and the grotesque occurring simultaneously; emotional involvement with the exotic music and songs; the transformation of the space with torches and living fire; the spatial relationship and proximity with the spectators; the variety of the performers' acting conventions and the choral use of their voices, or simply solitary whispers.

Ur-Hamlet is a performance about the times I am living in. Hamlet's castle is not besieged by ghosts or kings, but by rats – carriers of the plague, crawling from the subsoil. These enemies of the human race surface as miasmas from the dark underground of an orderly society. Other intruders also creep into this tidy society: hungry, wretched people looking for refuge. Are they also carriers of the plague, or will they be infected by it? The trespassers are eliminated methodically by the castle's dwellers – a mere territorial cleansing operation. The gravediggers try to keep order in this kingdom in which lethal forces scurry around. While corpses burn after a mad night of revenge, Hamlet proclaims new rules, invoking the name of his father. It is not his father's ghost that appears, but a child, ready to fight for his New Order.

Was this Ur-Hamlet *an exception in the history of Odin Teatret because it was so massive compared to your other work?*

This performance committed us to a working process we had never experimented with before. Preparation started in 2003 and continued in Holstebro and Copenhagen, then during the ISTA sessions in Seville (2004) and Wroclaw (2005), in the villages of Batuan and Ubud in Bali (2004 and 2005) and, in its final phase, in Ravenna, where we first presented it in July 2006, moving then to Holstebro and Elsinore. In each of these places, the rehearsals had dissimilar characteristics because of the multiplicity of habits, ways of thinking and acting styles of the performers. Also, tasks and objectives were different. At times, we concentrated on the single characters, at other times on adapting the story as Saxo Grammaticus tells it; still at others, inventing and improvising the castle's infiltration by the foreigners.

You did not choose Shakespeare's text but preferred to go back to the chronicle by Saxo Grammaticus, the first to write about Hamlet. Why?

The first account of a hero, later to become the prototype of the wondering and philosophical mind, was told in Latin by the monk Saxo Grammaticus, a good three and a half centuries before Shakespeare. In this chronicle, which takes place in prehistoric times, Hamlet is not the son of a Danish king, but of a Viking chieftain from Jutland. Saxo describes him as if he was our contemporary: a stealthy and crafty tribal chief, a professional in violence, a tyrannicide who becomes a tyrant.

In *Ur-Hamlet*, Saxo unearths Hamlet's skeleton from the basement of the castle, evokes his life and interprets it in Latin. He addresses the spectators in this archaic language, unveiling and commenting on the vile intentions of the characters and their deeds. He wanders through the performance, whose 'set' is made up of the Gambuh performers. He is the centre of the action, identifies with its development, and struggles to avoid its uncontrolled events, seeking a way to escape from them.

The space is lit by portable torches whose moving flames modulate the intensity of action and the perception of space. The actors move amidst this labyrinth of torches, carry them and use them to underline fragments or details of a scene, as in a painting by Rembrandt.

Did you have a structure of the performance in mind when you first started the work?

Let me tell you the plain facts. I started working in Hostelbro and Copenhagen with eight of my actors; in Bali, with my actors plus thirty-three Gambuh performers, the Japanese Noh master Akira Matsui, and Indian, Brazilian and European singers and musicians. We all met up in Italy with forty-three actors from twenty-two countries who participated in a seminar guided by me and my actors and who were included in *Ur-Hamlet*. In the performance, they were the trespassing immigrants driven by hunger, war and plague who sought shelter in Hamlet's castle, where the winds of revenge were blowing.

The whole process began from this web of meetings and the interweave of diverse conventions and people. You could call it a multicultural dramaturgy, but let us speak about that later and concentrate now on another aspect of this dramaturgy, the 'political'. It builds a provisional *polis*, a theatrical country which professionals, aspiring professionals and masters from different ethnic origins, cultures, languages, competences and stage traditions co-inhabit. It is a well-organised and efficient floating island, able to keep its autonomy and sail among the demands of economy and fashion.

What do you mean by 'multicultural' here?

The multicultural is a practical solution for contemporary theatre. The theatre, in any geographical and cultural context, is a small and minority genre of performance. It can escape its isolation and recover the central position once held by ancient populations when it spins fragile threads from one side of the planet to the other, connecting experiences and professionalisms which, in the past, did not feel the need to be connected. Or else, they were motivated by the opposite need: to prevent the different traditions co-existing closely in the same context from making a broth in which peculiarities and stylistic contours were obliterated.

In our daily life, multiculturalism is considered to be a value or an invasion, a subversive threat or a fertile revolution. In the theatre field it becomes a condition of survival, preventing the dispersion of technical patrimonies and know-how. If we did not have a vision able to unify them, these different technical patrimonies and know-how would find refuge only in a museum. Or else they would end up isolated and forgotten, minute and almost invisible, crushed by the hegemonic performance media.

How did you work as a director *with performers used to different conventions and styles?*

The multicultural situation is a fundamental premise of my work, but I do not aim for any stylistic syncretism. Nor am I keen to make amazing artistic effects from bringing together heterogeneous elements, thus generating a suggestive tension or an imagined dialogue between cultures. I am not interested in showing how various traditions can embrace each other in spite of their differences – plunging, for example, a Shakespeare text into the form of Chinese opera, or vice versa. On the other hand, I do not ask performers from different traditions to strip away their own stylistic conventions in order to recover an actor *in statu nascendi*, who becomes a beginner beside other beginners.

These approaches sometimes lead to memorable results, but I follow another path. Working with actors trained inside different traditions, I respect meticulously the scenic behaviour that characterises the professional identity of each of them. I compose the performance with heterogeneous fragments and integrate them in a new context. I practise a dramaturgy that is based on the intertwining of autonomous styles. I do not intervene in the fragments, but choose and connect them. A performance composed of fragments remains fragmentary if it does not dig a path towards a deeper unity. In order to reach this point, I have to work within the domain of technique, of scenic presence, at a pre-expressive level. Thanks to this approach, the actions of the actors can interact and create a new context in which

32

they change their nature. The fragments which started off as bits of separate worlds turn into necessary parts of a story, which neither I nor the actors would have been able to foresee.

Your reference to a 'deeper unity' suggests that you are speaking about theatre anthropology again?

Yes, we have come back to theatre anthropology, which investigates the recurrent principles of various traditions and performance practices. These principles allow us to locate a substantially unitary scenic *bios* (life) that exists under the skin of the numerous styles and conventions available. Recurrent principles give various artistic answers, but ask the same basic questions. How do we attract and hold the spectator's attention? How do we modify daily behaviour in order to make the actor believable, despite the artificiality of the representation? How, by working on the material and what is visible, do we wipe out the self-referring reality of the stage and let another reality, intimate and foreign, come into view?

I feel that, still today, a personal mythology drives me. It was present from the very first day of my apprenticeship, and I have called it Eurasian Theatre. Eurasian Theatre is an ideal region rather than a material geography. It is a mental panorama and, at the same time, a technical one, made up of curiosity and fertile misunderstandings, creative distortions and original interpretations. But this panorama is an important part of the horizon within which the 'small traditions' of the theatre reformers grew. I am just one of their epigones.

When, at the beginning of the twentieth century, a handful of dissatisfied actors or rebels – Stanislavsky, Meyerhold, Vakhtangov, to name only a few – began to shake their craft, they followed two directions in search of models and inspiration. One was intracultural, which rediscovered the theatricality of the circus and the music hall – manifestations of European popular culture – or the religious ceremonies and liturgies of Europe. The other direction was intercultural, which consisted of performative situations, types of representation, ritual and the religious cults of other cultures. This double horizon – this Eurasian dimension – had, and still has, a deep impact on many of us who do theatre. 'Eurasia' is for theatre what Africa is for painting, dance and music.

Chronology of selected productions

The productions below were devised by Odin Teatret and premiered at the Odin Teatret performance space in Holstebro, Denmark, unless otherwise stated.

1965   *Ornitofilene.* Oslo
1967   *Kaspariana*
1969   *Ferai*
1972   *Min Fars Hus*
1974   *The Book of Dances.* Carpignano, Italy
1976   *Come! And the Day will be Ours*
1977   *Anabasis*
1978   *The Million*
1980   *Brecht's Ashes*
1982   *Brecht's Ashes II*
1984   *The Story of Oedipus*
         Marriage with God
1985   *Oxyrhincus Evangeliet (The Gospel According to Oxyrhincus)*
         The Rooms in the Emperor's Palace. Lima, Peru
1987   *Judith*
1988   *Talabot*
1990   *Memoria*
         The Castle of Holstebro
1991   *The Castle of Holstebro II.* Wellington, New Zealand
         Itsi Bitsi
1993   *Kaosmos*
1996   *Ode to Progress*
         Inside the Skeleton of the Whale
1997   *Doña Musica's Butterflies*
         Judith
1998   *Mythos*
2002   *Salt*
2003   *Great Cities under the Moon.* Bielefeld, Germany
2005   *Ester's Book*
         Andersen's Dream

Eugenio Barba (b. 1936)

2006   *Don Giovanni all'Inferno*. Ravenna, Italy
       Ur-Hamlet. Ravenna, Italy

Selected barters (excluding the barters held regularly at ISTA meetings)

1974   Ollolai, Sardinia
       Carpignano, Italy
1975   Sarule, Gavoi and Monteisisi, Italy (Iben Nagel Rasmussen)
1976   Caracas with the Yanomami, Venezuela
1977   Brittany and Paris
1980   Lampeter, Wales
1982   Upper Volta, Burkino Faso (Roberta Carreri with anthropologist Mette Bovin)
1987   Montevideo, Uruguay
       Bahia Blanca, Argentina
1988   Santiago, Chile
1992   Tvis, Denmark
2000   Rinkeby Folkets Hus, Sweden
2004   Holstebro, Denmark

Barter videos

In Search of Theatre: Theatre as Barter (1974), directed. by L. Ripa de Meana, Odin Teatret Film

    On the Two Banks of the River (1978), written and directed by Torgeir Wethal, Odin Teatret Film

    Theatre Meets Ritual: Odin Teatret in Amazonia (1976) produced by Kurare

Selected bibliography

Andreasen, John and Annelis Kuhlmann (eds.) (2001), *Odin Teatret 2000*, Aarhus University Press

Barba, Eugenio (1979), *The Floating Islands*, Holstebro, Denmark: Odin Teatret Forlag

    (1985), *The Dilated Body*, Rome: La Goliardica–Zeami Libri

(1986), *Beyond the Floating Islands*, trans. Judy Barba, Richard Fowler, Jerrold C. Rodesch, Saul Shapiro, New York: PAJ Publications

(1994), *The Paper Canoe: A Guide to Theatre Anthropology*, trans. Richard Fowler, London: Routledge

(1997), 'An Amulet Made of Memory: the Significance of Exercises in the Actor's Dramaturgy', *The Drama Review* 41: 4, 127–32

(1999), *Theatre, Solitude, Craft, Revolt*, trans. Judy Barba, Aberystwyth: Black Mountain Press

(1999), *Land of Ashes and Diamonds: My Apprenticeship in Poland*, trans. Judy Barba, Aberystwyth: Black Mountain Press

(2007), in conversation with Maria Shevtsova, 'Reinventing Theatre', *New Theatre Quarterly* 23: 2, 99–114

Barba, Eugenio and Nicola Savarese (1991), *A Dictionary of Theatre Anthropology: The Secret Art of the Performer*, trans. Richard Fowler in association with the Centre for Performance Research, London: Routledge

Bovin, Mette (1988), 'Provocation Anthropology: Bartering Performance in Africa', *The Drama Review* 32: 1, 21–41

Christoffersen, Erik Exe (1993), *The Actor's Way*, London: Routledge

Hastrup, Kirsten (ed.) (1996), *The Performers' Village – Times, Techniques and Theories at ISTA*, trans. Judith Barba and Leo Sykes, Graasten: Drama

Watson, Ian (1993), *Towards a Third Theatre: Eugenio Barba and the Odin Teatret*, London: Routledge

(1987), 'Third Theatre in Latin America', *Drama Review* 31: 4, 18–24

(1988), 'Eastern and Western Influences on Performer Training at Eugenio Barba's Odin Teatret', *Asian Theatre Journal* 20: 1, 49–60

(2000), 'Training with Eugenio Barba: Acting Principles, the Pre-expressive and "Personal Temperature"' in *Twentieth Century Actor Training*, ed. Alison Hodge, London: Routledge, pp. 209–23

Watson, Ian and Colleagues (2002), *Negotiating Cultures: Eugenio Barba and the Intercultural Debate*, Manchester University Press

Zarrilli, Phillip (1988), 'For Whom is the "Invisible" Not Visible? Reflections on Representation of the Work of Eugenio Barba', *The Drama Review* 32: 1, 95–106

2   Lev Dodin (b. 1944)

Although Lev Dodin had staged a number of important productions in the 1970s, notably at the Leningrad Theatre for Young Spectators (LenTYuZ), one of the most innovative Russian theatres of its time, it was not until he became the artistic director of the Maly Drama Theatre in 1983 that he was able to create the conditions necessary for the full development of his work. From then on he was able to build up a repertory company, incorporating in it the students whom he continued to train at the Leningrad State Institute of Theatre, Music and Cinematography, renamed the St Petersburg Academy of Theatre Arts after the collapse of the Soviet Union in 1991. Equally, he was able to generate an ethos in which the incoming actors as well as the ones already established in the company could strengthen and expand their resources and grow not only as individuals, but as an ensemble bound by shared practices and goals. Today, the Maly Drama Theatre of St Petersburg is one of the closest-knit ensembles in the world, and one of the few surviving companies of this kind in Russia where the ensemble tradition stemming from Stanislavsky and Nemirovich-Danchenko at the Moscow Art Theatre became legion, but has now virtually disintegrated under the pressures of a free-market economy.

The continuum between pedagogy and professional work first gave rise to the epic *Brothers and Sisters* (1985), in which more than forty actors on stage at any one time, many of them transferred directly from Dodin's class into the company, performed scenes from the life of villagers in the Archangelsk region during the closing years of World War II and the years immediately after it. Performed on the eve of Gorbachev's accession to power and the reforms of 'perestroika' and 'glasnost', *Brothers and Sisters* seemed to presage these calls for reform, and is still in repertory today, a number of its roles having been assumed by a succession of younger generations of actors. *Gaudeamus* (1990) was developed exclusively by students, although it was directed by Dodin, as a final-year production and travelled across Europe and to the United States as part of the Maly's student ensemble. The same group devised *Claustrophobia* in 1994. Since then, Dodin has preferred to integrate students early in their training, intermixing them with the experienced actors to various degrees in productions – the chamber-like *King Lear* (2006), for example, or the potentially epic but honed back *Life and Fate* (2007), set in the context of the siege of Stalingrad, the persecution of the Jews in the Soviet Union, German concentration camps and the Soviet gulag.

This integral approach has the advantage of giving the younger actors a greater sense of collective responsibility and purpose and, as well, of placing them on an equal footing with the rest of the company right from the start. And this gives a greater sense of freedom and flow to a working environment that, since 1983, has been conducive to cross-influences, all actors motivating and learning from each other in the spirit of consensus rather than competition and according to the principle that training is uninterrupted or, as Dodin frequently puts it, 'without end'. Training thus understood is group training and continues, moreover, as productions in repertory are rehearsed and performed over the years not as a matter of routine, but of openness to new possibilities. Meanwhile, new productions are developed, and the discoveries made in them tend to filter through to the older ones, affecting the actors' perception and performance of them. This too keeps the works in repertory alive. The structure and blocking of productions, or what Dodin calls their 'drawing' or 'design', essentially remains the same, but their quality, tone, mood and atmosphere, and the dynamic between actors and between actors and spectators, change with time as the actors mature and change as human beings. In this way, life experience and the making of art are intertwined.

Devising is key to Dodin's work with the Maly and is adapted from Stanislavsky's system of *études*: actors imagine and play actions, incidents, situations, or whatever is required of their own making, probing and testing what they do as they go and thereby nurturing their creativity and receptivity as well as the technical aspects of their craft; and, while this type of exploration has been central to the Russian school of acting since Stanislavsky, only Anatoly Vasilyev in his laboratory theatre in Moscow has succeeded in pushing the outer limits of play – and pushing actors beyond their limits – as far as Dodin. Dodin's method also involves improvisation. It visibly drives *Gaudeamus*, which is a collage in perpetual motion of verbal and physical fragments, its script also devised by the students. Improvisation, when used for pre-existing texts like *Uncle Vanya* (2003), so subtly underlies the composition that its importance in the shaping of the production is barely perceptible at all. *Uncle Vanya* is one of four Chekhov plays staged by Dodin relatively late in his career, starting with *The Cherry Orchard* in 1994.

Dodin's method of *études*–devising–improvising is all–encompassing, involving free form inspired by dance and opera, as happens in *Claustrophobia*, playtexts and novels, which in many respect are his preferred source for productions: *Brothers and Sisters* (from *The Pryaslin Family*, a trilogy by Fyodor Abramov published between 1958 and 1978); *Lord of the Flies* (1986, from the 1954 novel by William Golding); *The Old Man* (1988, from the 1978 novel by Yury Trifonov); *Gaudeamus* (from the 1986 *The Construction Battalion* by Sergey Kaledin); *The Devils* (1991, from Fyodor Dostoevsky's novel of 1871–2); *Chevengur* (1999, from the dystopia written by Andrey Platonov in 1926–9, but which fell foul of the authorities and was not published during the author's lifetime); *Life and Fate* (by the Stalingrad war correspondent Vasily Grossman, which was completed in 1960 but not published until 1980, and then only abroad because its critique of the way the Soviet powers conducted the war and of institutional anti-Semitism was thought to be too damaging to the Soviet state). Indeed, the role of novels in Dodin's corpus of work is significant, vying in importance during the 1980s and 1990s with the contemporary Soviet plays, all critical of the Soviet regime, on which he had focused during the preceding decades when he was a freelance director. This is due to a large extent to Dodin's choice of novels according to issues that he believes have a contemporary resonance or illuminate current concerns in some way, as did the themes of power, manipulation and terrorism in *The Devils* for the re-evaluation of politics during the 'perestroika' years, leading to the end of communism.

Dodin's 'theatre of prose' differs from the work of other Russian directors on novels – Yury Lyubimov, Kama Ginkas and Pyotr Fomenko most prominent among them – in its particularly extensive as well as intensive devising process. Where other directors will usually adapt a novel and come up with a playscript then performed by actors, Dodin or several of his actors extract a playscript from their multiple devisings. The text, then, grows out of the performance, and the actors perform the novel in its entirety from beginning to end, crafting sequences on their feet rather than in discussion around a table and becoming co-authors of the emergent production rather than interpreters of preordained parts. The process generally takes several years. *The Devils*, for instance, took three years, and then another three after it was first performed during which time it was pruned back to nine hours of performance – the longest Maly work, followed by *Brothers and Sisters* which lasts a mere six hours. Dodin's role as a director is to cull, cut, combine and shape the performed material and to offer alternatives or suggest different lines of attack until the long and organic process eventually leads to a production ready to be shown to audiences. Even then, it is never still since Dodin continues to review and readjust it during its life in repertory. He also treats every rehearsal at every stage of the work's evolution as if it was a prime performance. The voice, music and dance teachers who belong to Dodin's pedagogical team at the Academy of Theatre Arts continue to coach the actors and participate in rehearsals, as do his designers – all part of the company's collaborative practice. Technicians and administrators also come in to watch and have their say, as they see fit.

His work with the Maly, which has become an inspiration for directors across the world who seek ensemble principles, sustains Dodin's productions of operas, seven in total to the present day. Here he treats singers as actors, calling forth from them the emotional power as well as nuances of feeling and seeing as regards characters and their circumstances that have contributed to the Maly's international fame. By the same token, he seeks ensemble acting from these singers, discouraging extravagant gestures, hieratic positions, conventional postures and impressive solo turns in order to reach his goal of a more simple, natural style of play and presentation, as in his theatre. Music is, of course, an integral part of the drama of opera and Dodin refuses to illustrate music with action and vice versa on the grounds that this is a doubling up of sense and sensation, making one or the other redundant when both are indispensable. As a consequence, he works the drama in counterpoint to the music so that action is quiet and movement is restrained when the music is at its most turbulent. While this is effective in all his opera productions, it is especially powerful in *Mazepa* by Tchaikovsky which Dodin staged at La Scala in Milan in 1999, conducted by the great cellist and conductor Mstislav Rostropovich. In wishing to make opera less 'operatic' and more like theatre steeped in comprehensible human life, Dodin joins the ranks of the foremost opera innovators of our time, Peter Brook, Peter Stein, Peter Sellars, Robert Wilson and Robert Lepage notable among them.

Maria Shevtsova: *You are known to have established a very close link between your school of acting and directing and your company. How do you choose the applicants who will become your students and eventually your actors? Do you have specific criteria?*

Lev Dodin: Our theatre is a necessary continuation of our school. It is often thought that a school simply prepares people for the theatre: students do something or other while they are there, but real theatrical life begins afterwards, when they start to play. In actual fact, any theatre aspiring to be artistic develops what begins in the school. A person rooted in a school, who has a deep sense of learning and integrity, carries this through. A school helps you to keep on finding something new, and there are no two courses from which you learn the same thing. The problems the younger actors face in a school stimulate the older ones in the company: often they can do what the older ones cannot. The older actors provide a frame of reference, which the younger ones push forward. Vakhtangov once put it in a wonderful triadic form: school–studio–theatre. This, essentially, is the best formula for an art theatre. The school is where the highest standards and responsibilities are set. The studio is a passage, in chamber-like conditions, from school to professional self-awareness. The theatre is concerned with immediate artistic decisions. The criteria for selection that you refer to are to be found in this interconnection and our sense of it.

The selection process takes several months of concentrated and exacting work. For our last selection, we looked at about 2,500 people. I wanted to take on about twenty people, but was persuaded by my colleagues to accept twenty-six. Our first meeting with the candidates lasts about fifteen minutes. We take them in batches of ten. They read a poem, a fable or some prose. They might sing something. We always have a short discussion. Discussion is crucial at every stage of the selection process, and the most important thing during it is to identify the interesting people. A person may not read a poem particularly well, or may not be particularly well educated, but there may be something terribly interesting hidden in him or her, something individual that outweighs whatever inadequacy is evident. I fear most of all the people who come 'prepared', who have been involved in amateur theatre, or whose voice has already been placed, and so on. All too often they are closed; they have an idea of what the theatre is, and this is difficult to break down.

During one of these discussion sessions, there was a young girl in a fashionably long, but unattractive dress and with a hideous bouffant hair-do around her small face. She read some horrible poems with a lot of pathos. It was intolerable. I was tempted to say, 'Thank you very much' and see the last of her, but my principle is to have a talk, so I thought I really had to, not really knowing why. I asked her what she did. She said she swam, and I asked her what she had achieved with her swimming. 'I'm a swimming champion of the Soviet Union', she said. It suddenly became interesting because, if she was a Soviet swimming champion, she had will power. She had won races in various countries. 'What did you see there?' 'Oh, we were kept in camps.' 'Are you used to working hard?' 'Yes, I work very hard.' 'What were your results at school?' She had nothing but fives [the highest grades in the Russian system], so she excelled all round. I said, 'Would you go and change your hair-do and swap your dress with

42

someone?' She came back a completely different person, with a normal face and a good figure. I asked if she could read some other poems – Akhmatova, Pushkin, Pasternak. She said, 'Yes, of course.' I took her into my course. She is Irina Seleznyova and played in London in *Stars in the Morning Sky* (1987). She's a wonderful person. She and her husband emigrated to Israel, where she became extremely famous, playing in Hebrew, which she had to learn; and she is not Jewish. So these discussions are very important because you see people's individuality in them.

In the second round, we ask them to read a range of different materials. We want to see whether they know Pushkin, Pasternak, Mandelstam. Do they know Shakespeare's sonnets? Not only Krylov's fables, but also those of La Fontaine? We talk again. They dance, sing. Sometimes they improvise. Then there's a third round, which is more complex. They whittle away as we go. The change of context in the different rounds shows up the less gifted ones, who had looked stronger in a weaker batch.

In the fourth round, we usually ask them to prepare part of a play in three days, and pair them off in twos or threes. At the same time, they have to do written work not about the theatre, but about something connected to life. I want to see whether they can write about their lives in an interesting way. After all, what we do in the theatre is to analyse our own lives and observe in them what the great dramatists write about. We start in April and end sometime in July. But the selection continues: we now have seventeen in the fifth year of the course out of the twenty-six we started with. You observe a lot as you go along – not only people's gifts and abilities, but also their staying power and capacity for work, which is always a sign of talent. I don't believe you can be talented but lazy. When people have a passion for what they are doing, they cannot be dragged away from it.

The whole process of working in the theatre is a matter of selection. The theatre disturbs your peace. How much can your nerves bear? What is your physical capacity? Your emotional capacity? Once again, we are talking about artistic and personal gifts. Some become finer, sharper, truer with the years.

How do you develop your actors' capacity for improvisation?
Gaudeamus (1990) for instance, was constructed out of improvisa-
tions by your students at that time. Later I saw many of them, now
established members of your company, improvise Chevengur *(1999),*
scene after scene, without interruption. How do you develop their
imagination?

The point is that they are thrown right from the start into an
atmosphere where things are continually tried out [*proby*] and where
they have to get an awareness of, and a feeling for, trying things out. I
don't like the word *repetsitsiya* [rehearsal] which comes from the
French *répétition* and which implies repeating something learned,
internalised and remembered. This turns a person into an 'interpreter'
of a role, and I really don't like this word at all. In my view, a person
plays a role, creates it, composes it. We try things out, one probe
[*proba* – singular of *proby*, as used above] after another. From the very
beginning of their studies in the first year, you would do the simplest
kind of probe, say, taking a shower. What if the water is hot? Cold?
Suddenly very hot? Boiling? Icy? You are constantly thrown. Later
on, the *proby* become more difficult, and none of them mirrors any
other. New components are constantly added, without end, as happens
in our life.

Students and sometimes even the company actors like to ask
how to play something – as if telling them is enough for them to play it
straight away. Nemirovich-Danchenko spoke of the 'second level'.
Stanislavsky called it the 'subtext' – a person says one thing, but thinks
another; and actors might ask what they are supposed to be thinking so
that they can play whatever they have to play. Nemirovich was asked
what he meant by the 'second level'. He said, 'It's the whole of a
person's life.' The whole of your experience and the whole of mine
stand behind our discussion today. How do we get all that in when we
play? You have to immerse yourself in the life composed and lived by
the great writers. You could spend years on a phrase by Dostoevsky
because it begins in one piece of dialogue, is picked up and contradicted in another, emerges in a third and ends with what it started
from. You have to understand the logic of this phrase and how it came
about. I remember when I worked on *The Meek Girl* (1981) with Oleg

Borisov [renowned actor of the Moscow Art Theatre] and Tatyana Shestakova [of the Maly Drama Theatre of St Petersburg, and Dodin's wife] – it was an endless accumulation of knowledge and understanding. We worked on it in the Moscow Art Theatre, then in another theatre, then on another version a year later, and every time we noticed something else. *Proby* were always involved, not simply words. New *proby* have a new quality, and this forces people to be flexible.

There has been a lot of talk in Western Europe about actor 'training'. What do you understand by the word?

Well, for Stanislavsky, training had to do with *dressage* [*mushtra*; Dodin first uses this Russian word and then, by way of commentary on it, creates a neologistic verb from the French *dresser* from which the equestrian term *dressage* is derived]. Training means preparing yourself for play, as footballers or jumpers do when they want to set a new world record. It's about setting tasks for yourself beyond what you have already achieved. It's a matter of continually maintaining your form as an actor; of constant rehearsal so as to extend your capacities and lift them to a higher level. Speech training, for example, would entail setting yourself extremely difficult tasks of the kind you would never encounter on the stage. If you can solve them while you are training, the most difficult situations on the stage will seem easy to you. Everything on the stage has to be easy. You know, ballet dancers, especially male dancers, sometimes wear a belt with weights attached to jump – up to thirty kilos – so that their jump is higher when they take these weights off. And they achieve the height they want when they perform because it is then easy for them.

Training can be physiological, physical, technological, musical and psychological. The *proby* we were talking about also involve psychological training. Anything involving concentration, emotional memory and even the development of your personality, of your capacity for empathy – all this can be subsumed under 'training'. An actor cannot be without empathy; a person without empathy cannot be an actor. You can train empathy in the sense that you can force yourself to help someone, to feel for them, to be attentive. Then there is also intellectual training – reading, trying to talk about what you have read. Sometimes my students and, even occasionally, some of my actors, say to me, 'I can feel it, but can't express it.' I say, 'That's not true. Everything that you feel has to be articulated.' The psychologists with whom I have discussed this have confirmed it. An unformulated thought is not a thought; it does not exist. If an actor tells me he/she understands something, but cannot say it, I think that he/she does not want to make the effort to formulate it. Actors have to *learn* to say it. I make my actors put their thoughts into words. This is part of an actor's work and culture – culture is essentially a matter of work, as well – and is integral to the actor's profession, which the theatre celebrates.

It is clear that 'training' for you is not merely a technical matter. Is there such a thing as 'training' the actor's heart and soul?

This is also a complex issue. All the training I have been talking about aims to sensitise, to refine and to create – how can I put it? – the feeling heart; to make the heart a feeling *entity*. An actor has to find opportunities for being moved, shaken.

The main task of the theatre is to give spectators the possibility of experiencing emotional upheaval. The spectators of the *polis* of Ancient Greece had a reasonably tranquil existence, but went for twelve hours or so to the theatre to experience powerful emotions. Human beings need this. They need to empathise with others and, in doing so, they learn to feel for themselves. This is very important because we increasingly seem not to know how to feel for others – or for ourselves, for that matter – in the space we live in, which is one of terrific speed, of computers and of mobile phones stuck to our ears. We are also told time and time again in this space that everything is OK. In such a space, we fail to listen to our own pain, or to recognise our own fears. There isn't a single person who isn't afraid of what life can bring. We are simply conditioned to hide it. The more we hide it, the less human we become. We have to open our humanness. The theatre opens it when spectators experience deep emotions, which they do when actors experience them too. The heart and soul are trained like this.

When the cast of *Brothers and Sisters* (1985) went to Verkola [in Arkhangelsk], it was not so much because we needed to learn the villagers' way of speaking, or their songs, or how they mow with a sickle and hold their hands, although it was also for these reasons. No, above all, we went there to experience the feeling of wonder and amazement that such people, places and beauty exist and that, in this beauty, people live in such a horrifyingly make-shift way; that these old women, who sing so gaily, recount the most horrifying things about their youth and about how the Soviet Union destroyed their lives. They're smiling and don't even realise how horrifying it is. They've forgotten, but the young actors who discover this and feel moved and surprised want to share it.

Working on *Life and Fate* (2007) we went to Narilsk, where millions of people died in the gulag. [The production was devised from Vasily Grossman's novel of the same name which was published first in the West in 1980 and in the Soviet Union in 1988.] Of course, we needed to find out certain details, but only one hundredth of them would go into the production, although for that hundredth to go in, we had to know a hundred times more. We have to see and know a lot. But, above all, we have to be astounded that such things happened, that such things were done to people; we have to shed tears. The heart's sensibility also has to do with having capacities, with being gifted. Capacities can increase as well as decrease. There are so many capable, gifted people who become less capable before your very eyes because their heart is being covered over with encrustations. Why? Because, in the theatre, a person is constantly imagining feelings, and, if you constantly only imagine them, you get used to the idea that they do not exist. Nowhere does the heart become so quickly encrusted as in the theatre.

Let us come back to Life and Fate *later and talk about Chekhov first. I remember asking, when you staged* Uncle Vanya *(2003), whether you hadn't given it a Shakespearean dimension. Do you think Chekhov has Shakespeare's range and breadth?*

Yes. These two theatre worlds appear to be at opposite poles, but, in fact, are closely connected. Both, although in different languages where their historical times are concerned, explore the full range of the contradictions that make up human beings.

Perhaps Dostoevsky would have had the same kind of human complexity without end if he had written plays. His novels certainly have this quality, which brings them close to Shakespeare. Chekhov, like Shakespeare, was open to the maximum, and each created a new theatre for his time. Chekhov breaks the rules concerning character. You cannot say that Uncle Vanya is weak. He is weak and strong at the same time.

The great scope Chekhov gives to passions is Shakespearean. He writes, as does Shakespeare, about certain laws of human nature, about the fate that hangs over people's heads. Doctor that he was, who was also fatally ill, he felt especially keenly what mortality was, and the value of life. This feeling of mortality, which human beings overcome in every second of their lives, and which shapes their sense of the value of life – as well as their love of life – is essentially Shakespearean.

Chekhov's is not at all the story of small people, or of boring people, or of failures. What constitutes people's failure in *Uncle Vanya*? They all exist meaningfully. It's simply that they make *demands* on life. Many would have been totally happy to live the wonderful life of a professor – become famous, publish masses of books and then retire on a pension. It's normal. Yet, suddenly a tragedy occurs. Serebryakov, the professor, doesn't want to finish up his work or his love, or his life, and, from this very thing, he grows into a big and significant figure. Vanya – he worked hard all his life and achieved a considerable amount, but he wanted something more. What he experienced was not merely a mid-life crisis, but an intimate sense of life evolving and of his desire to make greater demands on it. These are truly tragic aspects of human nature, and are Shakespearean motifs. Equally, it seems to me that, today, we cannot *not* hear Chekhovian motifs in Shakespeare. If, today, Shakespeare's range of passions and contradictions in Chekhov is very important for me, it is just as important for me to hear Chekhov's subtlety and detail in Shakespeare. The theatre has got used to a Shakespeare of crimes and grandeur, forgetting that his plays are also composed of the smallest details.

When we worked on *King Lear* (2006), it was the almost-Chekhovian world of finesse and detail, and of the fragility of human relations that was of such importance to us. A new, fresh Shakespeare, today's Shakespeare, immediately seemed to emerge from the play.

Lev Dodin (b. 1944)

Lev, this is your *understanding of Chekhov, but how did the actors come to share your view when you worked on* Uncle Vanya?

Uncle Vanya was our fourth Chekhov production, and that's very important. We had accumulated some experience of him by working on *The Cherry Orchard* (1994), *A Play with no Name* (1997) [also known as *Platonov*], and *The Seagull* (2001), each one done with different degrees of success. You can't be on tenterhooks when you are facing a great author. You have to love and respect him/her knowing that the work is very close to you. By *Uncle Vanya* we had absorbed a good deal of Chekhov's world and so felt really close to him. I think that, as a result, we were more relaxed than we had been for the preceding productions. *Vanya* is bewitching. It is such an impeccably beautiful play, and its tragic story is so impeccably harmonious. Yes, we discussed it quite a bit at the beginning, but the point is that our hearts were ready for it. We didn't even rehearse it for very long by our standards – only several months, although we performed it frequently afterwards and it has grown considerably since its opening night.

During our English tour (2005), we gave twenty-five performances one after another, and five dress rehearsals – thirty performances in all. But we rehearsed and discussed it almost every day, so we had a whole rehearsal cycle in which we discovered many new things. In the meanwhile, we had been working on *King Lear* – we spent three years rehearsing *Lear* before it was 'ready' to be shown – and Chekhov became absorbed in that. Our new experience rubbed off onto our old one. In the theatre, today and tomorrow influence the past. This is a law of theatre-making in that the most important work is not the creation of individual productions, but of theatre as such – its life, its spirit, its capacity to seek the new. This is particularly true of the Maly, and our repertory is crucial. It is good that we have *Brothers and Sisters* and *The Devils* (1991) and *Vanya* and *Lear*, and that *Life and Fate* is being born, but the most important thing of all is to have them together.

In the sense that all the Maly productions sustain each other. Isn't this the best argument for a repertory theatre?

I'd say that a repertory theatre is the only way for art theatre to exist. It provides *development*. An artist must necessarily develop – or isn't an artist. You're not an artist because you have painted one picture. An actor cannot develop by going from one company to the next – a new company, new director, new roles, and all this with the constraints of short rehearsal periods. In such conditions, you can only mobilise your energies to use what you know. There is no time to try out what you don't know because someone is always at you to do something quickly. I am convinced that this is a catastrophe for contemporary theatre. Yes, of course, there can be dazzling examples of commercial theatre, musicals, brilliant showbiz, but this is not the same as development.

I am not saying that repertory theatre is without its problems, but it's not an accident that Germany is the only country in Europe today where theatre really is developing. Repertory theatre has not been destroyed in Germany. Permanent companies survive, and there are serious government subsidies to support them not for the sake of maintaining buildings, or of collecting a bunch of famous actors to show off their importance, but for the sake of letting troupes grow and for encouraging creative work. It's not for nothing that [Thomas] Ostermeier is enjoying such success at the Schaubühne [in Berlin], which, after all, was nurtured by [Peter] Stein. Ostermeier has his own working principles, but the theatre still has actors from Stein's days and that is fundamental for its creative development.

Given the cumulative experience and cross-pollination between productions at the Maly, how did you start *on* Uncle Vanya?

I usually like to read a play aloud. The actors have already read it, of course, but I like to communicate my own feelings about it and let them hear something else. Stanislavsky said that, to be receptive to a play, you have to encounter it in the right circumstances; you can't read it in a car. For our first meeting, we create an atmosphere, have flowers, silence. We freely tell each other about our impressions and sensations – what surprised us, infected us, cast doubts – and then, quite quickly, we start trying things out in our own words. We don't use the play. We try situations out, to see what this or that one might be. Strangely enough, in the case of *Uncle Vanya*, we started out with Serebryakov, which is not where people usually begin. I had a personal sense of Serebryakov. About a year before, I was quite ill and Tanya

Lev Dodin (b. 1944)

[Shestakova] and I were at a holiday resort in Finland. It was incredibly hot, about 30° all the time, and everybody was going about in shorts. But I continually had the shivers and went about in trousers and a sweater and sometimes a jacket, looking quite eccentric. One evening, as Tanya and I were talking, I suddenly said, 'Everybody in *Uncle Vanya* laughs at Serebryakov because he walks about in a coat and galoshes. The point is that he's shivering; his nerves are in a bad way; he's going through major turmoil; he's in a depression.' Everything began to unravel from this.

We tried this and that in our own words, and then looked at the text; then, getting to know it better, we began to use it more. Gradually, we got down to the smallest details. Everything is important, but, at the beginning, it is essential to feel free and relaxed. Roles changed. Pyotr Semak first tried Uncle Vanya, and Sergey Kuryshev tried Astrov. [The roles were reversed for the production.] It seemed to me, later, that they could do both roles equally well. What is important in our company is that we have no division of roles as such. An actor might be Hamlet in one group of actors and turn out to be a Claudius in another: it depends on who is beside him at the time and how relations in a particular group take shape. There were long, relaxed *proby* in which the actors offered to try different parts.

Why was King Lear *your first Shakespeare production?*

I wanted to go to Shakespeare for a long time, but neither I nor the company was ready. I think the theatre shows us something about ourselves, but you have to have the right questions to get some sort of answer in reply. For a long time, I didn't think we had questions worthy of Shakespeare.

I think *Lear* is one of the most powerful if not the most powerful Shakespeare play and, maybe together with *Hamlet*, it asks the most fundamental, the most substantial existential questions. I began to think in recent years that if I didn't tackle these questions now, I'd never have time to get there; and, secondly, they seemed to be very much of the moment, very pertinent to our time. We are living, today, at the turning point of a new epoch; our civilisation is changing character. The old generation says, 'What ghastly youths', while the new says, 'What ghastly fathers'. We thought that *Lear* would give us a

Fig 2 *King Lear* (2006). Directed by Lev Dodin. Sergey Kuryshev as Gloucester and Vladimir Seleznyov as Edmund. Photograph by Viktor Vasiliyev

chance to be at the epicentre of all these problems if we approached it honestly and sincerely.

However, to try and see inside Shakespeare we had to try and see ourselves *in* Shakespeare. We had to study the text well, and this was an immense and complex task. We had to study Shakespeare's time – not to play it *in* that time but to grasp the sense of what Shakespeare was writing. We also had to find analogies in our own time, so we did a lot of research on presidential matters, not least in Russia. We had to understand the relations between people who work in the same governments or administrations, as Gloucester does in Lear's kingdom. And we had to find analogies in our own life. An actor cannot just play someone called 'Lear'. He has to remember that he, too, is a father and has to respond as a *father*. We give in too easily to the lie that politicians have a different family life, which means that, when we see powerful leaders on the TV, we feel they are a different breed of people. But Shakespeare could never have become a great playwright if he had written only about kings. He writes about human beings and shows that they are the same, all with complex feelings.

King Lear [in the productions Dodin has seen] always starts from the idea that Lear is a normal but tyrannical king who, for some unknown reason, in an irrational moment, decides to give away his power. This seems, to me, to be a rather narrow view of things. I don't know of a single historical instance where a dictator willingly gave away his power. Either Lear is fooling people, or there are other, more serious reasons for what he does. During the three years or so that we worked on *Lear*, we probably spent the most time on the first scene [involving Lear's division of his kingdom into three parts]. In some rehearsals the first scene lasted one-and a half hours or even more. We tried to understand its mechanism. What was going on here? Why did this happen? We tried to understand how this mechanism was to be wound up so that the rest would unwind accordingly.

In the course of our rehearsals we slowly began to realise that the play essentially begins two steps away from its conclusion – when Lear cannot *not* give away his power because he no longer has the energy to hold it; he is leaving this life. And the young people cannot *not* take it: after all, how long is a person to wait? At the same time,

Lear cannot give it away because he is still alive. Giving it away would mean he was as good as dead. So he gives it away *without* giving it away. And his daughters take it without actually receiving it. From this emerges the madness of the situation itself. We had to gather this madness up at the very beginning: great plays begin with a high jump – so high that it is virtually impossible to jump up straight away.

And where is the Fool in all this?

The Fool is important. He is Lear's alter ego, in some ways, and possibly voices feelings Lear is unable to articulate. Why else does Lear allow him to say what he does? However, it is extremely difficult, today, to construct the relationship between them because we don't know what a Fool *is*. We don't have the profession of Fool. We approached the Fool with care, going through numerous variations. It seemed to us that today's Fool could be an actor. Actors are allowed many freedoms.

Even in the Soviet Union, where there was considerable repression and censorship, there were actors who said such unpleasant things in such a talented way that it was a pleasure for the government authorities to listen to them. There was an actor called Vladimir Vysotsky, who played Hamlet [in Yury Lyubimov's 1972 production in Moscow] and also wrote songs, many of which were blatantly anti-Soviet. [Leonid] Brezhnev, the ageing, tyrannical Head of State at the time and, in his own way, a kind of Lear, loved to listen to tape recordings of Vysotsky in his dacha. He knew perfectly well that Vysotsky was singing the truth, and it gave him pleasure to know that Vysotsky could sing on, while nothing in the state changed. Furthermore, here was a talented man also singing about *him*. That must have been pleasant, too. To some extent, this great actor turned out to be in the position of a Fool. We suddenly realised that a great actor of this kind could be by Lear's side. The idea of having the Fool play a piano stemmed from here, and so on.

Even something in the actor's intonation recalled Vysotsky.

Vysotsky or Bulat Okudjava [a famous Soviet ballad singer]. The main thing was to have our imagination triggered off. You know, our imagination is silent when things are abstract. One of the mysteries of Shakespeare is the Fool's disappearance after the storm on the heath. Here he is, one of the main protagonists, who suddenly vanishes.

There is a mass of interpretations about this, some technical, others to do with the plot. But they are only interpretations. We do not have any explanations. We thought that although *he* disappeared, his spirit could not. The idea of the piano playing by itself [at the end of the performance] came from this.

You shortened speeches – considerably in some cases – and cut scenes.

Yes, we left those parts in which we really found ourselves and saw ourselves, and the timelessness of our production comes from this, too. You cannot play Shakespeare in historical costumes. What does 'historical' mean? How do you dress your actors for the archaic times in which the story takes place? Are they supposed to be in animal skins? In Shakespeare's time, they wore Elizabethan costumes, that is, contemporary costumes. Playing in Elizabethan costumes today would be strange. We would feel like living zombies. It would look like a bad action movie. Doing Shakespeare in modern dress is a better solution but, even so, it narrows the scope of what you can do on stage. And, then, dressing characters in the modern clothes of our Presidents and Prime Ministers does not tie up well aesthetically with the words. You begin to lose faith and so you begin to rewrite the words, which is precisely what is happening in the theatre today, much of it not satisfactorily, where an Othello, say, swears away, as he does *not* in Shakespeare's words.

Your cast is a mixture of your current students and the established actors of your company. Putting them together like this is one of your fundamental working principles, isn't it?

Yes, because the young actors should be challenged intellectually, physically and spiritually, and they stand up wonderfully to this challenge. They learn by dealing with difficult material and they learn from working closely with the older actors. But they also stimulate the more experienced actors and push them along, making *them* rise to new challenges.

Why did you turn to Life and Fate, *where the majority of the actors are still students?*

It is another great Russian book. It analyses what happened to us and to the world in general in the twentieth century in such a powerful way, and it speaks in such a prophetic way about what is happening to all of us in the twenty-first. It makes us aware of human nature, which is of utmost importance for the theatre, and we learn about it through the history of a century. While people have biological and psychological beginnings, they have social ties and are heavily influenced by everything that goes on around them. People may resist, but they nevertheless change in some way, even if their fundamental nature remains the same. The problem of choice, which we all face in our lives all the time, becomes a veritable problem of choice of life or death in particular historical circumstances. These are the themes of the novel.

I first read this novel, which I had never heard about before, in 1985 in Helsinki when I was directing a production there [Aleksandr Ostrovsky's *Bankrupt*]. I found it in a bookshop which sold Russian books that had been published abroad. I read it in two nights and understood that it spoke great truth about contemporary human beings. What is great literature? It always speaks about contemporary people as part of eternity, but also in terms of their historical development. This is how Abramov seemed to us [Fyodor Abramov, author of the novel *The Pryaslin Family* from which *Brothers and Sisters* was devised], and Dostoevsky, too. Grossman is not well known in Russia, although his books are available and specialists know him. A lot of Russian history has fallen into oblivion. I think that people here have begun to forget many of the dangers from whose effects Europe has suffered, and this also applies to the rest of Europe. Thinking about all this made me feel I had to stage Grossman.

My choice was also tied up with the fact that I had selected a new group of students, and they had to be immersed in something. I thought that making them go through various stages, as we used to do in the past – exercises in the first year, *études* in the second, fragments of various works in the third – was not the right approach because we were teaching something that did not make emotional demands on them or challenge them with ideas. Our old approach did not give them a chance to experience substantial emotional excitement, and this is really where you have to start. When they are immersed in a book like Grossman's, they can learn how to drink imaginary water, or imaginary vodka, because the protagonist of the novel, who is going through so much, drinks this vodka. In other words, the simplest of exercises are subordinated to tasks of a very high level.

These young actors, like many young people all over the world, did not know the history of their own country, let alone of other countries, and it was important to bring them there. Young people are generally concerned with the now – with the latest music group, a current topic or problem; and they are not bothered about how this group or topic might well be connected to something in the past. Who among the young knows anything of significance about World War II? What the Holocaust is? What it means to be a Jew? That Hitler not only destroyed Jews, but that Europe supported him? There were remarkable individuals who helped the Jews, but not European *societies*. We have to remember these things today because, today, we are faced with new problems and new choices. I wanted my young students to be conscious of this history, but also to be aware of their responsibility for the future.

Apart from this, it is a wonderful novel activated by all kinds of human passions – love, hatred, disappointment, fear, the passion of creation and of knowledge. All this is a Shakespearean dramaturgy, and a Chekhovian one, too. Grossman's favourite writer was Chekhov, and a whole chapter in his book is devoted to the question of what, exactly, is Chekhov.

Which year of your student intake performs Life and Fate?

The fifth [and last].

Once again you have put them together with the older actors.

Yes, but when I first started working with the students, I warned them that it might not necessarily lead to a production; we were simply doing research. We needed to be immersed in the material, to read and know it. We read a mass of other books, went into the archives, found photographs and travelled to the former gulag Narilsk, which is in the zone of the Arctic Circle. To give you some idea of the distance: there is a seven-hour difference between London and Narilsk. Narilsk is an extraordinary city that should never have been built. People cannot, *should not* live there because of the climate and the conditions of the place. There are huge mineral deposits there, and Stalin said, 'Here will be a city'; and they started to build it on the blood and bones of millions of detainees. I wanted the actors to see what such a phenomenon was.

The city was born out of this Utopia, as you can see from its centre, which is a beautiful square. It was built by famous architects who were interned there especially for the purposes of construction; internment was the only way to organise a labour force. The whole city was a gulag and more than fifty nationalities were in its camps. Bits of the barracks of these camps remain. We also flew above the taiga in helicopters and spotted remaining barracks here and there, hundreds of kilometres away from living beings. Unfortunately, we do not have a memorial, a veritable gulag museum in Russia to this day. They are thinking of establishing such a museum in Narilsk – influenced, even, by our stay there.

Our work for the production was sponsored by Narilsk Nickel, which has a Cultural Foundation, and our costs were high. You know, flying to Narilsk is more expensive than flying to Paris. Then, we travelled to Auschwitz. The Polish government helped us a great deal, and organised our journey. We stayed a week, as in Narilsk, and even rehearsed there for some nights. The experience made a deep impression on us; it was quite terrifying and the actors understood everything: they had never played so well before. They were aghast, seeing what talent human beings can find in themselves to do evil to others.

We gave the world première of *Life and Fate* in Paris, and the Russian première in Narilsk. We felt indebted to it, and I wanted the actors to renew contact with a place where they had had such incomparable experiences. It was minus 47 degrees when we performed there.

Well, this could be said to be the training of the heart that we talked about before! Did the people who had been interned there come to see the performances?

A whole group of them came, all very old and mostly women; men die sooner than women. Only one man, a ninety-two-year-old, was still alive.

How did they react?

They wept, of course, although the production is not about the gulag. The gulag is only a small part of a story that encompasses more than the gulag. An eighty-two-year-old woman and her daughter came to see our dress rehearsal, as well as two performances – three times in a row. She brought us photographs taken in the gulag. She was part of a group of young women detainees sent into town to do a job in a photography workshop and had asked permission for them to be photographed. Permission was granted: in any case, you couldn't run very far in that snowy emptiness! They gathered together a blouse or two, and other bits of clothes from other detainees, threw off their camp uniforms and were photographed seated. They wanted to look beautiful and hoped the photograph would come in handy. It's fantastic. She showed me her rehabilitation papers. She was rehabilitated only in 1991, her papers stating that she had been interned for nine years, six months and four days. Her internment was cut short by five years and twenty-six days when Khrushchev started freeing people from the camps. She does not know to this day why she had been interned. She had just finished high school in West Ukraine. The Soviet authorities simply took people – young people, who were sixteen or seventeen and especially huge numbers of peasants – because they needed a labour force. Many of them went back home, but could not adjust; everything was strange to them, so they returned, living out their life here, for this was what they knew.

It's quite horrific. You build some of the book's gulag motifs into the production, though, don't you?

The book is a kind of *War and Peace* [described thus by Grossman]. We took its 'peace'. Grossman also talks about peace in war, and we took this motif because war requires battle scenes, which we didn't want to do; and, secondly, what happens inside people was more important for us. We had the impression from the novel that what happens in not-war is far more difficult and frightening for people. War is governed by more ferocious, more integral and more comprehensible laws: you know who your enemy is and who is with whom. However, when, in times of peace, the enemy is among those who are close to *you*, among friends and colleagues, and when the enemy is inside yourself – *this*, we thought, was more important. Even the scenes we selected from the parts concerning the war involve issues of moral choice – a theme that has become silent in the consciousness of the Russian intelligentsia today; and, I think, not only in Russia. I know that these words about 'moral choice' ring of preceding eras, of past centuries, and yet I think that our epoch should recall them.

It's a huge novel, so how did you devise the text for your performance?

Together, as always, though with my leadership. We performed the whole novel several times. I must say that I had formulated a group of themes in my head that were important to us all. It was a complicated process. We even drew up Strum's genealogical tree so as to construct our thoughts around something definite. [Strum is a Jewish scientist in the novel whose mother is exterminated in a Nazi camp.] It seemed that everything could be linked organically to him. So we performed *études* on Strum's story, then we condensed them, then I began to hone them by working with the text. We took bits of text for an episode from other places in the novel when they had a particular resonance for that very episode, or clarified a thought we had about it. It's very meticulous work, and even after two premieres I see that several things need to be pinpointed and refined.

You are co-authors of the production, and I know this to be true of your earlier work. Do you make directorial decisions at the last minute?

No, I make them at every moment in the process, and the actors also feel that they can contribute to the selection as we go. I keep selecting – suggesting that we remove something, condense it, rework it, try something else, return to the theme and the context. Then, during the summer, I sat down and wrote a series of scenes according to our *proby*, connecting those points that you cannot link when you count them out orally on your fingers. We always had to keep in mind the fact that we were not performing a play, but a novel. I cannot stand adaptations, which imply that, yes, you have read the novel, but *now* you are playing the play. This approach narrows things down. Whereas, you have to have knowledge of the whole in the parts that remain; then you are aware that you are playing a novel and can alter things at any moment. Just recently, in Narilsk, we made a major operation on the second Act, which, I think, was compositionally useful. We could change the composition of the work because it was *part* of the novel. The actors knew it was a concentration of something bigger.

The actors, then, accept your directorial authority. Do they ever tell you that you are wrong? Are there any conflicts?

We don't have conflicts. Sometimes the actors say, 'It's a shame', or ask why I've done something. I also try to listen to them, to understand their feelings. When I am convinced of something I don't say, 'You have to do it like this.' I explain why I've come to that conclusion so that everybody understands it fully. I also suggest that they try a new possibility, and nothing is lost if it turns out to be no good because we have the earlier version. This calms everybody because the work that they have done before does not seem to be superfluous. It's not easy for actors when they are deprived of scenes that they have worked on. The essential thing is that they understand why those scenes need to be cut, why whatever is being done is done.

Who are you as a director? What is your role?

It's very difficult to analyse yourself. I like to know, to think, to get to know the theatre, and I seek to draw the company into this knowing. Some sort of leadership arises from this act of drawing people into an expedition. It's a relatively risky thing to do because you have all sorts of inner doubts and you are drawing people in when you yourself do not know the road or where you will arrive. Yet, it seems that everyone must assume that you know both the road *and* the destination. If the road changes, then everyone has to see it as a discovery and not as a defeat. Columbus sailed and sailed, and sailed to America, which did not turn out to be such a bad thing. It was important to sail with confidence.

Many underlying aspects emerge from your being a director. You become a pedagogue, an organiser, a friend, a psychologist and often a psychiatrist because the profession has its maladies and sometimes you have to have real insight into why somebody finds a task difficult; and people's lives are complex.

Translated from Russian by Maria Shevtsova

Chronology of selected productions

Dodin began his directing career in 1967 with *After My Execution, I Ask You* by Volf Dolgy at the Leningrad Theatre for Young Spectators (LenTYuZ). He directed various works at this theatre and at the Bolshoi Drama Theatre (BDT) in Leningrad (*The Meek Girl* devised from the novel by Fyodor Dostoevsky, 1981) as well as at the Moscow Art Theatre (*The Golovlyovs* devised from the novel by Mikhail Saltykov-Shchedrin, 1984). The chronology below lists only productions that Dodin directed with the Maly Drama Theatre (MDT) while he was working in a freelance capacity, and those he directed with the MDT after he became its Artistic Director in 1983. All productions listed were premiered at the Maly Drama Theatre of St Petersburg unless otherwise stated. Since 1998, the MDT has been known as the Maly Drama Theatre – Theatre of Europe, a title conferred by the Union of European Theatres.

1974   *The Robber* by Karel Čapek
1977   *The Rose Tattoo* by Tennessee Williams
1978   *The Appointment*, devised from the novel by Aleksandr Volodin
1979   *Live and Remember* by Valentin Rasputin
1980   *The House*, devised from the novel by Fyodor Abramov
1984   *The Bench* by Aleksandr Gelman. Directed by Eugene Arie and artistic co-ordination by Lev Dodin
1985   *Brothers and Sisters*, devised from the trilogy *The Pryaslin Family* by Fyodor Abramov
1986   *Lord of the Flies*, devised from the novel by William Golding
1987   *To the Sun*, devised from one-Act plays by Aleksandr Volodin
        Stars in the Morning Sky by Aleksandr Galin
1988   *The Old Man*, devised from the novel by Yury Trifonov
        The Returned Pages, directed by Lev Dodin and Valery Galendeyev
1990   *Gaudeamus*, devised from the novel *The Construction Battalion* by Sergey Kaledin
1991   *The Devils*, devised from the novel by Fyodor Dostoevsky. Festival Theaterformen, Braunschweig

Lev Dodin (b. 1944)

1992   *Desire Under the Elms* by Eugene O'Neill
       The Broken Jug by Heinrich von Kleist. Directed by Veniyamin
       Filshtinsky and artistic co-ordination by Lev Dodin
1994   *The Cherry Orchard* by Anton Chekhov. Odéon-Théâtre de
       l'Europe, Paris
       Claustrophobia, devised from texts by Vladimir Sorokin,
       Ludmila Ulitskaya and Venedikt Erofeyev. MC93 Bobigny,
       Paris
1995   *Elektra* by Richard Strauss. Salzburg Easter Festival, Salzburg
1997   *A Play with no Name* [*Platonov*] by Anton Chekhov. E-Werk,
       Weimar
1998   *Lady Macbeth of Mtsensk District* by Dmitri Shostakovich.
       Maggio Musicale Fiorentino, Teatro Communale, Florence
       The Queen of Spades by Pyotr Ilyich Tchaikovsky. De
       Nederlandse Opera, Amsterdam
1999   *Mazepa* by Pyotr Ilyich Tchaikovsky. La Scala, Milan
       Chevengur, devised from the novel by Andrey Platonov. E-Werk,
       Weimar
2000   *Molly Sweeney* by Brian Friel. Premio Europa, Taormina, Italy
2001   *The Seagull* by Anton Chekhov. International Chekhov
       Festival, Moscow
2002   *The Moscow Choir* by Lyudmila Petruschevskaya. Directed by
       Igor Konyaev and artistic co-ordination by Lev Dodin
2003   *The Demon* by Anton Rubinstein. Théâtre du Châtelet, Paris
       Otello by Giuseppe Verdi. Maggio Musicale Fiorentino, Teatro
       Communale, Florence
       Uncle Vanya by Anton Chekhov. Piccolo Teatro di Milano, Milan
       Salomé by Richard Strauss. Paris Opéra Bastille, Paris
2006   *King Lear* by William Shakespeare
2007   *Life and Fate*, devised from the novel by Vasily Grossman.
       MC93 Bobigny, Paris

MDT collaborations. Performed by MDT

1994   *Roberto Zucco* by Bernard-Marie Koltès. Directed by Lluis
       Pasqual. Odéon-Théâtre de l'Europe, Paris

1996   *Reflets* by Georges Lavaudant, Jean-Christophe Bailly, Michel
        Deutsch and Jean-François Duroure. Directed by Georges
        Lavaudant. Odéon-Théâtre de l'Europe, Paris
1997   *The Winter's Tale* by William Shakespeare. Directed by Declan
        Donnellan. Maly Drama Theatre, St Petersburg

Selected bibliography

Baltiiskiye Sezony 11 (2004), (*Baltic Seasons*: special issue of the journal
    for the sixtieth anniversary of the Maly Drama Theatre)

Davydova, Marina (2005), 'Lev Dodin: zhizn pakhnet senom i dozhdem'
    ('Lev Dodin: Life Smells of Hay and Rain') in *Konets teatralnoy
    Epokhi (The End of a Theatre Epoch)*, Moscow: The Golden
    Mask, OGI, pp. 97–107

Dmitrevskaya, Marina (1986), 'Ishchem my sol, ishchem my bol etoy
    zemli' ('*We Seek Salt, We Seek the Pain of This Land*'), Teatr 4,
    89–102

Dodin, Lev (2004), *Repetitsii* Pyesy bez nazvaniya (*Rehearsals of* A Play
    with no Name), transcripts by Anna Ogibina, St Petersburg: Baltic
    Seasons

    (2006), *Journey Without End: Reflections and Memoirs*, ed. John
    Ormrod, trans. Anna Karabinska and Oksana Mamyrin, London:
    Tantalus Books

Galendeyev, Valery (2006), 'Metod i shkola Lva Dodino' ('Lev Dodin's
    Method and School') in *Ne tolko o stenicheskoy rechi (Not only
    about Stage Speech)*, St Petersburg: St Petersburg State Academy
    of Theatre Arts, pp. 218–70

Maly Drama Theatre (1992), '*Gaudeamus*', *TheatreForum* 1, 63–80

Shevtsova, Maria (1997) 'Resistance and Resilience: an Overview of
    the Maly Theatre of St Petersburg', *New Theatre Quarterly* 13:2,
    299–317

    (1998), 'Drowning in Dixie: the Maly Drama Theatre Plays Chekhov
    Untitled', *TheatreForum* 13, 46–53

    (2000), 'War and Ash at La Scala: Lev Dodin Rehearses *Mazepa*',
    TheatreForum 16, 95–104

Lev Dodin (b. 1944)

(2001), 'The Life of a Production: Lev Dodin's *Queen of Spades* – from Amsterdam to Paris', *Russian Theatre Past and Present* 2, 139–58

(2004), *Dodin and the Maly Drama Theatre: Process to Performance*, London: Routledge

(2004), 'Lev Dodin's "Musical Dramatic Art" and the World of Opera', *New Theatre Quarterly* 20: 4, 341–53

(2006), 'Lev Dodin and the Maly Drama Theatre: *Uncle Vanya* to *King Lear*', *New Theatre Quarterly* 22: 3, 249–56

3   Declan Donnellan (b. 1953)

Among the wide range of different voices speaking from the stage today, that of Declan Donnellan is inflected with his singular position as a director with a dual role – not so much a transcultural role, which might be said to be the case of Robert Lepage, as a 'dynamic "two"' (Donnellan, *The Actor and the Target*, 2005, p. 54). The latter phrase is Donnellan's very description of how the actor must play for twin stakes simultaneously rather than be confined by one of them: this *or* that, love *or* hate, hope *or* fear. Not only does the search for 'one' block the actor, it is a mirage, for 'there is no magic "one" that will solve everything. Life comes in opposed "twos"' (*ibid.* p. 52).

    Thus it is that Donnellan is the only director in Britain to have a consistent working relationship with Russia, the first after Edward Gordon Craig whose famous 1911 *Hamlet* with Stanislavsky at the Moscow Art Theatre promised continuity, but was a one-off – and a stymied enterprise, at that. And he is the only director to lead two companies concurrently: Cheek by Jowl, which he founded in 1981 with his partner and designer Nick Ormerod after both had graduated in law from Cambridge University, and the Russian company, left with the functional name of the Chekhov International Theatre Festival after the event where it had made its first appearance in Moscow in 2000. *Boris Godunov* by Aleksandr Pushkin, the quintessentially Russian poet, was its inaugural production. However, although the Russian company is billed as 'in Association with Cheek by Jowl', the temptation to see it as the Russian arm of Cheek by Jowl – or, to borrow Donnellan's words, as the other half of the 'dynamic "two"' – is very strong indeed, primarily because of the stylistic cross-fertilisation between them, the one taking on the colouring of the other. In addition, both are touring companies; and Cheek by Jowl's beginnings as an international touring company rather than solely as a national one indicated quite clearly the international reach envisaged right from the start by Donnellan and Ormerod for their artistic work.

Cheek by Jowl, while starting out as an ensemble company, thereby running against the individualistic politics of the period dominated by Margaret Thatcher (Prime Minister from 1979 to 1990), was disbanded in 1998 and resumed in the early years of 2000 with a different, project-based, remit. It now gathers actors for a particular production, many seeking opportunities in film and television, which prevent them from long-term commitment to theatre work, especially when it involves extensive touring. The Russian company, by contrast, came together as an ensemble and remains an ensemble (for how long in Russia's rapidly changing economic and cultural conditions?), providing Donnnellan with the continuity he needs, as he explains here in the interview. This company was founded on the confidence inspired in both the theatre profession and the public by Cheek by Jowl tours in Moscow and St Petersburg, whose first huge success was the 1991 all-male *As You Like It*. Adrian Lester, in the role of Rosalind, was subsequently able to build his strong international reputation in film as well as the theatre on the basis of his achievements in this production, seminal for its celebration of love in the pristine clarity of word, gesture and image that Donnellan, a great admirer of Peter Brook's simple acting in simple space, had begun to make his own.

Donnellan's work as a director comes well into focus not only when the productions of his two companies are twinned but when, additionally, his work with French actors in France is brought into the picture. His productions in the 1980s, while foregrounding Shakespeare, also paid attention to Racine, Corneille, Ostrovsky and Lopé de Vega – all in translation but all integral to his ambition to make European classics accessible in what was fundamentally an inward-looking and even at times insular theatre environment. The drive to make such classics central to the British scene certainly widened his own horizons, eventually taking him to Corneille's *Le Cid* in French at the Avignon Festival (1998) and Racine's *Andromaque*, also performed in French, in Paris (2007). The formal elegance of these texts of the classical age, with their alexandrines – twelve-metre rhyming couplets – and strict rules of prosody lend themselves well to Donnellan's sense of the shape of words and how they contain emotion. It is this very containment that provides him with the challenge to find, with his actors, the means for breaking passions open so that they are expressed with intensity, but always without heroics and histrionics – something he continually explores through the verse of Shakespeare and to which his ongoing work on Pushkin (*Boris Godunov* is a repertory piece) contributes significantly.

The resulting spaciousness of utterances, of dialogue that breathes whether performances are in English, Russian or French, gives Donnellan's text-based theatre a limpid quality not usually found in this genre. A similar kind of transparency is at work in its visual compositions where several locations and events overlap – the King's court, his daughter Imogen in disguise in a cave, the forest in which war is waged in *Cymbeline* (2007), for example. Or else it is achieved through how outside and inside spaces converge, as occurs in *Andromaque*, where the shifting number and position of chairs, the only props on an otherwise bare stage, not only conjure up place and time, but also pinpoint the emotional struggle within and between characters, and the social status on which they insist in their deadly jousts of power and desire: Andromaque, who is usually in perpetual motion, sits on a chair to assert her royalty and independence as well as her rejection of Pyrrhus's seductions, while half-seduced by them, nevertheless; Pyrrhus, in what is also a ploy to win Andromaque, sits to cradle Astyanax her son, played by a grown actor who, by this discrepancy, introduces humour into a gamut of tones and moods that draw out the tension and excitement embedded in Racine's formal verbal structures; and so on, including the final scene where Andromaque and Astyanax appear as if they were a bride and groom (chairs now arranged differently to suggest a church).

The final image of Donnellan's production implies that because of Andromaque's forced marriage to Pyrrhus and the latter's murder immediately afterwards, Astyanax inherits the power that Andromaque has regained (although over a foreign territory) and which she believes is his right. The ambiguity of the image is such that it hints at Astyanax's possible future: he could well become another version of Pyrrhus, reproducing the tyranny and bloodshed of this son of Achilles who helped to destroy Troy. By making Astyanax a character – *not* the case in Racine, where he is simply referred to – Donnellan shows his skill in going to the heart of a drama through what is neither textually visible nor said. In this way, he succeeds in unsettling canonical material, offering spectators a fresh view of it.

Comparably bold strokes in how he abridges texts for the sake of finding their inner core abound in Donnellan's *oeuvre*, and is a way of clearing the path for his actors' attentive, precise work; and the discoveries made by the Russian company, for example, wash over into Cheek by Jowl productions or into Donnellan's interaction with French actors so that, irrespective of their uniqueness, *Andromaque*, for instance, gains in power from his experience of *Boris Godunov*. The wash may not carry cultural overtones – Racine is not Russianised, nor is Shakespeare, for that matter – but the sheer engagement with actors in different cultural contexts appears to have allowed Donnellan to explore more fully than he may have done otherwise the intricacies of acting and the complex connections to be made by actors about which he writes eloquently in *The Actor and the Target*. Of the many observations in his book that illuminate his relationship as a director with actors, his advice to actors on keeping their distance from their parts sheds the most light on how they produce the feeling of spaciousness characteristic of his stage. For, apart from the space-effects achieved by the means noted above, and apart from Ormerod's minimalist design, which liberates space, this spaciousness comes from the distances, often considerable, that the actors keep between themselves. The purpose is to see each other and their characters more clearly. Furthermore, keeping a distance encourages the actors to look outside of themselves towards the targets aimed for by their characters – a result to be attained, an action to be done – rather than to go introspectively into themselves in the manner of Method actors or, for that matter, in the 'affective-memory' mode developed in his early years by Stanislavsky.

While Donnellan's selection of plays has been predominantly classical, he has shown a lighter touch with Stephen Sondheim's *Sweeney Todd* (1993), Noel Coward's *Hay Fever* (1999) and Verdi's *Falstaff* (2001) in Salzburg, his only opera production, although he has several musicals behind him. His tougher side responded to the corrosive issues of Aids, the witch-hunt of homosexuals and the endemic corruption and greed of the Ronald Reagan period exposed by Tony Kushner's *Angels in America*, drawing parallels with Thatcher's Britain. He gave this play's two-part British premiere in 1992 and 1993 while he was still an Associate Director of the National Theatre in London (1989–97), returning to Kushner in 2002 with *Homebody/ Kabul*, which he rehearsed in New York in the aftermath of 9/11, the acrid smell of the destroyed Twin Towers and the human lives lost in them invading the rehearsal room. Some of that terrible confusion discreetly underlies the production's restrained presentation of Kushner's religious and political concerns – Afghanistan viewed with the eyes of an unprejudiced North American, and *before* 9/11.

Recipient of numerous awards, including three Laurence Olivier Awards, among them the Olivier for Outstanding Achievement in 1990, Donnellan has had similar recognition from Russia and France, the in effect three – rather than two – parts of his creative life symbolically coming together. In 1999, his production of *The Winter's Tale* (1997) with the Maly Drama Theatre of St Petersburg received the Moscow Golden Mask Award, the equivalent in prestige of the British Olivier. Directing the Maly, which is symbiotically tied to Lev Dodin, was Donnellan's first Russian engagement, preparing him for the Russian company he was to assemble soon after. In 2004, he was made a Chevalier de l'Ordre des Arts et des Lettres for his work in France. Yet, over and above these signs of institutional approval is Donnellan's contribution to opening out British theatre to the pulsations beyond the country's borders, *and* vice versa – an achievement whose nearest comparison would be that of Simon McBurney, although accomplished in different ways.

Declan Donnellan (b. 1953)

Maria Shevtsova: *What does 'actor training' mean for you? You formed an Academy at the Royal Shakespeare Company in 2001. What did you do there?*

Declan Donnellan: I think that to run any theatre well there has to be a going back to the roots, and, while the director has many functions, one of them is to look after the health of the acting of the ensemble. In other words, not only to help the actors to act, but to help the actors to act together and to help the actors to act with the audience. For me it is important that the director be in there, making connections all the time, helping the actors and the audience to make connections. But making the connections and maintaining the connections is really important: that's why theatre is so labour-intensive. An American author once said to me, 'Tell me when the show's going to be fixed', and I said, 'Well, I can't imagine it being fixed because then it will be dead.' So the production changes slightly, just as the wings of the aeroplane must move slightly otherwise the whole structure becomes unstable. If the wings don't move, the aeroplane is actually more dangerous.

Actor training is very important to me. There is, inevitably, a contingent of youngish actors in most classical companies - with my company in Moscow about 40 per cent of the actors will be in their twenties and thirties. It is important, for me, to think of the work as always being in flux, always in process and developing, as opposed to being somebody who creates and shows product. So I think of myself as being somebody who is coaching the acting – rather than teaching – from the very first day of rehearsal until the very last performance. It is really within that context that the actors' training takes place, but not of course with a formal pedagogical structure, as you might have in a drama school. In other words, not a regime of movement at 10 o'clock, improvisation at 11 o'clock, something else at 12 o'clock, and so on. So, when I was asked by the Royal Shakespeare Company if I would start an Academy in Stratford, I said I would do it for one year, as an experiment. We gathered a group of drama school leavers and took them through the experience of doing *King Lear* (2002) in a rehearsal of about twelve weeks, which was extremely long for an English rehearsal period. I toured with the company and kept rehearsing, as

71

I do always. I have just come back from Milan, where we did a rehearsal for *Cymbeline,* and am going to New York, where there will be another rehearsal; I had a rehearsal in Moscow two days ago for *Three Sisters,* and have another one in Cambridge at the end of this week, so it's a continual process of rehearsal. I have too much work on the road at the moment!

I think I realised that I didn't much like working only with students. I would like training to take place always in the context of a company with older actors, middle-aged actors and young actors so that the whole thing is taken holistically forward, rather than have a bunch of very inexperienced people, although the Academy was a very happy experience. At this moment in my life, it would be quite strange for me to direct a play where I don't have the experienced, mature actors with whom I can bring on less experienced actors.

How do you develop fully fledged actors within your two companies, Cheek by Jowl and your Russian company?

Oh, it's like the way you develop anything else: you can develop everything through attention. There is no particular technique. The most important technique in life is just paying attention. I don't mean it in the sense of 'That person needs attention.' Attention is everything. Occasionally you develop the actor by sitting there and witnessing the performance and talking to the actors about it afterwards, maybe very informally over a bottle of wine. That's at one extreme because normally we have an intensive, full set of notes in rehearsal about once a week. I don't train actors in a vacuum. What is important to me is a sense of development, of looking forward and deepening interest in the quality of what is happening. For example, we're continuing to rehearse *Cymbeline* (2007), which presents us with extraordinary events, like a woman [Imogen] who wakes up next to a headless corpse, which she assumes is that of her murdered husband [Posthumus]. It is a very important moment in *Cymbeline,* but how does a human being *experience* that? Incidentally, this might not be the most useful example because it is sensational.

Well, can you give me other examples?

What it is like for Posthumus to be separated from Imogen, actually really to experience what separation is like? There are many moments of loss in the play. The last scene in *Cymbeline*, when the King is told that his wife is dead, is often played for laughs. But really to try and act that as well as possible, you have to experience it as humbly as possible, rather than arrive at rehearsal with a preconception that it is a funny scene. It is good to remember the Rabbi who, when asked why no one could see God any more, replied that it was because no one could stoop low enough. In theatre a greater part of this 'humility' is accepting our ignorance.

The way we have done the end of *Cymbeline* is based on really trying to experience each moment. We put a lot of work into that last scene and we are still working on it to experience as well as we can what it might be like to see for the first time somebody whom you love – a brother or sister whom you have loved, or a father whom you have loved but never seen. It's an ongoing process, but it's not an intellectual process. In many respects, it's a rather *anti*-intellectual process because sometimes our intellects are not very useful, especially when they give us preconceptions. We have to meet the world as it really is, not as we intellectually perceive it ought to be.

Does this anti-intellectual, anti-preconceptions approach explain why you don't have an outright funny Malvolio in Twelfth Night (2003) – usually the case, at least in all the productions of the play that I have seen – but a tragic, even deeply tragic, one?

As a performance develops you have to throw out elements that aren't useful any more. Keeping something fresh also has to do with keeping your head empty. For example, the actor must remember that the character has never played the scene before, has never used these words before, and does not know how the scene will end. All of these things are permanently under threat by a long run of a production, so, almost inevitably, decay sets in and the stakes go down. It is very important to see from the inside what the stakes would be for Malvolio. We have to see clearly. However, if we arrive burdened with a preconception, for example, the idea that Malvolio must be a funny character, whatever that means, we will hamper our search. We will be like a scientist who commits the classic error of starting from his conclusion. Instead we have to let go of this control, this need to see the end at the beginning. Perhaps it will be funny to some, perhaps it will be sad to others, and perhaps it will be both. The actor needs to experience the situation from within, and if the audience wants to laugh, they do, and if they don't, then they don't; they might want to cry, or whatever. So you *allow* the audience to have an ambivalence towards the action. Some might say, 'Oh, that was an extraordinary idea for Malvolio to break down when he reads Olivia's letter' [after he sent her his love letter] – and it's great when people like it! – but it doesn't spring from an idea. It's got nothing to do with an intellectual concept, worked out before rehearsal – it doesn't work like that.

In the rehearsal room, we go through the process of what it would be like to be in a particular situation. We had to really experience what Malvolio has to experience, and to help him experience, and to have the experience with him. What would it be like to be incredibly, deeply in love with somebody? What would it be like to receive a letter from them saying that they were completely in love with you? (Of course, the Malvolio story is much more complex than that because, for example, the whole issue of class gets mixed into it.) And, as soon as you really experience that love, you find that the words that you thought meant one thing actually mean something else. You have to rid yourself completely of your preconceptions and sometimes that is very difficult to do. I've seen very wonderful Malvolio speeches that are very funny, but I thought that, this time, I would like to explore this different, rather more tragic path. So it's not an idea, it's an experience.

When I first started thirty years ago, I was much more controlling, having an end-game plan, and thinking how I wanted things to come out: how it should finally look, how it should feel, what effect it should have. But slowly I learnt to work in a different way. There is sometimes an honour in ignorance! Increasingly it seemed to me that what is important is to reflect as much as possible the actual experience, however unpredictable, uncomfortable or unexpected that may turn out to be. Recently there has been a slight shift in how I see the work that we do. I always thought that there was 'text' and that, under the text, there was 'story'; and the text and the story were often different. It's like in real life, where somebody says one thing, but does something else, and this conflict is often deeply painful. And this pain slowly teaches us that if what someone says is contradicted by what they do there is a simple rule. The rule says that we must pay more attention to what people do and less to what they say. In real life text and action are not equal. Actions always speak louder than words. It's what a person does that really matters. So it's the situation, it's the *story* that really matters because a text can mean one thing, or something else: fifteen words can read one way or another way, be used to mean completely different things. A text can mean many different things – otherwise how could theologians disagree in matters of religion? The context changes everything. What Hamlet says is important, but it matters less than what he does. I always thought of it as a double structure: the walls depend on the foundations; the text depends on the story underneath. Now it seems to me that there is something else buried underneath the story: there is a deeper layer. The story is actually made up of fragments of experience.

If I had said this to myself a few years ago, I would have said, 'Well that's completely obvious. Why are you making such a song and dance about this "experience"?' There are many reasons. For example, now it seems to me that this quality of experience measures the difference between *really* doing something and pretending you're doing it. This touches on one of the great conundrums in theatre. In rehearsals, what we seek is the *ambivalence* of things, and most of our work, including the scene with the headless corpse, has been about trying to discover the ambivalence of an event.

What should be our attitude towards Juliet? I don't know. You've got a trillion different attitudes towards Juliet. It is not about trying to control her. What you need is to see Juliet in all of her different manifestations and then let the attitude fill itself in. But what you need to do is really see, really experience, this person who is an independent person outside you. We really need to try to see her without delusions, without illusions; try to understand that the thing outside is unpredictable and changing. I remember asking Adrian Lester in *As You Like It* (1991), who was playing Rosalind: ' If you were a woman, what would it be like if your shoulders were too broad, or your feet were too long, or you were too tall to look like a woman?'

In the early stages of rehearsal if an actor asks, 'What am I playing here?' it occasionally helps to say, 'You're trying to do this' or

'You're trying to do that.' But, really, in the end, I find this quite constipated. It can block the actors with theory because they start trying to find lots of different interesting verbs. It tends to become a rather cerebral exercise. In *The Actor and the Target* I suggest that it may actually help the actor to loosen up a bit on the idea of action as something which I decide, when I plan what I am doing; where I have a policy on what I am doing. It helps more to see what the character sees. The problem that we are struggling with is to see the world without clouding it by our own filters too much. Rather than have actors try to work out policies and attitudes on what they're playing –'I'm doing this here', and 'I'm doing that now', and 'What do you want me to do here?' – I try and get them to go a bit easy on this sort of questioning and focus much more energy specifically on what it *is* that they see outside them; to focus also on *seeing* how difficult it is even for the characters to see things. When something dangerous happens in our life, when the stakes go up, we try to see what is happening rather than think what our attitude towards it is.

When the actor sees things as they are seen by the character, then action tends to look after itself. It's not really helpful for the actress playing Imogen to decide in advance what her attitude will be towards the headless corpse. The *experience* might even be like saying good-bye to somebody. People are always saying good-bye to each other in *Cymbeline* and, in the end, gloriously, they say 'Hello' to each other. But what really happens when you say 'Good-bye'? What happens in this specific moment when we are forced to separate? To find this out we have to ditch our preconceptions.

Do you think that your strong sense of experience now has something to do with your own Russian experience? Is it tied up with the fact that you have worked with actors coming from a different cultural perspective?

Possibly. It's always interesting to see the same mountain from different angles. It's more three-dimensional. I don't really think Russian actors are intrinsically different from British actors. What is very different is the culture they live in, and that is utterly, utterly different.

Declan Donnellan (b. 1953)

*Before I ask you any more about your Russian actors, let me ask
you why you consistently stage Shakespeare – seventeen productions,
including* Troilus and Cressida *coming up in 2008? You could almost
be described as a Shakespeare director, couldn't you?*

Well, I have an intense relationship with the work of
Shakespeare. There's something in that sensibility, I suppose. One of
the things I love about Shakespeare is his obsession with human love,
and one of the ways of looking at his plays is to investigate all the
different aspects of human love in them. The heroines, like Hermia,
love but have to disobey the living father, and they do well as long as
that father is alive. One of the few daughters who obey the living father
is Ophelia, and she is condemned to an ambiguous suicide. On the
other hand, Rosalind has a dead father to whom she is loyal. I also
think it useful to work on Shakespeare's missing mothers. They're
often dodgy and kept off stage, but they're so important. Some of these
shadowy mothers are highly ambivalent. Othello's mother gives him a
handkerchief and says, 'Take the handkerchief and if you ever want to
test your wife's fidelity, use this.' 'That's a nice present, Mummy,
thanks.' Then there's Malcolm's terrifying sainted mother, Mrs Duncan, who died every day she lived. She was another charmer.

A few of the mothers who actually come on stage are strange,
like Gertrude, or Lady Capulet, or Volumnia. Gertrude is so strange
because she has no real voice. I think Shakespeare tries to write a
passive–aggressive, withdrawing mother in her, but, of course, you
can't really stage that in a great public seventeenth-century play
because all these characters exist in their text and it is hard in such a
convention to write somebody who exerts power by not speaking.
Gertrude is so much about what Gertrude doesn't say.

The mothers are all dead by the end of *Cymbeline* and there are
four of them. Shakespeare's mother, Mary Arden, died the year he wrote
it. There is Cymbeline's first wife, the 'mother to the birth of three',
as Cymbeline will describe himself [at the end of the play]. Then
there's Posthumus's mother who is mentioned over and over again
(once as the subject of Shakespeare's rather obsessive mother-fidelity
jokes), but she's a dead mother. Then the other dead mother is Euriphile

who, again, is a carefully kept-offstage mother, who is Belarius's wife, and who adopted the two boys for whom 'Fear no more the heat o' the sun' is actually written to speak at her death. Then there's the Queen, Cloten's mother, whom Cymbeline describes to Imogen as her mother: 'Thy mother's dead'; and one thing that the Queen isn't – is Imogen's mother! After that dialogue comes Cymbeline's 'O what am I / A mother to the birth of three?' which is an amazing thing to say. It's very odd that a man refers to himself as a mother. Men on the whole very rarely refer to themselves as mothers, in my experience. And women very rarely refer to themselves as fathers, even in our modern times – it's still a line to cross. And for a father to describe himself as a mother in this period was highly subversive to the status quo then, and even now. The whole play appears to be about fatherhood, as do many of Shakespeare's plays, although you can't discuss fatherhood without implying something about motherhood, even if the mothers are hidden. I often do a lot of work on the missing mothers in Shakespeare, who are deafening by their absence. What happened to King Lear's wife? It would be extraordinary to attend to those three girls and their father and not do an enormous amount of work on this woman. We also have in Cordelia another disobedient daughter, as is Imogen to Cymbeline.

Let's talk for a moment about the sons. Why did you choose the same actor to play Cloten and Posthumus?

Well, because we had an actor who could play the parts. There are problems in the structure of *Cymbeline*. It is without question the most difficult play that Nick [Ormerod] and I have ever done. Posthumus is only with Imogen at the very beginning of the play and Shakespeare has not written a separation scene for them. Then we don't see them together again until the end of the play. I've done everything to keep him and their relationship alive throughout the play. The fact that the same actor plays Cloten means that Posthumus's presence is felt through the play so that, when he comes back in the fifth Act, you don't think, 'Who is this?' This double casting gives us two sides – perhaps like the 'shadow' figure to Jung – which is interesting to a certain degree. But the most important thing is Posthumus's continual, substantial material presence, although in another guise.

Fig 3 *Cymbeline* (2007). Directed by Declan Donnellan.
Photograph by Keith Pattison

I think the suggestion that Shakespeare was a Catholic is probably true. I'm completely fascinated by the fact that he never writes the play that everybody else was writing, with an evil Cardinal and a Spanish/Italian Catholic court, which were so popular at the time. And when he *does* write a tragedy, it's either pre-Christian or set in Denmark and Scotland – or Ancient Rome, so that doesn't count; but he's as far away as possible from being put in a position where he has to be propagandist against Roman Catholicism. The only contemporary Mediterranean tragedy is *Othello* and there is nothing more secular than the Venetian state in *Othello*. Othello was obsessed with his Christianity, so, in this contemporary play, the Catholic question shouts by its absence. *Romeo and Juliet* is a Mediterranean tragedy, but meddling friars apart, there is no sense of a corrupt Church. Besides, Shakespeare wrote it when he was young. When he gets a bit older, he really avoids the whole area.

I'm interested in what you said about Russian actors not being very different, but that their culture is. Well, they may not be different, but is your approach to them as a director different?

I had stars in my eyes when I first went to Russia and worked with Lev Dodin's company, directing *The Winter's Tale* (1997). I met Lev and the Maly Drama Theatre in Finland in 1986 and we became great friends. The Maly and Cheek by Jowl started to go around to foreign festivals together and we got to know them very well. I had an incredible longing for this marvellous thing that would be Russian theatre, and was thrilled when Lev asked me to work there. Before that, we were invited to perform in Moscow and these performances were among our best: the Russian audiences seemed to connect very warmly with our work. I felt a deep sense of personal connection. It was really one of the most unexpectedly happy periods in my life, suddenly feeling that I was really connecting to people who were basically strangers.

What I really like about Russians is the attention that they pay each other. Russians are very good at paying attention to each other. They're attentive to each other, not in a particularly intense, but often in a sort of lightly worn and human way. At the beginning I was incredibly respectful, over-respectful. My assistant at the Maly said,

'Declan, you're meant to direct them.' You can begin a relationship by falling in love – like I was in love with Russian theatre. But in love doesn't last, only love does and that is based on living in reality. Marriage is all about remarriage. The shift into love is hard, but I think that I have actually managed this shift in my relationship with Russian theatre. Eleven years later and *The Winter's Tale* will soon be having its 200th performance in St Petersburg, and we will be there!

How did you form your Russian company? They were not an ensemble that you inherited, as I understand it.

Absolutely not. How they came together was extraordinary – they just did. I was worried, having gone from Dodin's ensemble company, who had all been together at the theatre school, and worked there under Lev. The Maly actors are one of the world's closest-knit ensembles – they work together like a dream. The Moscow actors were quite different; they were independent stars. And I was worried that that sense of ensemble might be difficult for these strangers to forge; many had only seen each other in the cinema. But astonishingly they became an ensemble just like that, and, suddenly it was as if we had been together forever. It was a complete gift. I have been given a lot of gifts like this in Russia. I am very grateful.

The company is a very central part of my life because those Moscow actors remain the same, whereas the British actors might remain for three years, at the most. I am a big one for continuity in my life and the *actor* continuity in my life is exclusively Russian. I feel very at home with Russians and feel very liberated working with Russian actors, so it's no coincidence that *The Actor and the Target* was first published in Russian. The Russian spirit attracts me; I don't like to talk about the 'Russian soul'. At a press conference in Moscow before the opening of *Boris Godunov* (2000) somebody asked, 'How can a foreigner understand the Russian soul?' I said, 'I absolutely agree that no foreigner can understand the Russian soul . . . but there again no Russian can either.' I was relieved when the audience agreed with loud laughter!

You started your Moscow company with Boris Godunov. *I thought the production was riveting. Why did you choose this rarely performed play?*

I think *Boris* is one of the greatest dramas of world theatre. It ranks with Shakespeare and Sophocles. What is completely phenomenal about Pushkin is that this young man suddenly starts to write, without any experience of stagecraft, this sophisticated chronicle play. There is absolutely no reason at all in the world why a poet, however brilliant, should have the stagecraft to manufacture a work like that. I think that such dramaturgy is an utterly different talent from being a poet. I guess it's like Chekhov, too. Why should a story writer have been able to write these incredible plays? *Boris Godunov* was never performed in Pushkin's lifetime; if he had gone on writing plays like that, perhaps we could have inherited a completely different Russian drama.

Some great plays have a problematic structure, like *Cymbeline* – although that may be part of its mysterious grandeur. However, Pushkin's *Boris Godunov* is as if it were written by somebody who had been working in the theatre all his life and knew exactly how to build a scene, develop the character, spring the surprise, exactly how to vary the pace, exactly when to put the comic scene in – and it was his first and last full-length play! Shakespeare was about twenty-six to twenty-eight when he was writing plays like *A Midsummer Night's Dream*; it's written like clockwork; he really knew what he was doing. Detractors might argue the play can be a little heartless but, my God, it is written by a *professional*. *A Midsummer Night's Dream* is the most brilliant piece of showmanship, and it's many other things as well. But Shakespeare had had quite an apprenticeship in a very busy theatre company.

Showmanship is one thing that Pushkin has – God knows where from. What was he reading? Which translations of literature? There was nothing to watch in the theatre that could possibly have given him that. It's what we ask about Shakespeare: 'Where did he learn that?' Yet Pushkin has an extraordinary understanding of what works theatrically, and he is able to read psychologically and delve deeply into the human soul: he just goes right in and penetrates it in a way that an audience can perceive through poetry – you know, the whole business of the ghost, the boy, Boris's soliloquies, Grishka's dreadful lies. It's just fantastic how it's written. Then there's the love scene in the fountain, which is one of the lightest, wittiest, most passionate, most beautifully written scenes ever written with its joyful, loving, terrifying tryst – all about identity and that moment of disillusion and dissolution of identity.

You said Boris Godunov *was one of the greatest tragedies. What makes it a tragedy?*

Oh, I think *Boris* is a matter of despair, and about Boris despairing. He is the man who gets everything and ruins everything for himself. He is crowned at the beginning of the play and then learns that what he got was not worth the loss of his own soul. It is a universal examination of someone hanging on to power and wondering what that power is – or was. The marvellously sophisticated thing about *Boris*, too, and this makes it endlessly relevant, is that it is about the manipulation of public opinion; about how we often like to think, when we are oppressed, that we are the simple victims of tyranny. Of course, it is much more complex than that because a tyrant can only be a tyrant with the will of people. *Boris* is very much about how tyranny has to be permitted. We don't like to think that tyranny is permitted, but I am afraid that it happens through permission.

And Pushkin explores that whole issue?

I think he's exploring the fact that even the deadliest tyrant, even Ivan the Terrible, needed public support. Even Stalin needed public support. I mean, he spent an enormous amount of time cultivating his image. The deadliest tyrant needs a cult. There can be something attractive about somebody with maximum power; perhaps they remind us of our parents when we were tiny. The powerful image makes us regress and gives us security. We don't like to look at the fact that somewhere we can find tyrants attractive.

Virtually all the male actors of Boris Godunov *perform in* Twelfth Night, *which is so different in colour, tone and cultural context. How did you work with them?*

One of our early performances in Moscow was our all-male *As You Like It*. It was hugely successful with the Moscow audiences and the Russian actors wanted one of their own! Their enthusiasm was so infectious that I said I would do *Twelfth Night*, which I had always done with women, but that I wanted to do *Three Sisters*, which I love.

They said there were forty *Three Sisters* in Moscow, and I said I didn't care. So it was a kind of swap, Chekhov for Shakespeare. The men were not used to playing women so it was hard, at times. I had no conflict with the older actors, but the younger Moscow actors often wanted to be pantomimic, and I very much did *not* want that. Anyway, I was very strict! It was my job to stay with it and keep them there; to get them to play the seriousness of the cross-dressing, the serious-ness of Malvolio and of all the seriousness in *Twelfth Night*. I like to explore a play with actors. Working like this was very intensive and they came up with something that I think was much better because it's *also* funny, but it's funny out of the dark, not funny out of circus.

Did the Russian actors bring something to Three Sisters *that was a discovery for you?*

All of my work is about what the actor brings – all sorts of things; it is difficult to describe what they are. They brought their vitality and their humanity and their warmth. We rehearsed for two weeks in the woods in log cabins; we'd sit around the fire at night, and cook shashlik, and rehearse quite hard all day long. We built it up while Nick designed it. Everybody had that experience of being together, we improvised, talked little, did exercises on the rhythms of the text as if it were verse. We investigated the rooms of the Prozorov house, the pace of life; we did a lot of work on the army of the time and on what this provincial town was like. We got one of the dancers from the Bolshoi to help the actors to waltz.

I think the key to Chekhov lies in the short stories because there he speaks with his own voice. In other words, although the stage directions are suppressed in the plays, they are copious throughout the action of the short stories. They are a firm clue to what Chekhov thought. One thing that a reading of the short stories underlines is that Chekhov never sentimentalises his characters. His characters have good points and bad points but they are never merely nice. Chekhov is scrupulous in his desire not to pass judgement. The artist's job is the clear opposite of the judge. It's tough not passing a judgement. Chekhov keeps a loving but cool eye on the world; he's the doctor with the knife.

Declan Donnellan (b. 1953)

Cheek by Jowl is not a permanent ensemble company so do you have a different way of working with them because of it?

Oh, yes, because in England we have to build an ensemble before we start to work together. We choose people very carefully, although actors are very generous people and, on the whole, they form groups remarkably well. There's normally a good cell going on from our previous work so an 'inoculation' carries over. I have very occasionally started work with a company of actors who are complete strangers. I must say I find it quite unsettling when there's no continuity of working together.

How do you get Cheek by Jowl actors to bond?

There's always the discipline. Getting people on their feet together is very important, and we do a lot of work on the verse with movement when we do a Shakespeare play. I do a lot of work with verse even when we do a Russian play. The rules should be few and good. So there are certain rules we have to start with. If it's verse you have to understand what that is and how to do that. Even when people have done verse a thousand times before, they may have to redo and redo because it's always going to slightly change. And then verse is best rediscovered through movement; it's connected through breathing and how the breath sustains the long thought, the extended thought. We do a lot of work on plastique, on the body of the actors, and how they act together; on how to wake up the sleepy body and how to understand and pay attention to every muscle and every nerve of our bodies and not just with our eyes, and how to come to an increasing awareness, which is mostly done by removing things rather than giving things. There are a few things you can give like a very few specific exercises on verse and maybe specific exercises on dance. I remember how, in *As You Like It*, for example, we built the whole thing around the tango and retained that tango until the end. When we started to rehearse *Cymbeline*, we did an Irish dance called 'The Siege of Ennis'. We never used that dance in the end, but it was a binding device that structured us through text, language, movement. It is not difficult to have a company come together when it wants to come together. Which thank God companies always do!

Do you do the movement work yourself or have a choreographer working with you?

I work very closely with Jane Gibson, my movement director, who is one of the great unsung heroes/heroines of British theatre. The Russians, interestingly, come with their own disciplines of movement, but I really depend on Jane in Britain. She helps the actors' bodies to move and to experience things in their bodies. People always think movement has to do with choreography, but choreography is just a minute aspect of it.

Speaking of movement, you directed Romeo and Juliet *with the Bolshoi ballet, which I saw at the Royal Opera House Covent Garden, in 2004. Now, what does a director* do *with a ballet?*

I discussed the choreographic text with the choreographer, Radu Poklitaru, which he invented, and talked to the dancers about the characters and the movement. I do workshops at the Bolshoi and have directed the acting in *Giselle* and *Swan Lake*, and so on, and give classes to the dancers to encourage them to remember the humanity of what they are doing on stage because it so easily gets buried underneath increasingly virtuoso technique. Dance technique now – it's almost sports. You feel that you're almost measuring how high they can jump, and the casualty of that is human contact. It's labour-intensive work. If you look at old film footage of the great old ballerinas, you see that they don't have anything like modern technique. They were often full of incredible warmth and humanity, and a lot of them wouldn't get into the chorus now.

Is it ever a problem working through an interpreter, although I know your Russian is improving, and you have said so yourself?

No, not really. It's quite an advantage because in English I often tell too many stories, so I have to keep to the point.

You also work in France. Do you use an interpreter there?

No, my French is fairly fluent, although I make sure my assistant is bilingual so that if I get tired by the end of the day, I can lapse. I get very tired; I find it hard keeping my lips pursed all day long!

What's the change for you when you work in France?

French actors do seem to be different. Although it's a Western culture, the actors are much more settled. There's less at stake, so they're not nervous that they are going to lose a job in Hollywood. It seems much more stable. French acting culture is strange, though. They work in families, so, you know, the film family is different from the theatre family. The theatre family is divided into the commercial and the private, the commercial and the subsidised, and they don't seem to mix. Even within the subsidised world, there are different groups of actors, so there's a lot of politics in French theatre and I like to keep myself entirely ignorant because I don't want particularly to know who's in which family. But I love working with French people. They give me fantastic conditions to work, and they're very enthusiastic.

You will direct [Jean] Racine's Andromaque *in Paris in November (2007) at the Bouffes du Nord, Peter Brook's theatre. You did* As You Like It *there and* Le Cid *(1998). Do you have a special link with Brook?*

I didn't meet him until I was already quite formed as a director, but before then he had been a huge influence through his work. He opened up a whole world of possibility and he had a vocabulary that released something in me. It was a great joy when I met him. I had been introduced to him a couple of times, but we kind of really clicked, I guess, when I was in my late thirties.

You said to me earlier, before we began this interview, that theatre was anti-performance. Could you elaborate on this?

I think that one of the curses of life is that we are often caught up in a performance. I think that one of the things, ironically, that theatre does is start to examine and question that 'performance' in real life and helps us see reality more clearly. And, when we see reality more clearly, we can 'perform' less. This performance in real life can be highly destructive. For example, we can end up performing ourselves; we can avoid being really present and often show things rather than experience them. In that sense, theatre, like any other art form, is anti-performance. One of the ironies in theatre is that we use a lie to tell the truth.

Chronology of selected productions

1981   *The Country Wife* by William Wycherley. Cheek by Jowl, Edinburgh Fringe Festival

1982   *Gotcha* by Barrie Keefe. Cheek by Jowl, Arenabergshouwburg, Antwerp

87

Othello by William Shakespeare. Cheek by Jowl, Fermoy Centre, King's Lynn

1983 *Vanity Fair* by William Makepeace Thackeray. Cheek by Jowl, Clockhouse Community Centre, London

1984 *Pericles* by William Shakespeare. Cheek by Jowl, Theatre Royal, Bury St Edmunds

1985 *Andromache* by Jean Racine, trans. David Bryer. Cheek by Jowl, Donmar Warehouse, London

Bent by Martin Sherman. Northcott Theatre, Exeter

A Midsummer Night's Dream by William Shakespeare. Cheek by Jowl, Northcott Theatre, Exeter

A Masked Ball by Giuseppe Verdi. Opera 80, United Kingdom

The Man of Mode by George Etherege. Cheek by Jowl, Town Hall, Hemel Hempstead

1986 *The Cid* by Pierre Corneille, trans. David Bryer. Cheek by Jowl, Seagull Theatre, Lowestoft

Romeo and Juliet by William Shakespeare. New Shakespeare Company, Regent's Park Open Air Theatre, London

1987 *Twelfth Night* by William Shakespeare. Cheek by Jowl, Liverpool Playhouse, Liverpool

Macbeth by William Shakespeare. Cheek by Jowl, Theatre Royal, York

1988 *A Family Affair* by Aleksandr Ostrovsky, in a new version by Nick Dear. Cheek by Jowl, University Theatre, Colchester

Philoctetes by Sophocles, trans. Kenneth McLeish. Cheek by Jowl, Brewhouse Theatre, Taunton

The Tempest by William Shakespeare. Cheek by Jowl, Villa Communale, Taormina, Italy

1989 *Fuenta Ovejuna* by Lopé de Vega. Royal National Theatre (NT), London

The Doctor of Honour by Pedro Calderon, trans. Roy Campbell. Cheek by Jowl, Midlands Arts Centre, Birmingham

Lady Betty by Declan Donnellan. Cheek by Jowl, Theatre Royal, Bury St Edmunds

1990 *Peer Gynt* by Henrik Ibsen, trans. Kenneth McLeish. NT, London

Declan Donnellan (b 1953)

Sara by Gotthold Lessing. Cheek by Jowl, Millington Drake Theatre, Montevideo

Hamlet by William Shakespeare. Cheek by Jowl, Theatre Royal, Bury St Edmunds

1991 As You Like It by William Shakespeare. Cheek by Jowl, Redgrave Theatre, Farnham

Big Fish. Short film, Channel 4, United Kingdom

1992 Angels in America Part One: Millennium Approaches by Tony Kushner. NT, London

1993 Angels in America Part Two: Perestroika by Tony Kushner. NT, London

The Blind Men by Michel de Ghelderode. Cheek by Jowl, Donmar Warehouse, London

Sweeney Todd by Stephen Sondheim. NT, London

Don't Fool with Love by Alfred de Musset, adapted by Declan Donnellan. Cheek by Jowl, Donmar Warehouse, London

1994 Measure for Measure by William Shakespeare. Cheek by Jowl, Arts Centre, Coventry

The Rise and Fall of the City of Mahagonny by Kurt Weill and Bertolt Brecht. English National Opera, The Coliseum, London

1995 The Duchess of Malfi by John Webster. Cheek by Jowl, Theatre Royal, Bury St Edmunds

1996 Martin Guerre by Claude-Michel Shönberg, Alain Boublil, Edward Hardy and Herbert Kretzmer. Prince Edward Theatre, London

1997 Out Cry by Tennessee Williams. Cheek by Jowl, Everyman Theatre, Cheltenham

A Winter's Tale by William Shakespeare, trans. Pyotr Gnedich. Maly Drama Theatre, St Petersburg. (In Russian.)

1998 Much Ado about Nothing by William Shakespeare. Cheek by Jowl, Everyman Theatre, Cheltenham

Le Cid by Pierre Corneille. Avignon Festival. (In French.)

1999 The School for Scandal by Richard Brinsley Sheridan. Royal Shakespeare Company, Royal Shakespeare Theatre, Stratford-upon-Avon

Antigone by Sophocles, in a new version by Declan Donnellan. The Old Vic, London

Hay Fever by Noel Coward. Savoy Theatre, London

2000 *Boris Godunov* by Alexandr Pushkin. Chekhov International Theatre Festival, Moscow. (In Russian.)

2001 *Falstaff* by Giuseppe Verdi. Salzburg Festival

Homebody/Kabul by Tony Kushner. Cheek by Jowl, The New York Theatre Workshop

2002 *King Lear* by William Shakespeare. Royal Shakespeare Academy Company, Swan Theatre, Stratford-upon-Avon

2003 *Romeo and Juliet* (ballet) by Sergei Prokofiev. Bolshoi Theatre, Moscow

Twelfth Night by William Shakespeare. Chekhov International Theatre Festival, Moscow. (In Russian.)

2004 *Othello* by William Shakespeare. Cheek by Jowl, Théâtre du Nord, Lille

The Mandate by Nikolai Erdman, adapted by Declan Donnellan. NT, London

2005 *Great Expectations* by Charles Dickens, adapted by Nicholas Ormerod and Declan Donnellan. Royal Shakespeare Company with Cheek by Jowl, Royal Shakespeare Theatre, Stratford-upon-Avon

Three Sisters by Anton Chekhov. Chekhov International Theatre Festival, Théâtre Les Gémeaux, Sceaux, Paris. (In Russian.)

2006 *The Changeling* by Thomas Middleton and William Rowley. Cheek by Jowl, Théâtre Les Gémeaux, Sceaux

2007 *Cymbeline* by William Shakespeare. Cheek by Jowl, Le Grand Théâtre de Luxembourg

Andromaque by Jean Racine. Théâtre du Nord, Lille. (In French.)

2008 *Troilus and Cressida* by William Shakespeare. Cheek by Jowl, Théâtre Les Gémaux, Sceaux

Selected bibliography

Borreca, Art (1997), '"Dramaturging" the Dialectic: Brecht, Benjamin, and Declan Donnellan's Production of *Angels in America*' in

Declan Donnellan (b. 1953)

Approaching the Millennium: Essays on Angels in America, ed. Deborah R. Geis and Steven F. Kruger, Ann Arbor: University of Michigan Press, pp. 245–60

(1996), 'Declan Donnellan and Nick Ormerod' in *In Contact with the Gods? Directors Talk Theatre*, ed. Maria M. Delgado and Paul Heritage, Manchester University Press, pp. 79–92

Donnellan, Declan (2002; 2nd edition 2005), *The Actor and the Target*, London: Nick Hern Books

Edwardes, Jane (1994), 'Directors: the New Generation' in *Contemporary British Theatre*, ed. Theodore Shank, Houndmills: Macmillan Press, pp. 206–9

Giannachi, Gabriella and Mary Luckhurst (eds.) (1999), 'Declan Donnellan' in *On Directing: Interviews with Directors*, London: Faber and Faber, pp. 19–23

Reade, Simon (1991), *Cheek by Jowl: Ten Years of Celebration*, London: Absolute Classics

Shevtsova, Maria (2005), 'Declan Donnellan' in *Fifty Key Theatre Directors*, ed. Shomit Mitter and Maria Shevtsova, London: Routledge, pp. 231–6

4   Elizabeth LeCompte (b. 1944)

Elizabeth LeCompte began her directing career with *Sakonnet Point* in 1975, forming The Wooster Group from members of The Performance Group established by Richard Schechner in New York in 1967. The latter company owned The Performing Garage at 33 Wooster Street and, when it disbanded in 1980, this building passed on to LeCompte and her collaborators, providing them with a stable rehearsal and performance space that ensured both their artistic and financial survival. In a context of uncertain income and high rents, such guaranteed security is vital for work which depends on long periods of collective devising, productions taking months and even several years, some going through various stages of work-in-progress shown to the public before they are thought to be right. For this reason, it is difficult to speak of a 'finished' Wooster Group piece – additionally so because of LeCompte's practice of fine-tuning it as it is performed and reperformed in its supposedly completed state.

Wooster Group work is fashioned from found materials introduced by everybody involved in the making process: this includes technicians, assistants and translators. Materials can be printed matter – plays, reports, documents, photographs and so on. Or else they can be audio-visual, and are not necessarily recognisable or even visible at all in the made piece. There are bits of TV programmes – for example, 'Channel J', a late-night nude chat show, in *Frank Dell's The Temptation of St Antony* (1988), to which Peter Sellars had contributed dances in early rehearsals. Videos are used in order to play off of them as lip-sync, imitation or impersonation, as happens with the video of Grotowski's *Akropolis* for *Poor Theater* (2004, discussed with LeCompte in the conversation to follow). Films are significant, like the filmed version of Richard Burton playing Hamlet live at the Lunt–Fontanne on Broadway in 1964, a performance LeCompte had seen at the time. She uses it for *Hamlet* (2006), saying she thought 'an amalgam of Richard Burton's and Scott's [Shepherd's] stage personas would be interesting' (follow-up of 29 March 2007 to the interview in this volume). She 'liked Eileen Hurley's performance', and her choice of this filmed version rather than any other had to do, equally, with the fact that 'Richard Burton's Hamlet also signalled the last time a performance of Shakespeare could be done on Broadway without a major movie star in the title role' (*ibid.*).

The Burton *Hamlet* was shown in cinemas across the United States for two days in 2000, stimulating the Group's interest in this now-available 'text'. All materials, including non-verbal ones, are, in the company's language, 'texts'. The production reconstructs from the film a hypothetical theatre performance that plays on the ambiguities of presence – the Group's abiding concern. This involves the presence of the performers in the here-and-now put up against, and even in confrontation with, the imaginary as well as the virtual, technologically mediated 'presences' they display. Like all its other works, The Wooster Group's *Hamlet* is in the presentational style that is its antidote for interpretation and representation (narrative, character, psychological motivation for action) which LeCompte, in the forefront of the mid- to late-twentieth century avant-garde, terms 'naturalism'. In this she is very much like Robert Wilson and Richard Foreman, the second being one of her collaborators in the 1980s.

Other found materials include whatever suitably falls to hand from the tapes, sets, props and costumes stored in The Performing Garage. This 'archive' plays an essential role in the aesthetics of a theatre that is 'poor' in much the same sense as Grotowski meant it: a theatre of meagre financial resources and stripped-back scenic support, but rich in its fully physicalised, performer-driven and performer-concentrated explorations and discoveries. Costumes are often recycled but adapted to a new show. Sets or set-fragments are reused. For instance, a rail that spatially separates performers, performance and audience in the 1981 *Route 1 & 9* (a division that is the antithesis of Schechner's idea of shared spectator–performer space) becomes a table-with-a-ramp in *L.S.D.* (... *Just the High Points* ...) (1984). The raised platforms and 'corridors' of *Brace Up!* (1991) return more or less intact in *Fish Story* (1994), thereby also indicating the link between these two productions. (LeCompte's original intention was to have them performed together.)

These raised platforms, which appeared as walls or floors in productions preceding *Brace Up!*, return in an elongated configuration of the latter in *To You, the Birdie! (Phèdre)* (2001). Here the spatial composition is made complex by plasma screens, sliding screens, cubicles and images of the live performers on numerous television monitors – a constant feature of Wooster Group productions – which are juxtaposed as close-ups or as body parts against their immediate image in the flesh. This layering, brought about by a multiplication of images and multiple planes and perspectives, creates the visual density typical of the Group. Similar texturing is achieved through the combination of pre-given sounds (whether taken from the tape/record 'archive' or found for the occasion), sounds recorded specifically for the show, and the sounds of words in monologues or quasi-dialogues, many uttered through microphones for added layering effect. Singing is also a source of aural layering.

The Performing Garage offers an intimacy of space – without familiarity – in which spectators can see at close quarters the artifice of construction and not the verisimilitude of life. They see, in fact, how a piece is being constructed before their very eyes and this act of seeing consequently becomes the content of spectating – in parallel, one might say, with the performers' act of making the performance. As LeCompte puts it: 'The piece is about the making of the piece, always' (quoted in Cole, 1992: 96). Yet this making, although organic in that it grows from the elements feeding into it, is anything but a matter of sequential development. It is about resolution. When asked whether she had encountered any difficulties while rehearsing *Hamlet*, LeCompte replied that it had 'many, many difficulties, many problems to solve – as in every piece. That is what the work is made of – problem solving' (conversation of 29 March 2007).

A pragmatic approach like this is not without its own problems, and no more so than when it generates ambiguities of the kind that had *Route 1 & 9* accused of racism. Here four actors in blackface had performed a comedy routine by black entertainer Pigmeat Markham, juxtaposed against Thornton Wilder's *Our Town*. Despite the Group's protestations that the work contested racial stereotypes – *Our Town*, too, was used to expose small-town prejudices – the New York State Council on the Arts heavily cut its funding. No less contentious was the Group's *L.S.D. (. . . Just the High Points . . .)*, which intermixed various texts, notably Arthur Miller's *The Crucible*, Timothy Leary's record album *L.S.D.* (1966) on the joys of psychedelic drugs, and the family nanny's recollections of the Leary household. Its collage, in which Miller's denunciation of McCarthyism was set against Leary's dismissal of strait-laced norms, and this in a range of other, alleged criticisms of society, prompted Arthur Miller to withdraw the rights for his play. But the production, together with the notoriety surrounding it, upheld the reputation The Wooster Group had already earned as a group having radical opinions behind its radical aesthetics.

Nevertheless, the 'problem solving' to which LeCompte refers concerns aesthetic decisions rather than political ones, and Ben Brantley, the *New York Times* reviewer of *Poor Theater* picks this up when he observes that the Group has been 'internationally acclaimed for performances that are designed to disorient, to undermine the reassurances traditionally offered by artful theatrical illusion' (29 September 2005). In other words, by stressing the idea that LeCompte and the Group 'are all deliberate destabilizers, inverters of conventions and rules' of artistic construction (*ibid.*), Brantley is closer to the mark regarding the Group's foremost achievement than earlier claims about the primary importance of politics in its work. Disorientation is integral to the Group's collage reworking of established texts, which go from *Our Town*, *The Crucible* and Eugene O'Neill's *The Emperor Jones* (1993), among others it has chosen from the North American canon, to Chekhov's *Three Sisters* for *Brace Up!*, Racine's *Phèdre* and Shakespeare's *Hamlet* from the European one. Paul Schmidt's translations of *Three Sisters* and *Phèdre* (discussed here by LeCompte) are, in fact, not so much translations as new versions fit for the Group's purposes – something not possible with previously existing translations, which carry the intentions and views of the translators and/or of those for whom they were done.

How The Wooster Group disorients spectators through newly oriented canonical texts varies according to production, but the company's working methods have stayed remarkably constant, regardless of its changing composition. Over the years the Group has seen various performers come and go, notably Spalding Gray, eight of whose first monologues it produced, Peyton Smith, Willem Dafoe and Ron Vawter, who died in 1994. Katy Valk has provided continuity for later collaborators Scott Shepherd, Sheena See and Ari Fliakos, while LeCompte herself is the only remaining founder of the Group. Its methods are as intricate as its presentations, embracing the methods already cited (which are hardly exhaustive) as well as choreography, dance and music. The choreographies of Martha Graham and Merce Cunningham provide to a large degree the movement scores of *To You, the Birdie! (Phèdre)*, for instance, and are played off of the originals mostly invisible to the audience, in Wooster Group fashion. *Poor Theater* hinges on William Forsythe's unique style of dance, sequences off which the Group performs with surprising virtuosity, given the technical demands on the body of Forsythe's practice.

The dancers imitated are on the monitors that the Group performers watch and copy with intense concentration, adjusting their movements to the template as they go. They do the same with other videos/films – *Akropolis*, for example, or Burton's *Hamlet* – often to comic effect. In all cases, the technicians can wind back a tape or forward it, taking the performers by surprise. Their response, in the moment of doing, energises an already hugely energetic process and has it work on impulse, spontaneity and risk, all of which keeps performances alive despite their reliance on technology and its multiple mediations, and, indeed, *because* of it.

Maria Shevtsova: Poor Theater *(2004) has a three-part structure with three main touchstones: Jerzy Grotowski, William Forsythe and a small section that refers to Max Ernst. Going through Grotowski does not seem like the most obvious choice for you. The Wooster Group's approach is not anything like his, so why did you go to his work and* *allude to his essays* [Towards a Poor Theatre, 1968] *in your title? Moreover, you use the tape of* Akropolis, *which is a 'canonical' Grotowski work.*

Elizabeth LeCompte: It probably had to do with my thinking about why I was working, what I was doing in the theatre. I was really disappointed in the way many people spoke about *To You, the Birdie!* (2001), and I think I felt I had to examine what it was that attracted me to performance at all. I'm always wondering why I even got involved in live performance. I mean, why didn't I just go straight to film? Why didn't I stay a painter or a photographer?

So I thought back on things that I'd seen, and how I got involved in the theatre, and one of the main things still very present in my mind was Grotowski, when he came to New York in 1968. I saw several of his pieces. I'm not sure any more whether I actually saw *Akropolis* [first shown in Opole in Poland, 1962], but I definitely saw *The Constant Prince* [Poland, 1965]. So I guess that's what attracted me to go back and see why Grotowski's work was still there in my mind. I never had much to do with Grotowski. I never did a workshop with him, or with [Ryszard] Cieslak or with anyone [from his group].

And you didn't follow that kind of style, either.

But I was working with Richard Schechner in The Performance Group as Assistant Director at the time, and he was very into how Grotowski worked. So I had read *Towards a Poor Theatre*, or at least parts of the book. Richard Schechner was very interested in it, and was doing a kind of training of The Performance Group that was an amalgam of his ideas and what he thought were Grotowski's. It was a kind of hybrid training. So I was aware of it and I was interested in it, but it wasn't some place that I wanted to go.

Then why did you start looking back there rather than somewhere else?

To tell you the truth, I don't know.

Well, why William Forsythe? This wasn't going back anywhere: Forsythe is the 'now'.

Well, it *was* going back, because I had come in contact with Billy when we were touring to Frankfurt in the late 1980s before the [Berlin] Wall came down, and then in the early 1990s. I did not see his work then because the company was not performing, but I occasionally watched his rehearsals. We became friends through people in the Group. I was always interested in the way he worked because it seemed similar to the way *we* worked. He was working with a company in the way that I was working with a company. He was working from ideas of improvisation that he would then score, which is similar to my way. He was interested in performers as well as dancers. Dance was his base, but he incorporated performance in his pieces. Performance was my base, but I incorporated dance. So I think I probably identified in some ways with him as an artist, and with his company. When I read in the paper that they [Ballett Frankfurt] were disbanding in 2003, I thought that I would like to do something in honour of him: in honour of him *and* us because I felt that we were also embattled as a company. Funds for us are always very low, and it's very hard to keep a company together. And I think I deeply identified with what had happened to him.

At the time, I felt people thought we were irrelevant. They said, 'Why aren't you doing things that could play to more people? Why aren't you doing things that people can understand more easily? Why aren't you doing opera?' They're always telling me I should be doing opera. I don't have the money to do opera. The only way I could do opera is to have somebody else fund it. Then, we would have to do it the way they want it done. It's like asking me to do something that I don't do and that I'm not interested in doing. So I kind of understood what was happening with Billy Forsythe. He was working in a post-modern mode. The powers that were supporting him were looking for a more conventional dramaturgy – or they were just looking for a change. I've had the same feeling – that people moved away from what we were doing; or, perhaps, they just wanted a change.

Billy thought he had a producer who was deeply sympathetic to him, and then he lost his support. We didn't ever have the kind of money that Billy had, and I think that's inherent in 'poor theatre', too. That's one of the reasons I call our show *Poor Theater*. We produce ourselves. We didn't do what many people told us to do over and over again – get a big producer, leave the Garage, have someone produce you who has bigger spaces and can get you more money.

Elizabeth LeCompte (b. 1944)

This would have completely changed your work process and your art form. What was very striking about Poor Theater *was the way you had put Grotowski and Forsythe back to back. By doing this, you suddenly showed me the connection between them, which I had not seen before. Did you become aware of this link as you were working, or did you have this insight before you started working?*

I can't say that I saw it beforehand. I didn't articulate it in words. I just kept saying, 'Let's pursue these two things next to each other and see what happens.' The way we work means we don't have to know. We don't have to write a grant application saying why these two people are important. We own the space so we can say, 'We're working on these two things, and we don't know what's gonna happen with it.' More and more, people who are in the arts have to make connections like the one you made before they work on a piece. Sometimes that makes for pretty dull work. This is one of the things that put us in a different place from Billy, who often had to know ahead what he was going to do to 'justify' it to the people he depended on.

How do you work with the Group? You're a collaborative and collective group, and you improvise a great deal. Did you improvise more, or less, on this work than on, say, To You, the Birdie! *or* The Emperor Jones?

Well, you have to be careful when you say 'improvise'. We don't improvise texts. The texts are there. They're like a guide for us. When I say 'texts', I mean both physical and written texts. Our improvisation has to do with how we combine texts. We improvise around how our physical text will meet our oral text. I'll take a piece of music, a text, and a physical thing on the TV and I'll say, 'OK, you have to do all these three things together.' The performers take all these texts and make the associations, and they take off of them. They don't make anything up on their own out of thin air. The way they combine the material is the way they make something up on their own.

You could only have this kind of composition with a group of people who know you and each other well.

Well, I did the same thing with *Rumstick Road* (1977), and I didn't know those performers all that well. No, it's just a method of working, and some people like it and really enjoy it because it involves a certain amount of giving over. You can't stay with one text. You can't say, 'I'm going to do just the written text.' You have to be multifaceted. You have to have an idea of a physical world that you want to inhabit and an oral world, and dance all of it together. It usually takes a very particular kind of performer.

How long do you let the performers run with, say, a line or a TV image before you might say, 'You've gone too far'?

Ten seconds.

In other words, what I'm beginning to ask you is this: How do you work as a director in relation to this kind of improvisatory process?

I say, 'That worked.' After ten seconds I can see whether it works or not. Then I structure another task on top of that, which will take it someplace that I'm thinking of because they showed it to me. Like, they'll do something and I'll go, 'Ooh, that works.' I usually can tell very quickly whether it does or not. So then they'll go again with a new set of tasks, and then ten seconds later I'll go, 'Ooh, that works', and then restructure it again.

Do you video all this so that you can remember what worked and what didn't?

Yes. If something worked, and I go back and say, 'You lost what you had ten minutes ago', we can go to the camera and see what it was.

The fact that you layer in material, all along, as you prepare your work might suggest why so much of that extensive layering stays in when it is finished and shown to audiences. Am I right?

That's right. I'm sure it stays because we're able to videotape it and reproduce it, which we do in a lot of the pieces. We'll make a huge mistake, like I'll give them something to improvise off of the TV, the text, and some way of dancing, or some costume element that hinders them in some way. They'll do it, and they'll make a mistake. Something will go wrong: the tape will go fast forward by mistake and they'll all be stunned, and they won't know what to do, and they'll pick it up somewhere else. I have it taped on video, and we can go back and then reproduce the mistake if we want to use it. This is something you could never imagine getting any other way.

Elizabeth LeCompte (b. 1944)

Did you take part of the Akropolis *tape to start with for* Poor Theater, *or did you start with something from the TV, like a contemporary soap opera?*

The specific task for that piece was to try to reproduce the film in our space. And as they worked on it, I would go, 'We have to try something else. It doesn't work, it doesn't work.' We'd try something else each time until we came to something that, for me, felt like 'Oh, that's the closest I'll come.'

It's really difficult, this task, isn't it, because you're asking them to . . .

Fail.

Well, are you asking them to imitate without incarnating whatever they are doing? Asking them to be it and not be it, at the same time?

Well, no, because I think they naturally *do* fill it, although they start by imitating. In *Poor Theater*, they started by imitating. As they got more and more familiar with the Polish language, the physical tasks and with the meaning of the text, they filled it – slowly. Now, mind you, the question for me was always: Did they fill it beside the original text? And what would the piece be if you took that text away?

Have you tried it?

Oh, sure, we did it. It was uninteresting because it had no cultural relevance for me. I needed Grotowski's dialogue.

And you needed that cultural resonance?

Yes, for this particular piece. Now, it's not true for something like *To You, the Birdie!*, where Katie [Valk] did some massive improvisations on Merce Cunningham and Martha Graham. I didn't need to see the originals on what she was doing. What she was doing was beautiful, whereas, with Grotowski, I did have to see the original probably because I never really related to Grotowski's work as such. I loved seeing *Akropolis*. I thought the piece was just brilliant – and I thought the performance was brilliant – but I didn't relate to it deeply. I related very much to his idea of a company, and the work structure of a company.

Grotowski's work was extremely physical, which is why the back to back with Forsythe is so startling. Suddenly you see just how

Fig 4 *Poor Theater* (2004). Directed by Elizabeth LeCompte. Pictured (l–r): Sheena See, Kate Valk, Geoff Abbas (on video monitor), Ari Fliakos, Reid Farrington (on video monitor), Scott Shepherd. Photograph by Paula Court

much precise technique was involved in what Grotowski did. Do you do as much physical work with your own group?

Well, Billy has ballet to start with and Grotowski had the systems of training that he developed. We don't have that. We do a lot of physical work, but it tends to come out of the piece we're working on at any particular time. Right now, we're doing a lot of physical work around sword fighting and learning the language of sword fighting. We're doing it because it's at the root of part of *Hamlet*, which we're working on now. For *To You, the Birdie!* we got very involved in badminton. It became extremely heavy training. I think that some of the heaviest training we've ever done has been badminton. We had an Olympics badminton trainer, Chi-Bing Wu – a wonderful man. He trained us for two years. He still comes in occasionally to give us a training session. It was tough. Everybody did it. We would train with him once a week for three or four hours, and then every day we would do three or four hours of it.

Did the same apply to mastering the Forsythe material? Did you have the dancers come in to teach you?

Oh, yes, every day, for three hours, at least. But we're not doing his stuff. If we were really doing it, we would have to have trained for ten years.

You're doing Wooster Forsythe stuff.

Yes, but it was extremely difficult. We started before we did *Poor Theater*. At first I just said, 'Well, let's just do stuff like Billy. Let's just imitate him and see what happens.' I wasn't thinking that we would ever learn to dance. I didn't care that much. I just knew that there were certain signs that made a Billy piece. My strategy was: If somebody put a gun to my head and said, 'Do a Billy piece now, or you're gonna die', what would I do? So every day I would say, 'There's a gun to my head, unless you do a Billy piece, I'm gonna die.' So the actors would do what they could, and they got more interested in it. They started watching things. People came down from Billy's company and helped us, and we got kind of into it, the way we did with Polish. We studied Polish the same way. Like, 'OK, put a gun to my head, you have to speak Polish.' So they tried, and did their best, but then they got interested. We all got interested in Polish.

After imitating the Polish we heard in *Akropolis* for a long time, we finally brought in a Polish teacher, Zenon Kruszelnicki, an actor and director who had worked at Grotowski's Laboratory Theatre in Poland. We got into the structure of the language, and actually several of the performers learned to speak Polish. I could have done the Grotowski section in some kind of gibberish. It wasn't about the Polish, per se. In *Poor Theater*, it's not about the Polish language, or about the Forsythe technique, for that matter. It's about the juxtaposition of these ideas – 'Grotowski' and 'Forsythe'.

If you had done it in gibberish, it wouldn't have been half as interesting.

You don't know. It may have gone in a different direction. It would have been different.

Look at it this way: the fact that they were doing it in Polish added another dimension. It was like perspectives in painting; you had more perspectives on the work with them speaking Polish. I was amazed by how good their Polish was and how fast they were using it. It takes mastery to get a language at that speed.

They worked really hard. They liked it. It was the same as studying badminton, only they were doing it with their mouths. It was like an athletic thing with their mouths because they had to learn how to reorient their tongue. It was the same with badminton. They had to learn how to go against all their natural instincts about how to approach certain badminton moves. It took a year, two years, before they would naturally make the right trajectory with their racket. It was the same thing with the tongue, so I just saw it as the same.

Where did the badminton idea come from for Phèdre, *of all things [the basis of* To You, the Birdie!]? *Racine's text does not have a badminton image to work from.*

I had several new performers who I hadn't worked with before, and I always look for some kind of a physical theatre language that links everybody so that they are, in some way, in the same world, physically as well as verbally or orally. We didn't have a link because we had so many different kinds of performers. Some people were comfortable just standing on the stage, others kept having to wave their arms. I saw everything you normally see when you go to a theatre. I saw a lot of people with a lot of different kinds of training, and no one thing linking them to make one world. Usually I go to something outside all the performers that they all have to come to. So we started with table tennis just to try to link people to a task where they had to make the same moves, and I could see how their bodies were making these moves. I also needed to see how they attacked that task so I could get some sense of how to work with them. Some would be all about how good their stroke looked. Others were about winning the game. Each approach made a different thing on their bodies. I would get to know them by watching that, and I would have a sense of what task to give them to bring them into the world together.

Then I went on to badminton because it was so much more physical; it was more interesting to watch on the stage. We worked out of that to Merce Cunningham and the Marx Brothers and their different films. All these different kinds of performers would look at a Marx Brothers move and they'd do the same move. So at least I had that unity. They didn't have the same way of doing it, but they were doing a move that was similar. It's just a way of bringing everybody into the same space. Billy has a base line with ballet. I don't have it, so I had to find something else.

It's like having some sort of common sign system.

Yes, exactly. They all have that to begin with, so they move from there to something else. We discovered a few months in that the French court had actually played it.

Yes, jeu de paume. I don't remember any Marx Brothers being screened during To You, the Birdie!

Oh, you don't see it. It's only there for the performers: they're improvising off of it.

Do you mean that it's playing, but the audience can't see it, only the performers can?

Yes. There are TVs on the sides in the wings and on the sides of the stage and up above, which the audience can't see. Well, they can if they really look: if you're sitting very house right or house left, you can see the stage right or stage left TV, and you can see those images.

Is that why you use so much technology? The whole aesthetic requires this process of imitation, which technology secures?

Well, it's a system for co-ordination. I don't even think of imitation because sometimes we just use it where the TV will go 'Flash', and that means there's a change of something. We use it as a kind of sign system, as well.

Apart from that, what else is the purpose of all this machinery?

To bring everyone into the same space together. It also brings in outside influences. I think this is what Billy does. He doesn't want everyone to go immediately to the training that they've had in ballet. Something coming from outside puts them off of their routine. It's a conversation with something that you can't control. This means it gives a certain kind of immediacy to the performance, which you only get from taking impulses off of something that you're not controlling.

Does that mean that each performance changes quite radically from night to night?

The structure doesn't necessarily change, but the way the performers relate to it does. I think the actors try to get that immediately by saying, 'You take the impulse off of the other actor.' Then the actor doesn't give you the same cue back that he or she gave you the past fifty nights! A lot of times you are routinised, and you just give the same thing back, no matter what. You have to break that routine every night to stay totally alive and, at the same time, be able to repeat the same thing. You have to stay very alive in the present.

What about the paradox of the immediacy of the performer and the repetition of the image. Or does the tape change?

Yes, it does. All the time. The technicians can improvise and put up whatever they want, so every night the tape is different.

Was the tape very different every night for To You, the Birdie!*?*

The tape was the same for certain sections, and different for others. For example, there would be a section of the Merce Cunningham dance that Ari [Fliakos] would be following, and the technical people could throw in a cheerleader from MTV, a music thing, in the middle of it. He would have to stay on his track but incorporate that new bit, and go on. They would try to fool him.

That's an obstacle race!

Well, they like it. It's more like when jazz musicians are improvising. They have a structure, a really clear structure. Then another musician will take a turn, and they have to go with it. If they know their world and understand it, it's a very exciting way of performing. But you have to think of it as music.

Yes, of course. When you think of it as music, you also think of it as the dynamics of the process. You're scoring it, but you're scoring it with the living moments. Now, what about the use of technology as a distancing device? We have been talking so far about its 'aliveness'.

Well, I don't use it like that because, for me, it's very live. It's just different. It's not the same live as 'live' live, but, for me, it's live.

There were a lot of split images in To You, the Birdie! *There were screens; there were plasma sheets – semi-opaque sheets where you saw and didn't see the action. What were the purpose and challenge of using them?*

Well, a lot of that just has to do with beauty. I like the look of it. Things like that are simple. I like playing with special volume and playing with it so as to bring it up to a flat, picture surface. TV can do that, you know: it can suddenly make a flat surface and then, all of a sudden, it's a three-dimensional surface. It's something that painters can't do; and film-makers can't do it. It's something I can do in the theatre.

I was reading about your earlier work, and what really struck me was the fact that you were constantly readjusting the space, like an architect might. You've got up space, down space, short space, and you place your audience differently – and that's the connecting link with Grotowski.

That's interesting.

Playing with space – among other things – is exactly what he did.

And he played with how you looked at it. I don't actually enjoy the rehearsals until I have the space. You know, rehearsals before that to me are just a muddle; I don't know what is happening. I do them, but, until I have the space, I don't really engage deeply with the text.

What about the relationship of your performance to the spectator?

Frontal.

The actors frequently address the spectators. That's a frontal address as well.

Well, only if the text allows that. For instance, even though Katie and Sheena [See] spoke towards the audience, they weren't really speaking to the audience. I'm not really that interested in the audience seeing it from a different place, because I adjust what they see over the whole picture, playing so carefully that, if you are on the side, you wouldn't see. Because so much about what I am doing with the text has to do with the space, I like to control how you see it.

That's the painter in you.

Yeah, absolutely. And the photographer.

Isn't the relationship to the spectator partly why you do several versions of the work? I think your term is 'run'. How many runs did you have for Poor Theater, *for example?*

Four runs [November–December 2003; February–April 2004; November–December 2004; September–October 2005].

Do you readjust the work in response to how the audience reacts?

Oh, yeah.

Does the work shift a lot in terms of its interaction with spectators?

Well, it does depend on the piece a lot. For *Poor Theater*, I had decided to take audience suggestions. So, every night, we'd take the suggestion box. We'd give them paper to write on and, in the next day's rehearsal, the first part would address what they had written; and, if they had complaints, then we would try to fix it according to what the complaints were. I never did that before, but it was a lot of fun. So the audience that didn't like the piece kind of made it happen. I would try not to judge, you know, and say, 'Well, I wasn't trying to do that.' I'd try to go, 'Well, that's interesting' and, 'If I were to do that, what would happen?'

You're remarkably open as a director then, aren't you?

Well, I have the ability to be open because nobody said, 'You have to produce this.' I think anybody would be like me if they didn't have to produce something on a certain schedule and to a certain idea that is prewritten.

Do you show sections of your work to the public before you put it on as a production? Do you have open rehearsals?

Elizabeth LeCompte (b. 1944)

I usually show a section that we've been working on, but I wouldn't call them open rehearsals. I don't speak in them. I don't go out and do what I do in a rehearsal. It's a showing of something we've been working on. With something like *L.S.D.* (1982) – we just showed *The Crucible* section without all the rest of it. I'll show a section that hasn't been integrated into the whole piece, and just ask the audience to understand that this isn't the whole piece; this is only a section of it.

This leads me into questions I wanted to ask you about 'text'. Why did you use The Crucible *for* L.S.D. *(. . . Just the High Points . . .)?*

Well it's hard, really, to remember that far back, but I do know that I had some issues with people about using Kate passing as a black woman on the phone and using blackface in one section of *Route 1 & 9*. And I was just concerned about why that was so disturbing, and what made it so disturbing. I was working at the same time on a record interpretation of an LP by Timothy Leary. That led me to Timothy Leary's babysitter, who, we knew, was a writer in New York, to tell us about those days outside Boston. She said that she was there, baby-sitting, when the Learys went to a play. I think she mentioned that they'd gone to see *The Crucible* in Boston. So I guess I thought of that, and I remembered that Miller had written a black character. He was a white man writing a black character, and we'd been told over and over again that we weren't allowed to do a black character: it was not right; it was hurtful and it was somehow racist – in effect, if not in intent. I was curious about that, so I wanted to see the trial scene with Katie playing Tituba, a black character. Katie also played one of the young girls, but she didn't take off her makeup. So she was two black characters. We had no trouble at all with that. The only problem we had was that people would say, 'Why couldn't you get a black actress to do that?' Then I would have to explain that we didn't cast out, that this was a company and, if we didn't have that persona in there, we would try to do it; that's what theatre was. So I found that I was trying to explain theatre when I was trying to explain racial politics in theatre, which was interesting to me.

It is interesting. Did you somehow connect LSD with repression?

I didn't until after. The two things came together fortuitously.

You have used quite a lot of North American classics: You used Our Town *by Thornton Wilder,* The Emperor Jones *by Eugene O'Neill,* The Hairy Ape *by O'Neill, and T. S. Eliot. Is it because the Americans were saying something to you about America? I mean, how strong was the sense of cultural roots in your work?*

I tend to look around and see what's in front of me because I also have that luxury. I don't have to cast out and go and find things. It's always that someone wants to do something. Spalding Gray was very interested in the O'Neill and T. S. Eliot and in *Our Town,* so I kind of hired him on those and just said, 'OK'. I didn't have a theatre training, so I didn't have a background in these texts, and he did. They were all new for me. I remember *The Crucible* being done in high school, so my connection to that was different from the *Our Town* connection. But, you know, pieces like the Flaubert one [*La Tentation de Saint Antoine,* used for *Frank Dell's The Temptation of St Antony* on which work started in 1985] – it was Peter Sellars who wanted to do it and he said he'd give us money and would be able to help us out. It was wonderful in the early days, in the middle 1980s: he helped us tremendously. He was interested in that text because we were going to collaborate on a piece, but, of course, he didn't have the time or the patience. He's not as patient as I am; he thinks a lot faster. He came in and did some dances that I later incorporated into the piece. I took a long time to make it because I was so distant from it: it's Catholic, it's French, it's translated. But I enjoyed it immensely, and it took us in a new direction because I went on to another translation after that, which was Chekhov [*Three Sisters* used by LeCompte for *Brace Up!* (1991)]. Ron Vawter thought of the Chekhov text, as I recall, and so we started reading it in various translations. [LeCompte was not taken with any of them.]

Chekhov is a very particular universe and very alien, I would have thought, from yours in New York. How alien was Three Sisters *to you when you started working with it?*

Not at all. We found Paul Schmidt right away, who is a friend of ours. He came down with his translation, which hadn't been published yet. We read it and it was just so close to me that I loved it immediately. I just reverberated to everything that was spoken. I just loved listening to the words. I still think it's one of the most beautiful texts I've ever read.

Why did you call your production Brace Up!*?*

Well, I couldn't believe we were actually going to do a text because I'd never done a full text before. At the very beginning we worked a lot with Japanese forms that didn't necessarily have to do with Chekhov, and we were making a little Japanese documentary about a Geinin theatre troupe at the same time as we were working on *Three Sisters*. I called the project *Brace Up!* because I started with the Japanese theatre forms first. Then the Chekhov came into that project, and it kind of stuck. I never thought we'd be able to do Chekhov. We didn't have enough people; we only had four people and it was a huge cast, but slowly things accumulated and people came in, and then Paul played a role and translated it and a lot of the technical people took over roles. So, gradually, I just staged the piece more completely than I expected I would.

I didn't know Masha was the main role. I mean, I didn't know much about theatre so I thought all three sisters were equally important. People were coming and saying 'Who is playing Masha?' and I'd go, 'Why are they asking that?' The woman playing Masha couldn't always be there and it was just too hard to rehearse without her, so I cut two, three pages out, in the second Act. I cut a couple of tiny sections here and there, but basically nothing until the end. I didn't finish the piece. I got to where Vershinin comes up to say goodbye, and then we stopped the piece there. I didn't finish the piece until *Fish Story* (1994) [after *The Emperor Jones*]. *Fish Story* was just the last Act of *Three Sisters*.

So you used three and a half Acts for Brace Up!*, and the last half of Act IV in* Fish Story*. What was* Fish Story *about?*

It was a culmination and a combination of all the work we'd done on this Japanese Geinin theatre company [Sentaro Ichikawa Troupe] and theatre in Japan. There was a documentary that we found about it at the Japan Foundation Film Library. So people in the company took on the personae from this documentary. Geinin is a kind of popular theatre, although its practice comes from Kabuki and Noh – you can see all of that in it. They'd go from theatre to theatre. It was like a travelling theatre company in the sense, maybe, of troubadours. I went to see a Geinin troupe about fifteen years ago, but they were one of the few that were left. It may survive outside of Tokyo in smaller places. So we enacted pieces from the documentary where the Geinin are preparing a performance to show in the hotel: they live in a hotel because, in the end, the Geinin troupes didn't have theatres. Hotels would hire them, and they'd come and do their performances for tourists. The conceit of *Fish Story* is that this troupe of Japanese, which is actually The Wooster Group, are performing their version of Chekhov.

The reason it's *Fish Story* is because they spend quite a bit of time in the documentary talking about fishing and bringing the fish home, and how symbolic the fish is. So that becomes the metaphor for making the piece, in a way. It toured to Europe. We're definitely going to revive it. It's very difficult to do because it has a dance structure. The Japanese dances in it are extremely difficult, and all the [Wooster] performers are tied down. They have apparatuses around their waists that are attached to their heels, and they can't stand up straight. They have to perform like that to keep them low and on the same level, without training them for twenty years. It was a method for us to get a Japanese stance and be able to do these very low Japanese dances.

Well, there's another answer to my question about technology. Actually you use technology not for any highfalutin' reasons, but for very practical, technical purposes.

Yes. I have to say that *Fish Story* was a success, here, in America. It was just the Europeans who didn't like it. But we didn't have a larger theatre at the time, so we only played to eighty or ninety people a night; and we had a relatively short run. It's a wonderful piece. It's just expensive, it takes a big staff. It has a lot of the same people who were in *Brace Up!* because of the same characters.

How did you work with your actors for Brace Up!?

Well, I had Katie as the interlocutor. I thought of it as a silent film, say, a Japanese silent film, and that Katie was explaining the story and playing all the characters. So whenever we didn't have a character there, Katie would just take on the voice and do it.

How did you start working with the text? Did you sit around reading it? Did you discuss it?

Elizabeth LeCompte (b. 1944)

Well, yes, at the very beginning, because we had to choose a translation. So we spent a week choosing the text, but once we got the text we just went downstairs and put it up on the stage immediately. I knew right away that Paul would play the doctor because he was going to have to be on video because he wouldn't be there all the time. And he was the translator, so it made sense for him to be the doctor.

Did you ever stop and ask him about what words meant, or how they sounded in Russian, or why he had translated in a particular way?

Katie did within the piece. She would ask him: that [asking] was part of her persona. She would say, 'I don't like the way that sounds.' That's how we developed the translation. He retranslated it, as we were working, to make it work.

On what criteria would he change something?

I don't know, really. I think he would listen to the performer, sometimes, and say, 'The performer wouldn't say it like that.' Sometimes he would listen to the text itself and say, 'Oh, it's not playing right.' I think it was just an ideal way for him to work to complete the translation.

I presume you said Katie's 'persona' because you don't have characters in the traditional sense of the term? You don't interpret texts.

I guess not. On the most basic level, I try to put the play on its feet, so to speak, with whatever I have available. I think that the text says everything that the character has to say. If you inhabit the text fully and do it as a task fully, you can't help but inhabit the character. The character, for me, in theatre is the text and the persona of the person, and if the person isn't truly connected to the text on some level that's beyond the analytical, then it's probably not going to read.

When you say 'inhabit the character' are you referring to a Stanislavskian idea about the biography of a character? Do you ask questions like 'Do the sisters remember their father's funeral?' 'What was life like back then, when he was alive?'

I didn't know much about Stanislavsky, so I got a hold of some of his notes from a production in Germany, and I tried to follow them to see how he was analysing it. I don't think it's easy to say, when you cross cultures and languages like that, 'This is what motivates someone.' At least, it isn't for me because I think everything's a translation, even emotion. Emotional ideas about what motivates character is a translation. So, no, I didn't try to say to the performers, 'What did Chekhov's character "do" '? 'Why did that person do this?' I tried to understand from the text what it seemed like the person was doing. Was the person near or far away? Was the person thinking or saying? Was the person in conversation, or was it rhetorical? You know, pragmatic things like that.

You weren't looking for the 'subtext'?

Well, the subtext is in the performance. I don't need a subtext if the text is good. You need a subtext if there's no text. If the text is that good, the subtext is there naturally with the performance.

What about Phèdre? *You move from Chekhov to a seventeenth-century text and to Racine, of all people.*

Well, Paul [Schmidt] talked with us a lot about doing another piece, and he wrote several things for us. One of them was *Phèdre*. When I first read it, I didn't see anything in it for us, so we put it away in a drawer. His translation was specifically for us, for The Wooster Group. Paul took out a whole lot of characters, and he got rid of the rhyme. He really changed it a lot more than he did in his translation of Chekhov. We came to *Phèdre* because Paul was very sick, and we wanted to do something that just made us think about him, so we started working on it, as he was dying.

It's a kind of tribute, isn't it?

Yeah, because a lot of it had to do with my trying to imagine what character he wanted to be and how he was identifying with it. I think he wanted to be Phèdre. So I thought of Katie as both a man and a woman. I thought that her voice would have to be bigger than just a female character. It would have to be a metacharacter, of sorts. Scott [Shepherd] did quite a lot of the lines for almost every character except the nurse [Oenone]. She did all her own.

What was the point of doing it like that, with one person speaking almost all the lines?

I think to take that metacharacter out of the realm of naturalism into something else that felt closer to what the text was about for me than turning it into a kind of soap opera.

Racine's text is very formal. Was this a way of formalising it?

The way Paul Schmidt writes the text *isn't* very formal, but it was a way for *me* to formalise it. The original is very formal, but Paul's text is very conversational, and I needed a way to take it out of that. I didn't like that conversational quality because, when we did it like that, it just seemed like doing *Hamlet* as if Hamlet was an adolescent boy at a prep school. It might be an interesting way into certain parts of Shakespeare, but, somewhere, you have to know that Hamlet was supposed to be a prince. I guess I was trying to find something about the French court and what it might have been like. You know, that kind of formality, that way of behaving. I didn't want to bring it to us. I wanted to go to them.

Do you mean that you didn't want to make it contemporary?

When we were doing it as a contemporary piece, it seemed trivial to me because you couldn't understand why it was happening. I had to keep the formality somehow, to say 'These people aren't real.' I mean, we don't know them any more. They're far away. They're distant beings.

Is this partly why you had the badminton game going through the production so much? Was that also a way of formalising the piece – and distancing it?

No, I think that was to give it a structure.

And what about those perpetual enemas? Was that a central metaphor?

I did quite a bit of research, with everybody around, about what people did at the time – what the king and queen did, and they did do a lot of emetics. That kind of purging was a huge thing in France. So I thought that was a way for us to do something pretty violent. It was also a way of poisoning yourself, of committing suicide, too.

[Kate Valk comes into the room and hears the last bit of the dialogue.]

Kate Valk: There wasn't a central metaphor for you, just, 'asshole'?

Elizabeth LeCompte: No, no. Just asshole. As a portal. Asshole rather than the vagina. I was thinking of that because I was thinking of what Paul was going through. Paul was Catholic and he was always struggling with his homosexuality and certain ideas about who he was.

I guess I was trying to come as close as I could to him. And, again, he wanted Katie to be Phèdre.

Kate Valk: Well, also it's all the whole sado thing about ass-fucking and taking it up the ass. And that relationship to sex and sexual compulsion – like plenty of women and other characters in de Sade. I mean, the same impulses would be toilets that run, you know, and they could take a shit wherever they wanted.

Elizabeth LeCompte: Like Marie-Antoinette taking a shit under the staircase at Versailles.

Were there any theatre-makers you were particularly interested in when you left painting for the theatre?

Very early on, mostly performances from television. But, over that time [during the 1960s], I saw a couple of pieces by the Living Theatre – *Frankenstein* – and I saw The Performance Group's *Dionysus in '69* [directed by Richard Schechner], and I was very interested in them. Not too long after that I saw a number of Robert Wilson's early pieces at the Brooklyn Academy, which was huge for me. I saw the original *Deafman Glance*. And the dancers that I used to go see – Balanchine, early Cunningham, Grand Union and Meredith Monk.

Did you then, and do you now, think of your work as political?

Well, that's hard because everyone sees politics in a different way. And I guess politics are in The Wooster Group pieces. I don't think of myself as political in the sense that I'm a 'doctrine' director, or that I have an agenda. I'm really just trying to examine what my place is in the world, really. I get pretty political about it, as a woman. I'm just aware very personally of who I am in the world, and I think that this very fundamental kind of politics is in all the pieces. All the pieces are obviously going to be made by a woman, and from a woman's point of view.

Do you find that more attention goes to men directors than to women directors?

Yeah, but I think I grew up with that and I've accepted it – not happily, but I've accepted it. Hopefully, the next generation of women is doing better than my generation. I'm not saying that the pieces are saying, 'Look, women are in terrible positions.' I'm trying to be as honest as I can, and come from who I am and what I see. I feel that this is political because there are really so few female voices in the theatre in that way. I don't think people have really seen it very much because I often put a man in a very large role as well as a woman, and people can be very literal about that. They think, 'Oh, she's a female director. It must be about the man.' So I think people have sometimes missed that the heart of what comes from the pieces is very female.

Chronology of selected productions

This chronology does not list the productions shown in multiple forms as work-in-progress, parts or occasional open rehearsals, as is typical of The Wooster Group. The dates below indicate the first performance of a 'completed' work at The Performing Garage in New York City unless otherwise noted.

1975   *Sakonnet Point*
1977   *Rumstick Road*
1978   *Nayatt School*
        Three Places in Rhode Island (*Saskonnet Point*, *Rumstick Road* and *Nayatt School*). Mickery Theatre, Amsterdam
1980   *Point Judith*. The Envelope, New York City
1981   *Hula* (performed under the alias 'Ray Whitfield and the Johnsons')
        Route 1 & 9
1982   *For the Good Times*. Danspace, New York City
1983   *North Atlantic*. Globe Theatre, Eindhoven, Holland
1984   *L.S.D. (. . . Just the High Points . . .)*. First performance of all four parts in Boston, Massachusets
        L.S.D. (. . . Just the High Points . . .) (with new version of Part II)
1985   *Miss Universal Happiness* (a collaboration with Richard Foreman and The Ontological-Hysteric Theater)
1988   *Symphony of Rats* (a collaboration with Richard Foreman and The Ontological-Hysteric Theater)
        Frank Dell's The Temptation of St Antony
1991   *Brace Up!*
1993   *The Emperor Jones*
1994   *Fish Story*

1996   *The Hairy Ape*
1998   *House/Lights*
2001   *To You, the Birdie! (Phèdre)*
2004   *Poor Theater*
2006   *Hamlet*. Festival Grec, Institut de Cultura, Barcelona
        Who's Your Dada ?! The Museum of Modern Art, New York
2007   *La Didone*. Kaai Theatre, Brussels

Video-film

1986   *Flaubert Dreams of Travel but the Illness of his Mother Prevents It* with Ken Kobland
1987   *Wrong Guys* (film – in progress)
1992   *White Homeland Commando* written for the company by Michael Kirby
1994   *Rhyme 'em to Death*
1999   *The Emperor Jones* with Chris Kondek
2004   *House/Lights* (DVD)

Selected bibliography

Aronson, Arnold (1985), 'The Wooster Group's *L.S.D. (. . . Just the High Points!)*', *The Drama Review* 29:2, 65–77

Arratia, Euridice (1992), 'Island Hopping: Rehearsing the Wooster Group's *Brace Up!*', *The Drama Review* 36:4, 121–42

Callens, Johan (ed.) (2005), *The Wooster Group and its Traditions*. New York: Peter Lang

Cole, Susan Letzler (1992), 'Elizabeth LeCompte Directs *Frank Dell's The Temptation of Saint Antony*' in *Directors in Rehearsal: A Hidden World*, London and New York: Routledge, pp. 91–123

Dunkelberg, Kermit (2005), 'Confrontation, Stimulation, Admiration: The Wooster Group's *Poor Theater*', *The Drama Review* 49:3, 43–57

Gray, Spalding and Elizabeth, LeCompte (1978), 'Rumstick Road', *Performing Arts Journal* 3:2, 92–115

Klaver, Elizabeth (2000), 'Scenes from the Popular Culture Debate: The Wooster Group's *Route 1 & 9* (The Last Act)', *Essays in Theatre* 19:1, 21–32

Knowles, Ric (2000), 'The Wooster Group: *House/Lights*, Landscapes and the Politics of Nostalgia', *Essays in Theatre* 19:1, 33–43

LeCompte, Elizabeth (1978), 'An Introduction', *Performing Arts Journal* 3:2, 81–6

(1979), 'Who Owns History', *Performing Arts Journal* 4:1, 50–3

(1985), 'The Wooster Group Dances: from the Notebooks of Elizabeth LeCompte', *The Drama Review* 29:2, 78–93

Marranca, Bonnie (2003), 'The Wooster Group: a Dictionary of Ideas', *Performing Arts Journal* 25:2, 1–18

Mee, Susie (1992), 'Chekhov's *Three Sisters* and The Wooster Group's *Brace Up!*', *The Drama Review* 36:4, 143–53

Quick, Andrew (2007), *The Wooster Group Work Book*. London: Routledge

Savran, David (1985), 'The Wooster Group, Arthur Miller and *The Crucible*', *The Drama Review*, Fall 1985 29:2, 99–109

(1988), *The Wooster Group, 1975–1985: Breaking the Rules*, New York: Theatre Communications Group

(2005), 'The Death of the Avantgarde', *The Drama Review* 49:3, 10–42

Schmidt, Paul (1992), 'The Sounds of *Brace Up!* And the Wooster Group's Staging of *Three Sisters*: Translating the Music of Chekhov', *The Drama Review* 36:4, 154–7

The Wooster Group (1996) '*Frank Dell's The Temptation of St Antony*' in *Plays for the End of the Century*, ed. Bonnie Marranca, Baltimore: Johns Hopkins University Press, pp. 261–314

5   Robert Lepage (b. 1957)

Among leading directors today, it is Robert Lepage – sometimes labelled as 'the alchemist of modern imagistic theatre'[1] – who best exemplifies the convergence of live theatrical performance with contemporary media and technology. In addition to the extensive use of video (sometimes on multiple screens, as in *Elsinore*, 1995), action-painting with light, or surrounding the actor with post-industrial mechanisms, flexible machinery and even robots (*Zulu Time*, 1999), he has also explored the cinematic structuring of dramatic material. Even the name of his Quebec theatre company, Ex Machina, implicitly ascribes creative powers to technology itself – referring to 'the god in the machine' of Greek comedy – thus putting technology front and centre: specifically the cutting-edge interactive technology of Softimage computer animation, CD Rom and 3-D TV. And notably Lepage has directed rock shows for Peter Gabriel (1993, 2002), as well as a striking multimedia and fully mechanised show for Cirque du Soleil in Las Vegas (2004). Coming from a bilingual society, Lepage's work uses multiple languages, extending beyond words; and language remains a major theme, extending to a piece like *Lipsynch* (2007) where voices exist independent of speakers, reproduced in the technological world represented by filmed background on the stage. As he has said: 'Everything begins with a text. But I find myself more than ever returning to the idea of the theatre as a meeting place for architecture, music, dance, literature, acrobatics,

[1] *Guardian*, 23 June 2001.

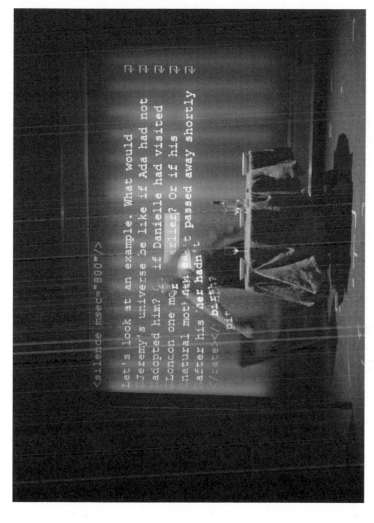

Fig 5 *Lipsynch* (2007). Directed by Robert Lepage. Photograph by Eric Labbé

play, and so on.'[2] In Lepage's terms, traditional theatre is 'vertical', translating physical existence to a 'higher' mental or spiritual realm. By contrast, in order to speak to modern ways of perceiving the world the new theatre has 'to become horizontal'. Since today's society has a film education, theatre must 'use the capacity of an audience to read things in fast-forward, jump cuts ... People have a new language, and it's not all linear.'[3]

Despite such commitment to popular performance, Lepage deliberately defines himself as an outsider in personal and geographical terms (specifically as a gay artist in a predominantly heterosexual culture, as a Francophone separatist and a Quebecois voice in an Anglo-dominated nation, and in opposition even to that as a voice speaking largely from outside the Province, indeed increasingly from outside Canada, and in a combination of languages). He also defines himself as an outsider in artistic terms. So, while backed by his own company of longstanding artistic collaborators, in his most identifiable productions he explicitly presents himself as a completely self-sufficient performer, an *auteur*, combining the functions of director, designer, lighting-engineer, lead actor and even dramatist.

At the same time, he is clearly linked with the international avant-garde of Peter Brook, Robert Wilson and Ariane Mnouchkine, all of whom he refers to often, and with admiration. Frequently compared to Brook (for instance by the London critic Irving Wardle, on first seeing *The Dragons' Trilogy* in 1986, or by Peter Gabriel),[4] Lepage's aim – like Brook's – is to evolve a radically non-traditional form of theatre; and the choreographed mime in *Geometry of Miracles* was explicitly based on 'dance-movements' created by Gurdjieff, whom Brook acknowledged as his own spiritual guru. Like Wilson, much of Lepage's work is self-referential, both in the way art and theatre itself become a dominant theme of the performances, and in the way so much of the material has autobiographical resonances; and both share

[2] Cited by Remy Charest, in *Robert Lepage: Connecting Flights*, Theatre Communications Group, 1999, p. 26.

[3] Lepage, cited by John Lahr, *New Yorker*, 28 December 1992, 190.

[4] According to Gabriel, Lepage 'is as much a transformational catalyst as Peter Brook' – cited in *Guardian*, 23 June 2001.

a move away from text-based theatre. Again, like Wilson, who works from storyboards in his productions, as one of his actors has described, Lepage's method of directing is to 'explain a scene visually'.[5] One of his standard rehearsal techniques, in fact, is an exercise that involves his actors sketching images of the play with magic markers on sheets of paper.[6] Similarly, despite differences in their theatrical approach, Lepage singles out Mnouchkine in the interview to follow, as one of the formative influences on his work.

A major theme in Lepage's work is art, particularly in his one-man pieces, which present artist figures ranging from Leonardo da Vinci (1986) to Hans Christian Andersen (2005), though also in larger scale pieces like *La Casa Azul* (2001) dealing with Frida Kahlo, or *The Seven Streams of the River Ota* (1994), which foregrounds different styles of performance. He also sees connections between his approach and the Surrealists, impersonating Jean Cocteau in one of his early pieces, *Needles and Opium* (1991). Another source is Bertolt Brecht, whose work Lepage has repeatedly focused on – *Galileo* and *Mother Courage* both in 1989, an extensive study of *Threepenny Opera*, which resulted in *The Busker's Opera* (2004). Parallel to this has been an abiding interest in Shakespeare. This led to several productions of *A Midsummer Night's Dream* – first in French (1988), then (staged in a sea of mud, with the main prop being an iron bed) for the Royal National Theatre in London (1992) and together with other dream-texts as *Shakespeare's Rapid Eye Movement* in Japan (1993), then as one of the first productions of Ex Machina (1995) – plus several versions of *Macbeth* and *The Tempest*, in addition to a bilingual co-production of *Romeo et Juliette* (1989), and his one-man version of *Hamlet* (titled *Elsinore*, 1995). There the highly complex mechanised acting area was typical of his technological focus in the mid-1990s. Revolving as well as rotating, and capable of separating into segments – all controlled by the actor – this compact but elaborate construct was integrated with multiple video screens linked to real-time

---

[5] Lothaire Bluteau, cited by Brian Johnson, *Macleans*, 11 September 1995, 62.
[6] For a description of this exercise, see K. Jan Gibson, 'Seeing Double: the Map-Making Process of Robert Lepage', *CTR* 97 (Winter 1998), 22.

minicams also controlled by the performer, allowing Lepage to play all the main characters in a psychological monodrama that in many ways could be compared to Gordon Craig's classic Russian *Hamlet* for Stanislavsky in 1911.

Throughout his career Lepage has alternated between one-man pieces (semi-autobiographical as well as initially starring himself, though in several cases subsequently handed over for touring with another actor) and large-scale epic works. These big multi-part, multilingual and increasingly multimedia performance-pieces have ranged from conjuring images through minimal props on an almost bare stage, as with *The Dragons' Trilogy* (1985, 2003), to technical *tours de force* like *Zulu Time*, or *La Damnation de Faust* (both 1999). Like almost all other leading directors today, he has also had a long involvement with opera, beginning with an untraditional deconstruction of *Carmen* (1987) possibly as a response to Brook's adaptation which had reached New York in 1984. A fantastically imagistic 1992 staging that turned two early twentieth-century operas, Bartók's *Bluebeard's Castle* and Schoenberg's *Erwartung*, into pyschodramas exploring the gender politics of the modern era, has been followed by his own version of Mahler's *Kindertotenlieder* (1998) and the development of a new opera, *1984* by Loren Maazel (2005).

However, the experimental complexity of much of his work has depended on having his own company, which he achieved remarkably early in his career. On graduating from the Conservatoire d'Art Dramatique de Québec in 1979, and finding themselves without roles or contracts, Lepage together with Richard Fréchette co-founded their own company: the Théâtre Hummm (named after a popular comic strip). Joining and effectively taking over a theatre collective, the Quebec Théâtre Repère, in 1982, he became artistic director, together with its founder Jacques Lessard, making his name with the striking six-hour production of *The Dragons' Trilogy* (1985). For Lessard, Lepage in his development as a director was increasingly moving away from the founding principles of Théâtre Repère, based on a theory of intuitive creativity derived from the RSVP (Resources, Score, reVised, Performed) cycle of the 1960s designer Lawrence Halprin; and in 1989 Lepage resigned to take up a position as head of French Theatre at the

National Arts Centre in Ottawa, which he held, despite funding cuts and bureaucratic interference, until 1993. In 1994 he founded Ex Machina, and gave it a permanent base at la Caserne Dalhousie – a multidisciplinary production centre in Quebec city where he became Artistic Director in 1997 – and in 1995 he founded his own film and multimedia production company, In Extremis Images, together with Daniel Langlois. At the same time a number of key collaborators have remained as the core of a fluid acting group all the way from the 1980s: among them Richard Fréchette, Marie Gignac and Marie Brassard.

Christopher Innes: *If I could start right at the beginning: how did you get trained as an actor and a director?*

Robert Lepage: Well, actually, in the 1970s, there was no directors' training as such, at least not in French-speaking Canada. I was very interested in doing these things then, but I was also interested in being an actor and writer and all of that. So I put myself through the Conservatoire d'Art Dramatique in Quebec City, and my teachers, during my three years that I studied there, were always saying I was spending way too much time doing lighting and working on productions and observing other invited directors, and all that, where they wanted me to be more concentrated on my work as an actor. So, that's where the taste for directing really came from. When I came out, I didn't have a casting for anything, and felt that I would probably not have much of an acting career. So, very early on I started devising my own work.

In the 1970s there was a lot of political theatre in Quebec . . .

A lot of this was small street-groups, so directing was never really an official post because it was all about the collective, working together. Of course, everybody did a bit of everything, but I would always end up being the one doing the blocking, and designing the set, and coming up with concepts and so on and, eventually, I kind of identified myself as being a director. But there was no real training.

So, you didn't have any particular mentor or guru . . .

Of course, there are a lot of people that I looked up to . . . There was someone who connected me with how things were being done in the civilised world. This was André Brassard, who was a very important director in Quebec at that time. He'd done all of Michel Tremblay's work and also introduced Quebec to the work of Jean Genet and a lot of European directors. I'd say I was probably fifteen years old. There was a promotion going on when he was doing *Twelfth Night*, so the first real professional play that I saw was directed by him, and I was amazed by what the director could do. That was where I really understood that directing is writing and not just blocking or being the guy who does the traffic, and saw that directing was actually a very valuable form of expression.

Some of your published material says you trained in Paris at one stage.

Yes, people say, 'Oh he studied there for a year, or in that year he studied with Alain Knapp.' I did train in Paris . . . for about three weeks. At the end of our conservatory, the government would pay a kind of internship to go to Europe, not just for workshops to work with great masters, but also just to be in Europe where there's a lot of theatrical activity and get to see things there. And so we chose to go to Paris and see Alain Knapp. What was interesting about Alain Knapp was his technique. It was all about improvisation, but it was mainly about the director/writer. You write as you perform and you direct as you perform – it was about improvising not just the words, but improvising the *mise en scène*; and that meant having a very strong directorial vocabulary.

Of course several of your plays from The Andersen Project *to* Needles and Opium *deal with unsuccessful Quebec artists who end up in Paris . . .*

Well, yes, it's the kind of Woody Allen-ish joke-approach for inviting the audience into a show.

One of the things that is very difficult, I would say, in Canadian culture, is that as an audience member you always feel things that are presented to you are imported. So you never feel really invited in. I always give the example of Woody Allen because he's an incredibly cultivated and literate person, but he acts as a loser; and he does that thing of being Joe Everybody who suddenly discovers the world of the Greeks or discovers the Italian Renaissance. That's why in *The Andersen Project* there's a guy from the popular culture, and rock and roll, and he ends up in the opera world. Of course it's not me ... I know the opera world very well now, but it's a way of bringing reticent people to enter a certain world, to enter into the stories.

How does it work, when you're performing in a European context, as this Canadian from small-town Quebec? Because there you're not trying to inform them about Quebec.

It's interesting because Europe's just a bunch of ex-empires, you know, and the people who tried to impose their own culture, are now, I think, being redeemed by becoming very curious about other people's culture. In Great Britain, I think, people are more open now to foreign cultures, foreign languages – something that France developed maybe a bit earlier: that sense of de-colonisation. It's like one of Brecht's principles, this idea of the *Verfremdungseffekt*.

It's really unfortunate when that gets translated as alienation.

In French it's *distanciation*, which is even worse. Actually, what it means is making something look strange and, therefore, making it interesting. You take life as it is in real life, but the artist gives it a twist where suddenly it is so interesting because it's so strange.

You've done solo shows – you've also done mammoth epics like The Seven Streams of the River Ota *or* The Dragons' Trilogy. *How do you select which format a show will be?*

First of all, it's a question of equilibrium in the sense that my first interest is to work with people. I like doing big creations and take the time to tell a story. Right now I'm working on one of those big epics that's a nine-hour show. We have a working title called *Lipsynch*.

Can you take me through the process of developing this kind of show?

It's not necessarily about lip-synching but it's the working title we have. The subject matter that is chosen, the basic metaphors, are always things that I suspect are rich enough, or juicy enough for a group of people to embark on, and do research that I don't feel I can do on my own. I try to be as open as possible and let people express themselves and try to express myself, but, you know, it is a collective, and there is always a bit of compromise, a bit of putting water in your wine and saying, 'OK, well I don't agree with this but we're working in this together, and I agree that has to go forward.' So, a lot remains unexpressed – and the solo shows allow me to venture into those avenues and sometimes also they're too personal.

With Hans Christian Andersen there seems to be a lot of yourself in the title figure as well as in the young Quebecois musician.

It's no coincidence that it was Andersen who wrote *The Ugly Duckling*, a metaphor for the awkwardness of childhood and the blossoming of adulthood. I can identify with this. Too: where Andersen was tall and ungainly, I had alopecia. And a lot of artists in the nineteenth century felt that they had to travel outside their own country to be recognised . . . If you are a Quebecois artist, like me, you feel the same impulse.

But even the most personal solo shows I do are almost always also about someone well known – even *The Far Side of the Moon*. It didn't end up being a very a personal show; it was about Buzz Aldrin. The starting point was really about someone's uniqueness and someone's loneliness. I think a solo show is necessarily about someone's uniqueness and someone's loneliness.

That's a wonderful linkage of form and content. But they are also, almost all, with the possible exception of Buzz Aldrin, about artists.

Of course, because this is a solo show it is going to be about me at the moment where I do it, or some aspect of my life, so I cannot deny the artistic preoccupation that a solo takes. Artists, their lives and their work, are good triggers for my own reflection and my own expression. But I'm moving away from trying to quote these artists or completely reproducing parts of their lives. *Vinci* (1986) was actually much purer because it was absolutely not about Leonardo da Vinci. We saw a lot of his work, but he only came into the bit at the very end, in the bathhouse in Florence. His biography was very, very loosely connected to the rest of the story. That's also the case with Andersen. I only keep what's essential from the biography; and we get to understand more about Andersen if it's filtered through my personality, or the personality of the character that tells the story.

You talk about the metaphors and resources. Are those the first things from which you develop a production?

That's part of the playfulness of what I'm trying to do. I know that eventually there will be words and there will be lines and there'll be written text and there'll be all of that, but people have to have a picture of what it is they saw. In their lives they are reminded about what you've been trying to convey by details. You know, a few glasses of water . . . but I don't burden myself with realistic or anecdotal elements. It takes a while before you choose an object or an image to trigger those memories.

So the images in fact get fixed later in the process?

Everything happens at the same time. It's just that they're not connected for a while. I improvise with hours and hours of dialogue – that's on one side – but, at the same time, we do explorations with objects, and we try to find interesting new ways of showing or presenting things. And these are not connected. If we try to force a connection, it isn't really happening. There's a moment where all these kinds of ideas, whether they're textual or imagistic, naturally and eventually, connect. Suddenly, that specific image strongly conveys this thing that I was trying to say. So you could cross off that dialogue because the image says it better. Other things are better said spoken; so this image is redundant. It's not something that you know at the beginning. It's really a huge chaos at the beginning, but I've done so many of these shows, that I've learnt to trust that eventually the show will tell me that this is too long, cut this, and find an image instead. Or, remember what you did two months ago in the rehearsal room – that beautiful little object with a little bit of lighting actually said what you're trying to say but much, much stronger. It's trial and error and it's also part of a big game where you just kind of connect pieces of puzzle; and when you try to force them they don't work. It's really like sculpting.

But your shows keep developing, even after their first per-formance, even when on tour.

Yes. Just ask the crew! We bring in big trunks and we don't need one third of these things any more when we're doing the show, and they say, 'Can we leave that in Canada, because the shipping is going to be cheaper?' and I say, 'No.' Because I just know that we'll be performing somewhere, and we'll remember that scene we cut. Actually, material always re-emerges constantly. In the big shows like *The Dragons' Trilogy*, complete characters sometimes disappear, and then when we're touring, we go: 'Oh, this is where it should have been!'

Is that in response to the specific audience, their reactions, or their preconceptions?

You actually allow the audience to tell you what your show is about. If you start by saying, 'this is what I want to say, and it will not move', then the chances are it's going to be a one-way street. But if you listen, you find things you never saw before. Same thing for reviewers. All these people, these voices, come with what you're doing, and if you don't allow that to have an effect on your show, then the show's going to fall down, dry out. I did a show called *The Geometry of Miracles* (1998) and when we started touring, we were right in France at the moment they were burning cars. Then the character [of the spiritual guru Gurdjieff] takes on an importance in meaning that you never thought. Or, in London, on the day we opened *The Andersen Project*, there was a big controversy about cartoons in the Danish newspapers, so when I do the whole bit about Denmark suddenly it doesn't resonate the same way.

So your shows change for local context – but they must also change in important ways depending on the language you are performing in?

Yes – absolutely. What I do right now with *The Andersen Project* in London is not the same at all as in Paris. There are a lot of common points, but in French it's all about a French-Canadian guy who has to deal with this patronising French character, but acts like a coloniser when he goes to Copenhagen. The whole comedy of the scene is the fact that he cannot speak English. That's when I do it in French. It's very funny, but you can't do that in English; so in London, it's about something else.

You've always played with language like that, right back to your Roméo et Juliette *in 1989, which was half French, half English, I believe.*

Yes. It wasn't a conscious decision to do that. At the time, I was really interested in Juliet, because her part revolves a lot around a very closed society. She's more locked up in her room and locked out in the Capulet house. Romeo is more of an adventurer and goes all over the place ... But I thought it would be interesting to do a piece where they converge in Juliet's room and the spectators are around the set, and we only do the Juliet parts. That would mean that even the balcony scene, we would overhear, because what's happening during the balcony scene is that the nurse is making the bed; and that's all we would see. She would be overhearing what's happening on the balcony.

So when we were offered to do something in Saskatoon for what they call the Jeux Canada Games – this was during the Meech Lake affair – Gordon McCall said it would be nice if we could find a pretext to do a bilingual thing.[7] So I said, 'I will do the Juliet part in French, and you do the Romeo part in English and let's not consult. You do your thing with your actors, and I'll do my thing with my actors.' And I told him from the start, 'What I'll be doing is extremely insular because of the Capulet household, so I think that whatever you decide to do, I'll be able to come in' – and it was great actually.

Flexibility is obviously a key for you.

You have to follow theatre's crazy anamorphous nature – say you have an idea about a big subject, and if you want to cover the whole thing, how long's it going to be? Probably twelve hours ... OK, how do we produce a twelve-hour show? Where do we find the money? After first month of rehearsal you are approached by the Japanese government, and decide it's not going to be twelve. It's probably going to be seven, because seven's a more important number for the Japanese.

I'd always thought the numerology in The Seven Streams of the River Ota *was symbolic?*

I also have a kind of mysticism. I don't know how to translate it, but for some reason there's a twenty-eight-year cycle. The Berlin Wall lasted twenty-eight years. There is a thing about twenty-eight years, which is four cycles of seven years.

Do you find that patterning in your own career?

---

[7] Meech Lake was the venue for federal/provincial talks in 1987, designed to bring Quebec into the Canadian constitution, which, while successful, were eventually vetoed by Native interests, and abandoned – causing an outcry in Quebec – in 1989. Gordon McCall was the Artistic Director of the English-language Centaur Theatre in Montreal.

Oh, completely. It's all over the place.[8] I don't believe in anything magical, or fate. But I think there are signs, convergences of energy that, as an artist, you have to be in tune with.

Apart from the problems of financing, can you talk about some of the other challenges, now that you run your own independent Quebec centre, la Caserne?

Almost ten years ago, when I left the National Arts Centre to come back to Quebec City, it was a big challenge to create a system that would be organic and flexible enough to be an incubator for half-baked projects that find their own shape by being nurtured by people who can adapt very quickly. Of course it varies because of money reasons, but the fact that I was very successful abroad means we don't spend all of our energy like most theatres in Canada trying to sell tickets. So we're very, very focused. Resources are focused on development, and we produce so many things. In general, directors work on one big project every two or three years. I find it's better to do fifteen different productions because some of these ideas will dry out, and you'll shed them like old skins, but they may come up with prototypes that will be used for another project. So it's a pool of creative elements. A lot of things in *The Andersen Project* came from another project that never happened.

One of the things that struck me is that at la Caserne you've done a very wide range of work. Zulu Time *(1999),* Casa Azul *(2001),* The Busker's Opera *(2005): they're totally different kinds of show. How do you train your company to meet such diverse demands?*

We don't have a company in the traditional sense – although we try to employ the same people, we don't have people paid by the year to perform. But we do have that equivalent on the technical side. We have a group of technicians in carpentry, administrators, and research

---

[8] Serendipitously, perhaps, *The Dragons' Trilogy* (1985) comes almost seven years after Lepage's professional debut; seven years after that he mounts his first production outside Canada (*A Midsummer Night's Dream* at the Royal National Theatre (NT) in London, 1992); and the next period is marked by two key shows, *Zulu Time* and *The Far Side of the Moon* (1999, 2000) – suggesting the time is ripe for a new departure in Lepage's work.

people who follow all of the work and who develop a system, so we can afford to do all these things at the same time.

I just came back from Paris, where I spent a day with Ariane Mnouchkine. The way her company works isn't my way. They embark for three, four years on one big project, but it's also a kind of a school, almost like a college: it's a system. They are training in the workshop, and they have classes. We cannot afford to do just one thing every three years, so we've replaced that training by all these different productions. For instance, *The Busker's Opera*: it wasn't really intended to be a show, it started by us trying to do *The Threepenny Opera* and having people learn German. You have to sing; you learn to play instruments. And in the course of that our regular collaborators were suddenly going through these workshops because we were doing this production.

So how do you select your productions?

What I'm trying to say is that sometimes we say yes to a project that doesn't have a great potential commercially; but there's something creative about it. There's something that suddenly changes how we do things. This thing called *Lipsynch* [a piece under production at the time of the interview, premiered 2007] is all about the spoken voice, the sung voice or the borrowed voice, dubbing, and so on.

For all the emphasis on language, your shows tend to deny verbal communication: for example in Zulu Time there's a cabaret singer, who sings in Spanish and in German to the French audience. How many can understand?

That was the point about *Zulu Time*: that you do a complete comical number in a language that you know people don't understand. People laugh and then they go, 'OK, well, what is comic about this? Is it really about language? It's about energy.'

You have at some points worked closely with writers. Marie Brassard, Jean Casault ...

They're not writers actually. We officialised our collaboration by saying written by ... because they wrote the scripts. But that's not their first thing. They're actors. I did work with writers a long time ago on a project called *Alanienouidet* [National Arts Centre, 1992 – the writer of record was Marianne Ackerman] but that didn't turn out very well, I've also worked with Adam Nashman from Toronto, who was there for *The Far Side of the Moon*.[9] But, they don't write things for me; they're there, like Marie Gignac, as dramaturges more than writers, to ask the right questions.

And now you are actually working with John Mighton,[10] having done the film of his play, Possible Worlds. *He told me it was about string theory?*

Yes. It's an interesting thing because John, of course, will not be in control of the whole thing. At first that was a bit of a difficulty, but [*Elegant Universe*] is about science, and he's a physicist and mathematician, so he used the idea of trying to translate what the scientists were working with and are talking about. But the project is actually a tripod. It's a scientific discourse. It's really a conference crossed with music – a [live] concert by the Emerson Quartet – and then there's a third action, which dramatises the life of one of the speakers at the conference, using some of the music. It's trying to find a new way of looking at storytelling, linked with the actual concepts of string theory.

This sounds like something outside of your normal range: hugely experimental. How will it fit in with your normal pattern of performance at la Caserne, followed by tours?

It has its problems. It is something we'd like to tour but chances are the Emerson Quartet won't be that available; and the scientists, of course, have their own laboratories ... We want to keep this authentic, so how do we do that? Do we change the quartet? Do we change the people?

You have talked a lot over your career about the integration of theatre and film and in your recent Barbican post-show talk, you

---

[9] Adam Nashman is the director and writer for the 3D Cabaret in Toronto, who also worked with Lepage on *La Celestina*, 2004; Marianne Ackerman, co-founder of Montreal's Theatre 1774, is an award-winning theatre critic and author of over a dozen plays, including one co-authored with John Mighton and the dramatist Judith Thompson, as well as the bestselling novel, *Jump*.

[10] John Mighton, winner of the prestigious Siminovitch Prize in Theatre (2007) and founder of the JUMP (Junior Undiscovered Math Prodigies) programme, is the author of mathematics texts as well as plays.

spoke of film techniques becoming more user-friendly in the sense that film and theatre would approach each other in the future. Can you expand on that?

Well, let's not call it film and theatre, let's call it live performance versus recorded performance or live storytelling versus recorded storytelling. They never seem to be able to live together very well – on a basic level it's due to the fact that the lighting system of a play and the way you light a film are different – two different technologies, two different vocabularies. But this new high-technology world, this computer world, is reconciling the two. People who do sound, people who do images, used to be recognised as two different crafts; but now, if you edit a film, it's the same language, the same computer using the exact same tools to do both sound and vision. And it's the same thing with theatre and film . . . we're starting to speak the same language. And because the tools that we're using have the same words, then, suddenly, it's easier to say, 'Oh how do you tell a story?' For this subject, maybe I should be using more film with my story. I personally think that there are open channels right now that we didn't have ten, fifteen, twenty years ago.

To survive, I think that theatre has to embrace the vocabulary of its audience and the vocabulary is now that of film. It used to be, when we went to the theatre, our narrative vocabulary was very limited. But now people see films, TV, rock videos, commercials, and stories are told to them all day, in different vocabularies. So people live in a language of jump-cuts and sound-bites; and if you're not going to use that as a storyteller in the theatre, they're at the end of the story before you are. Not because the action is slow, but because the art of storytelling in theatre is aged and slowed down. You have to bring youth back to storytelling by being aware of how people understand storytelling now. If you look at rock videos, you go, 'My God! These are conveying expressionistic themes with no beginning, middle or end . . . ' Where people in film have actually embraced that, they've been actually extremely successful: people like Tarantino are tight with narrative structures, and the audience are ready for that.

So when you come to restoring and reviving something like The Dragons' Trilogy, *which you performed in London in 2005, but first*

*produced in 1985 – a whole generation ago – did you find that you
needed to do very different things with the story?*

Strangely enough, what had aged in *The Dragons' Trilogy* was
not what I thought had aged. It was exactly the opposite. The historical
first part was almost untouched when we did it, because it was still
very fresh and modern – contemporary. The second part needed a bit of
change, but more of a dramaturgical kind of shifting. The third part we
almost rewrote. That had aged a lot, because it was taking place in
modern times when we did it in 1985. Set in 1985, it had been like a
contemporary comment about the time. Now, it came across as yet
another period piece. So that needed a lot of refurbishing in the way we
did dialogue, the way we edited, and the way technology was used in
the third part . . .

Why did you choose to restore The Dragons' Trilogy *– to revive
that one, as opposed to, say,* Tectonic Plates?

I would say it's one of our founding productions. It contains the
lexicon of everything we've done after that.

We were very young when we did *The Dragons' Trilogy*, and it
was a very long show, like an early Mozart piece, you know: tons of
things and unfinished ideas and quotes and tryouts, and all that. It was
completely crazy, something that could only happen when you know
very little, and you do what you know without any doubts, so you just
go for it. The more you know, the more you doubt; and we felt we
needed to rejuvenate the company's work by going to the very, very
early stuff we had done and bringing it out and refreshing it. Not just to
give it another life. I would look at scenes and think, my God, the
audacity that we had in those days! I mean nobody knew us in those
days. We were only just starting out back then, so we weren't bothered
by critics. We were just trying to do some things, which we felt were
important. But you could really see the beginning of *The Polygraph*
(1987). You could see the thread that eventually led to *The Seven
Streams* (1994). You could see the thread that led to *The Andersen
Project* (2005) . . . all these themes are within that work.

So it's important for the company to do that piece. We're trying
to move forward, and it's blocked; so we have to stop just doing shows

and shows and shows. Then you think, 'What's the next idea going to be?' And then you think . . . 'Where does all this come from?'

You're using the term 'we' a lot there.

Well, because I'm just the spokesperson. I'm the face you put on the work and on the signature. It is a group, a tiny group of people, but it's still a 'we' – collaborators like Marie Gignac, who helped evolve this idea, and are still around. There's someone like Michel Bernatchez, who is the executive producer, and has been there from the very beginning, who had the genius of saying: 'OK, so you want to do this in this way, so how do I find the money?' Just like in film, the directors and producers are the most important people because it's always 'How do you bend the rules . . . How do you reinvent the structure for this particular thing?'

One of the things that wasn't there in your beginnings is your work with musicians. You've done two Peter Gabriel tours (1993 and 2002), now the Emerson Quartet, and Laurie Anderson, then there's all the recent opera work, like 1984 (2005). You've said that working with writers was difficult, what about working with musicians?

1984 was particularly interesting because I got to follow the creative process on writing the music and libretto. I didn't have any kind of participation in that other than being at a meeting and giving my opinion once in a while. The thing that was interesting was to understand that process, because there was no pre existing recording of this opera like there usually is, the only exposure to the music was Loren [Maazel] rehearsing with the piano, and I realised that we were all trusting that the day would come that certain ideas would be expressed by the orchestra, but you don't know that. Then the orchestra came in, and put everything Lorin had sculpted into a three-dimensional soundscape. For me it was a very, very interesting process. And it's not over, because the production is still very virgin, so there is much editing still to be done and a lot of cleaning up. But I felt this is probably how it was when Mahler or Schoenberg wrote, and there was a lot of controversy.

You've also worked with Laurie Anderson, who has her own style of music but creates something for your piece The Far Side of the

Moon (2000). Do you go to her with a completed conception that she provides some music for?

We were supposed to work together on another project, and it didn't work out. So we'd met before and that's where I learnt that she had been training to be an astronaut. She was very, very into this whole idea of the moon.[11] So, when I embarked on this project, I thought, 'Oh, she would be a perfect candidate to do this.' And the way she works is so amazing. She never said, 'I'd like to see what you do.' She knew that it would be better if she sent me stuff that I used for improv. So she would only send little thirty-second loops, allowing us to do a patchwork, or to take stuff and repeat. She was in New York, e-mailing me these little snippets with titles that were appropriate.

It must be very different, when you're doing shows with someone like Peter Gabriel.

Yes, because all his songs are worlds in themselves, you know. So you have to cater to already existing things. Peter is an extraordinary Renaissance artist. He is as much interested in the world of engineering and new tech, and geography, and politics, and he tries to make sense of that through his music. Sometimes he reconciles that in a brilliant way, sometimes not ... but he's an extraordinarily playful person. I've learnt a lot with him on that level, too. With him everything has to be a sensual experience, and he knows that a show is just an option to do something different to the recording. He's a great theatre person; and one of my early tastes for theatre came from seeing his shows – like *Genesis* – where he'd inhale helium to change the pitch of his voice and create characters, wear costumes, sing in drag. He'd work with masks. So, that through playfulness and theatricality, rock performance was very connected to Shakespeare. It's a way of seeing theatre that the modern stage has lost, where

---

[11] The performance artist Laurie Anderson also composed music for Robert Wilson's *Alcestis* at ART and for Spalding Gray's films, as well as collaborating on the opening of the 2004 Olympics in Athens. In 2003 she became NASA's first artist-in-residence; and subsequently wrote her own performance piece on the subject, *The End of the Moon*. A central theme in Anderson's work is exploring the effects of technology on human relationships and communication, which links closely to Lepage's theatrical approach.

people would be dressed as minstrels and come on stage with an electric guitar, and they'd have visuals and they'd have explosions, and tell stories, and take characters, and change voices.

How do you approach directing this sort of material?

It's a dialogue, which starts with Peter's unrealistic visions, because Peter comes out, forgets the cost, the practicality of the thing. He says, 'Let's start with that, and then we could do this' – so there's a lot of bringing him back down to earth. But coming through this craziness, there are challenges that you want to live up to. I mean, you say, 'Yeah, that's a great idea, but the roof of Earl's Court would collapse if you did that!' But it haunts you.

Gabriel's shows always seemed very fluid. Does he keep on trying new stuff throughout his tours?

He drives everyone crazy on tour. He'll say, 'Tonight let's shift these two songs.' And all of the songs each need twenty-five people moving a piece of set here; and you can't just do that. Well, so they have to come in much earlier that day, and we finally do it.

You, too, talked about performance as a substitute for writing. So, do you face your technical crew with exactly the same problems? 'Let's do these two scenes the wrong way round' and so on . . .

Of course, my shows are not as heavy as big rock and roll shows, but yeah, I do that all the time. Sometimes, at the beginning, I radically change absolutely everything, and we don't have time and the show crashes, and we pick up the pieces and we continue from there. But there's a moment where the show is in a shape where you can do certain things safely, and you can say, 'Well, let's shift these two scenes tonight and not do this and put this in or not put that in' – and people are challenged, they're on their toes.

Like Peter Gabriel shows, Zulu Time (1999) or Elsinore (1997) were technologically challenging, with huge robots and rising catwalks, or that extraordinary machine that completely surrounded you as the actor – I always wondered whether the work with Zulu eventually took you to the Cirque du Soleil, KÀ, for Las Vegas?

A lot of people have doubts about the artistic value of things like *Zulu Time* because it was a very expensive project and took just forever to come to fruition and got entangled with a lot of technical problems. But I've learnt so much from looking for languages and vocabulary within the new tools that are available. So when I was approached by Cirque du Soleil, I knew that the difference with an experience like *Zulu* is that they would want to indulge in all this new technology, looking for new ways of breaking codes and usual ways of presenting spectacle. But they have the money and the time that we don't have. There's no limit and also you have absolute artistic control on everything.

But surely you have to be conscious who your audience is: that it's Vegas. So there must be some compromise.

Yes, half of the things we invented for this show have not been used. They are just prototypes. But that's the whole point. Cirque du Soleil has become a real experiment: they say, 'You want to try this? OK. However much it's going to cost – fine, do it. It's not going to be in the show? OK. Let's do it somewhere else in another show.' You know, They're not putting their investments in tradition; they're putting them in avant-garde because that's their only basic principle: what can we present that hasn't been presented yet? They always start there.

The thing is, you don't just invent gadgets. You invent ways of working. It becomes the philosophy of what you do . . . So, some of that I use in my own shows, like *The Andersen Project* where we say to the technician, 'This is an interesting thing that Cirque didn't want to do.'

Does the technology give you freedom, or does it actually limit the amount you improvise during the show itself?

We still change everything, but these shows take a much longer process before they become human. It takes a long, long time before we master those things; and very early we burden ourselves way too much and the editing process is very, very, very long and cumbersome.

One of the things I notice is that your more recent shows like La Casa Azul *(2001) are really low-tech in some ways – in contrast to those highly mechanized shows from the 1990s. Was that a phase, or does your approach alternate?*

I think I pretty much learned from the mistakes [in *Zulu Time* and *Elsinore*]. I'm still learning, but there was something crazy and adventurous in *Zulu Time* that was very promising. So now I think I've swung the other way, to the point where I think I would do something like *Zulu Time* again ... Rock and roll was the same thing. Yes, there's soul-searching theatre where you create from your own experience – it's important and finds its place on stage. But what makes the theatre change and evolve is its technology, its materialistic reality. And though absolutely nobody got the point, in *Elsinore*, the thing that always interested me in *Hamlet* was the fact that Shakespeare was a man of theatre, not just of the written word. In his time, he was a man of spectacle. He was a man who would have been as interested in all the technologies of my time. How can I write for them? The actual problems of staging something produces poetry, and I'm sure that *Hamlet* is all about that.

Your one-man shows have always had a strong personal connection, yet you handed on Elsinore *to an American actor, Peter Darling.*

The first time I did that, it was with *Needles and Opium*, and then *The Far Side of the Moon*: it was a guy called Yves Jacques who took that over, and I think he performed it more than I did – he's still performing it.

So there are clones of you all over the place. To what extent do they study and repeat your performance in the piece?

I hope they're not clones. Someone like Yves Jacques, he's a fantastic actor but also an impersonator and it was a danger in the beginning because he had seen the show so much. He felt so privileged to be able to do this that he did start to impersonate me ... But there's a moment where a performance has to be your thing; and when he started doing his thing with it, then it became fantastic. I'm not an actor. I'm an actor–writer–director. I'm not empowered enough as an actor to define these characters. I do what I can, but once that's done, and I've toured it, and the show's found not a definitive shape, but a strong shape, then it's good that actors – who are actors – come in and say 'OK, give that to me.' And that's what happened in *Elsinore* when Peter Darling came in, the same show that had been panned by everybody suddenly gained a huge effect. Of course, also [once the part is handed over] I'm in the position of a director, which helped; but it was because there was a real performer there with a real voice who could sing.

Did these actors, Yves Jacques or Peter Darling, have a director's book that codifies the production? Was one made at any stage of your own performance in the roles?

No, not really. As I say, the piece morphs itself into the personality of the person performing – that's what theatre-ship is all about. The directorial language imposes itself with time, and as the choices are made.

And those choices are recorded? The lighting changes; the changes of shape and revolves of the machine in Elsinore *– at what stage do those things get written down, fixed?*

It's difficult to say because, even today I'm still rewriting parts of *The Far Side of the Moon*. One of the important elements is distance. And then the fact that I'm training someone also helps me correct things; and that pretty much writes it down. But it's really done with a production that's not touring, when it's all over, we sit down and rewrite it.

That seems the opposite to most writing techniques.

Of course a lot of writers think that should be the first thing we do. But I always come back to Ariane Mnouchkine. Ariane has always had a huge influence on me, but when she came to see *The Seven Streams*, she was pretty flabbergasted; and she really wanted me to see her last show, *Caravansérail* [*Le Dernier Caravansérail (Odyssées)*, 2005] because she said, 'You have to see the influence you had on that.' For that show she used writers the way I do – for dramaturgical support. Before then Ariane rarely improv'd or explored material in the way we do. But this was devised by the company. I went to the last performance, and was talking to some of the performers, and they said, 'Well, now they're going to write it down.' It is certainly unusual to see this at Théâtre du Soleil, but it gave the show an extremely modern image, very strong, very contemporary.

Many of your shows start off in French and then transfer into English – what language do your actors work in?

They're pretty much all bilingual. It used to be compulsory. My assistant, a brilliant guy who is actually my stage manager on this [*The Andersen Project*], when I met him, he only spoke French, and I said, 'If you want to work as my assistant you have to learn English, because we're collaborating all the time with English people.' So he put himself through English classes all summer. That's not compulsory any more. It helps, of course, the more languages you speak, but now this *Lip-synch* thing is *about* language. So we brought in a German actor who only speaks German and English – and we have a Quebecois actor, whose father's Austrian, so translates into German for the other guy. Then there's a Spanish girl from Valencia who speaks Valenciana, she speaks Spanish, but she doesn't speak a word of French, and there's a woman from Quebec, who only speaks French. So you're trying to get this German guy to improvise with this Quebecois woman, or this guy from Spain who doesn't speak either English or German. You become an interpreter. It becomes about something else than just language.

Being part of Quebec, being part of Canada as a whole, makes you conscious of different languages. But what has always struck me with your work is that it's not the verbal language that's important. It's other forms of languages. It's the body language; it's the images. It's the movement. It's the music.

At the beginning, I don't know which of these elements is going to predominate. The piece tells you that as you work on it. By comparison, Brecht is all about writing. It's a literary world that keeps him alive, but in his day, it was all about writing at the same time as you direct, at the same time as you design, the same time as you work with costumes, the music, all that. And Brecht said all these things have to happen at the same time. Do not detach these things. That's why he became obsessed with the idea of taking pictures every thirty seconds.

That's right. All those Model-Books, published by the Berliner Ensemble as a guide for other directors of each play.

Yes, because Brecht knew at one point that the only thing that would be left, the truth that would be left, would be just the writing.

I've noticed that you sometimes videotape your shows. Do you always?

We try to record it as much as we can, but we're terrible at keeping archives. It's a pity because we don't write down what we do. But, once again, the recorded world and the live performance world don't always go together either.

At what point do you tape a show? What about The Andersen Project, *which you are still touring?*

We knew what we did in Quebec City last year will not survive very long, so we made sure that that last performance was taped. Then after that we moved on to Copenhagen and then on to Lyon, France, where other tapes were made. So, we do have something like a Model-Book, but being live performers, we never look at it. That's actually quite a joke, you know, when you think how theatre is now. They're all equipped with video cameras, and we record rehearsals, and all of that becomes lasting theatre once it is caught on video. We eventually use it to remember what the structure of this or that version was – because, at that point we might not have anything on paper ...

But despite using video projection frequently in your shows, I don't remember ever seeing any of these recordings as publicity.

The worst thing you could show on TV is an excerpt. I always avoid that. It's the worst publicity for what you do because it's so anti ... it's not in the nature of what you do. I don't know if you've read or you've seen Richard Eyre's series he did on theatre?

The BBC series on twentieth-century British theatre, Changing Stages, *which was broadcast around 2000?*

Yes. He really nailed it down, with the Michelangelo snowman metaphor. In that part of Italy, there'd be a snowstorm like once every fifteen to twenty years – it would be so rare that people would make it a big event; and supposedly, it snowed in Florence one day, and Michelangelo and some apprentices went up to a plateau where the snow was very mushy. That's an interesting material to be sculpting, and he supposedly sculpted his best work ever: this man made of snow that everybody was in awe of. And, of course, the sun came out; and about three hours after, there was not a single trace of this master-piece. No picture of it; no video. So, the only people you can trust are the people who were there and it's exactly the same with theatre.

So for a record of your work, in this technological age, what would you think of as ideal?

Still pictures and a recording of it.

A sound recording, rather than a video?

Robert Lepage (b. 1957)

Yes. Back when I was in theatre school, there was a new theatre magazine called *Jeux*, and we were all very excited because we were in Quebec City, and we didn't get to see the shows in Montreal. All the pictures of those supposedly crazy shows were all recorded in *Jeux*. If we got to see the shows, they had nothing to do with the pictures, but the thing is, I remember seeing pictures and imagining what the show was. They were prompting me to stage what was in my mind. That's why it's important sometimes to only have traces of things.

Chronology of selected productions

1979   *L'Attaque quotidienne* by Robert Lepage and Richard Fréchette. Théâtre Hummm, Quebec
La Ferme des animaux adapted from *Animal Farm* by George Orwell. Théâtre Hummm, Quebec

1980   *Saturday Night Taxi* by Robert Lepage, Richard Fréchette and Francine Lafontaine. Théâtre Hummm, Quebec

1982   *En attendant* by Robert Lepage, Richard Fréchette and Jacques Lessard. Théâtre Repère, Quebec
À demi-lune by Robert Lepage, Johanne Bolduc and Estelle Dutil. Théâtre Repère, Quebec

1984   *Circulations* by Robert Lepage, François Beausoleil, Bernard Bonnier and Lise Castonguay. Théâtre Repère, Quebec

1985   *The Dragons' Trilogy* by Robert Lepage, Marie Brassard, Jean Casault, Lorraine Côté, Marie Gignac, Marie Michaud. Théâtre Repère, Quebec
À propos de la demoiselle qui pleurait by André Jean. Théâtre Repère, Quebec
Comment regarder le point de fuite by Robert Lepage. Théâtre Repère, Quebec
Histoires sorties du tiroir by Gérard Bibeau. Les Marionnettes du Grand Théâtre, Quebec

1986   *Vinci* by Robert Lepage. Théâtre de Quat'Sous, Montreal
Le Bord d'extrême, adapted from *The Seventh Seal* by Ingmar Bergman. Théâtre Repère, Quebec

Comment devenir parfait en trois jours by Gilles Gauthier, adapted from *Be a Perfect Person in Just 3 Days* by Stephen Manes. Théâtre des Confettis, Quebec

1987   *Polygraphe (The Polygraph)* by Robert Lepage and Marie Brassard. Théâtre Repère, Quebec

En plein nuit une sirène by Robert Lepage and Jacques Girard. Théâtre de la Bordée, Quebec

Pour en finir une fois pour toutes avec Carmen, adapted from the opera *Carmen* by Georges Bizet. Théâtre de Quat'Sous, Montreal

1988   *Les Plaques tectoniques (Tectonic Plates)* by Robert Lepage. Théâtre Repère, Quebec

Songe d'une nuit d'été by William Shakespeare. Théâtre du Nouveau Monde, Montreal

1989   (Co-director with Gordon McCall) *Roméo et Juliette* by William Shakespeare. Théâtre Repère and Centaur Theatre (Quebec). Performed in Saskatchewan. (Bi-lingual.)

La Vie de Galilée by Bertolt Brecht. Théâtre du Nouveau Monde, Montreal

Echo, adapted from *A Nun's Diary* by Ann Diamond. Théâtre 1774, Montreal

Mère Courage et ses enfants by Bertolt Brecht. Conservatoire d'Art Dramatique de Québec, Quebec

C'est ce soir qu'on saoûle Sophie Saucier by Sylvie Provost. Les Productions ma chère Pauline, Montreal

1990   *La Visite de la vieille dame* by Friedrich Dürrenmatt. National Arts Centre, Ottawa

1991   *Les Aiguilles et l'opium (Needles and Opium)* by Robert Lepage. National Arts Centre, Ottawa

Los Cincos Soles. National Theatre School of Canada, Montreal

1992   *Alanienouidet* by Marianne Ackerman. National Arts Centre, Ottawa

Le Cycle de Shakespeare: Macbeth, Coriolan, La Tempête by William Shakespeare, adapted by Michel Garneau. Théâtre Repère, Quebec

Robert Lepage (b. 1957)

A Midsummer Night's Dream by William Shakespeare. Royal National Theatre, London (NT)

La Tempête by William Shakespeare. Atelier de Recherche Théâtrale d'Ottawa, Ottawa

Macbeth by William Shakespeare. Theatre Department, University of Toronto, Toronto

Bluebeard's Castle, opera by Béla Bartók, and *Erwartung*, opera by Arnold Schoenberg. Canadian Opera Company, Toronto

1993 *Shakespeare's Rapid Eye Movement*, based on a collection of dream texts by William Shakespeare. Bayerisches Staatsschauspiel, Munich

Macbeth and *The Tempest* by William Shakespeare. Tokyo Globe Theatre, Toyko. (In Japanese.)

National capitale nationale by Jean-Marc Dalpé and Vivian Laxdal. National Arts Centre and Théâtre de la Vieille 17, Ottawa

Secret World Tour by Peter Gabriel. Real World Tours, London

1994 *Noises, Sounds and Sweet Airs* by Michael Nyman. Toyko Globe Theatre, Tokyo

Ett Drömspel by August Strindberg. Kungliga Dramatiska Teatern, Stockholm

The Seven Streams of the River Ota by Robert Lepage and Eric Bernier, Gérard Bibeau, Normand Bissonnette, Rebecca Blankenship, Marie Brassard, Anne-Marie Cadieux, Normand Daneau, Richard Fréchette, Marie Gignac, Patrick Goyette, Macha Limonchik, Ghislaine Vincent. Ex Machina and Cultural Industry, London. Edinburgh International Festival, Edinburgh. Second development, Wienerfestwochen, Austria, 1995. Third development, Carrefour International de Théâtre, Quebec, 1996

1995 *Elseneur (Elsinore)* based on *Hamlet* by William Shakespeare. Ex Machina, Montreal

Le Confessionnal by Robert Lepage. Film version, Cinémaginaire-Enigma Films

Le Songe d'une nuit d'été by William Shakespeare. Ex

Machina, Théâtre Le Trident, Quebec

1996　*The Polygraphe* by Robert Lepage. Film version, In Extremis Images Inc., Montreal

1997　*Elsinore* by William Shakespeare, in a new version by Peter Darling. Ex Machina, Quebec

Nô by Robert Lepage. Film, In Extremis Images Inc., Montreal

1998　*La Géométrie des miracles* (*The Geometry of Miracles*) by Robert Lepage, Tea Alagic, Daniel Belanger, Jean-Francois Blanchard, Marie Brassard, Denis Gaudreault, Tony Guilfoyle, Rick Miller, Catherine Martin, Kevin McCoy, Thaddeus Phillips and Rodrigue Proteau. Ex Machina, Quebec

Kindertotenlieder by Robert Lepage, based on the Song Cycle by Gustav Mahler. Ex Machina, Quebec

La Celestina by Fernando de Rojas. Kungliga Dramatiska Teatern, Stockholm. (In Swedish.)

1999　*Zulu Time* by Robert Lepage. Ex Machina, Quebec

Jean-sans-Nom, based on the novel by Jules Verne. Ex Machina, Quebec

La Damnation de Faust, adapted from works by Hector Berlioz, Almire Gaudonnière and Johann Wolfgang von Goethe. Saito Kinen Festival, Matsumoto, Japan. (In Japanese.)

2000　*La Face cachée de la lune* (*The Far Side of the Moon*) by Robert Lepage. Le Théâtre du Trident, Quebec

Possible Worlds by Robert Lepage and John Mighton. Film version, In Extremis Films, Montreal

2001　*La Casa Azul* (*Apasionada*) by Sophie Faucher. Théâtre Quat'Sous, Montreal

2002　*Growing Up Live* by Peter Gabriel. Real World Tours, London

2003　*La Face cachée de la lune* (*The Far Side of the Moon*) by Robert Lepage. Film version, La Face cachée de la lune Inc., Quebec

The Dragons' Trilogy, in a new version by Robert Lepage, Marie Brassard, Jean Casault, Lorraine Côté, Marie Gignac, Marie Michaud. Ex Machina, Quebec

2004　*The Busker's Opera* by Robert Lepage and Kevin McCoy, adapted from *The Beggar's Opera* by John Gay. Festival Montréal en Lumière, Montreal

La Celestina by Fernando de Rojas. Teatro Cuyas de las Palmas de Gran Canaria, Ysarca, Spain. (In Spanish.)

KÀ by Robert Lepage. Cirque du Soleil, Las Vegas

2005 *1984* Opera by Loren Maazel, based on the novel by George Orwell. The Royal Opera House, Covent Garden, London

The Andersen Project by Robert Lepage, inspired from the stories of Hans Christian Andersen. Ex Machina, Théâtre du Trident, Quebec; Hans Christian Andersen Festival, Copenhagen

2007 *Lipsynch* by Robert Lepage. Ex Machina, Festival TransAmériques, Montreal

The Rake's Progress Opera by Igor Stravinsky. Théâtre Royal de la Monnaie, Brussels

Selected bibliography

Bienen, Leigh Buchanan (2000), 'Robert Lepage's Theater', *Triquarterly* Winter: 107/108, 304–27

Cummings, Scott T. (1997), 'The Seven Streams of the River Ota', *Theatre Journal* 49: 3, 348–52

Dundjerovic, Aleksandar Sasa (2007), *The Theatricality of Robert Lepage*, McGill–Queens University Press

Innes, Christopher (2005), 'Puppets and Machines of the Mind: Robert Lepage and the Modernist Heritage', *Theatre Research International* 30: 2, 124–38

Jirgens, Karl E. (2005), 'Chaos, Performance and the Novo-Baroque Skin Games of Brossard, Stelarc, and Lepage', *Open Letter* 12: 5, 100–24

(2003), 'Multi-stable Perception in Robert Lepage's *Tectonic Plates*', *Open Letter* 11: 7, 97–122

Knowles, Richard Paul (1998), 'From Dream to Machine: Peter Brook, Robert Lepage, and the Contemporary Shakespearean Director as (Post) Modernist', *Theatre Journal* 50: 2, 189–206

Lepage, Robert (1998), *Robert Lepage: Connecting Flights: Robert Lepage in Conversation with Rémy Charest*, New York: Theatre Communications Group

(1993), interviewed by Denis Salter, 'Borderlines: an Interview with Robert Lepage and Le Théâtre Repère', *Theater* 24: 3, 71–9

(1996), 'Robert Lepage' in *In Contact with the Gods? Directors Talk Theatre*, ed. Maria M. Delgado and Paul Heritage, Manchester University Press, pp. 129–57

Paul, J. Gavin (2006/2007), 'Border Wars: Shakespeare, Robert Lepage, and the Production of National Sentiment', *Upstart Crow* 26, 45–60

Rewa, Natalie (1990), 'Cliches of Ethnicity Subverted: Robert Lepage's *La Trilogie des dragons*', *Theatre History in Canada* 11: 2, 148–61

Skoll, Geoffrey R. (1991), 'Power and Repression', *American Journal of Semiotics* 8: 3, 5–29

Wolff, Tamsen (1998), 'Elsinore', *Theatre Journal* 50: 2, 237–40

6   Simon McBurney (b. 1957)

Theatre de Complicite – a French-without-accents label that nods to the key influence of French theatre in his early development, while recognising its English context – has been the vehicle for Simon McBurney's unique brand of physical performance. Founded in 1983 by McBurney, together with Annabel Arden and Marcello Magni, the company has kept the same name (stripped of its original French accents), although its members change frequently – in contrast to Lepage, for instance, who has changed the name of his theatre company several times while retaining a core of collaborators from the beginning of his career. The name focuses on the relationship between audience and performer, where spectators become accomplices in the stage action, in the sense of participating imaginatively. However, McBurney has also given a slightly different description: 'Complicite in French doesn't have quite the pejorative meaning it does in English though I like the idea that it's a partnership in an illegal action, that there is something wicked about it. It's meant in the sense that when the audience watch the actors the sense of relationship between the actors on stage might be so intimate that with a bit of luck the audience might whisper to one another in the middle of the show: "I bet they're fucking each other" ' (Cited in John O'Mahony, 'Anarchy in the UK', *Guardian*, 1 January, 2005). And the shock-effect of that metaphor points to a deliberate quality in the work devised by Complicite.

This is a deliberately uncomfortable style and focus, where form is set in harsh contrast to content, a concept is extended to the point where it becomes grotesque, or apparently unstageable material is transformed into a vehicle for theatrical virtuosity. So, for instance, in

Fig 6 *Mnemonic* (1999). Directed by Simon McBurney. Photograph by Sebastian Hoppe.

Simon McBurney (b. 1957)

A Minute too Late (1985) – one of their earliest pieces, remounted twenty years later at the Royal National Theatre (NT) (2005) in recognition of its status as a key turning point in the development of British theatre – the morbid subject of death was inverted into an uproarious slapstick event by satirising ordinary people's clumsiness in dealing with mortality. Alternatively, the violence of Fascism is set within whimsical fantasy, with inanimate objects and live people being interchangeable, like open books fluttering into a flock of birds, or actors turning their bodies into furniture in *The Street of Crocodiles* (1992), McBurney's dramatisation of Bruno Schulz's short stories. Or the completely abstract is turned into the physical and visual in *A Disappearing Number* (2007), a piece McBurney devised about the remarkable collaboration between two mathematicians, Srinivasa Ramanujan, a poor Brahmin from South India and a Cambridge don, G. H. Hardy. Throughout his career, his work has been marked by challenging intellectual exploration, as for instance with *Mnemonic* (1999), an investigation of memory which layered the present over the past, paralleling a contemporary story of lost love with the recent discovery of a Neolithic hunter, deep-frozen in Alpine ice – or with *The Vertical Line* (also 1999), devised together with John Berger (whose strong Socialist novel, *The Three Lives of Lucy Cabrol*, had formed the basis for one of his most fully developed pieces of physical theatre in 1994), where the significance of the excavation of Neolithic cave paintings at Vaux was evoked in the unconventional setting of the disused Aldwych London subway station.

While several of the directors interviewed here were influenced by Jacques Lecoq, only McBurney counts as a true disciple, attending L'École Internationale de Théâtre Jacques Lecoq in Paris for two formative years, at a time when Peter Brook was heading up the Centre for International Theatre Research in Paris, although he had already gained a reputation for wordless comic mime while studying at Cambridge, in the reviews presented at the Footlights theatre, where he worked with Hugh Laurie, Stephen Fry, and McBurney's then girlfriend Emma Thompson. McBurney has continued to privilege mime and wordless action in the pieces he develops. In the characterisation of some of his shows, the influence of *commedia dell'arte* can be discerned, which also derives from Lecoq, although McBurney rarely uses the masks that are one of the bases of Lecoq's work, except when directing works like Brecht's *Caucasian Chalk Circle* (1997) that require masking. Choreographed movement combines with naturalistic expression as well as stylised gesture in his productions, to create a striking physical comedy – to which after his earliest pieces, dialogue was increasingly added – and McBurney has also experimented with music both in *A Disappearing Number* where, as he has remarked, 'when Ramanujan is formulating his equations, the accompanying tabla music actually corresponds to the numerical patterns in his mind' (Kate Bassett, *Independent*, Sunday, 9 September 2007) – and through his collaboration with the Emerson String Quartet in *The Noise of Time* (2000).

Certain themes recur in McBurney's work: particularly the inhumanity of the modern world, depicted through characters crippled by stunted desires or unable to communicate verbally, where the stage offers a counterpoise of vibrant human potential through the high-energy and acrobatic physical performance. In many ways his 1997 production of Ionesco's Absurdist classic, *The Chairs*, where the elderly actors Geraldine McEwan and Richard Briers were choreographed into a bravura display of physical action, is a perfect illustration of Complicite's theatre, playing as the drama does on stage props (the chairs – which McBurney points to in the following interview as being particularly evocative) substituting for people, as well as an orator who is dumb and can only mime his message. And indeed, McBurney's work contains many aspects of Absurdist comedy.

Most recently, McBurney has been experimenting with the integration of modern media and live action, a new direction that first emerged in 2003 with *The Elephant Vanishes*, where his company visited Japan to work with the Setagaya Public Theatre of Tokyo. McBurney's extensive use of screens, video projections and light walls in this production was deeply embedded in the stories by Haruki Murakami used as a source. As McBurney has put it: 'Murakami puts his finger on something which we all feel. Sometimes people talk about an urban anomie or a dislocation, but I think it's much more specific than that. I think that in this ultra-consumerist society we live in, we are experiencing a disquiet particular to the way we are living'

(*Guardian*, 1 January, 2005) and the resulting mix of sliding screens, projected images, and video footage reveals the banal conformity of everyday life. Since then he has used projected images and video in his National Theatre production of *Measure for Measure* (2004 and 2007), as well as making a film of the production, in many ways raising the same issues as Lepage's cinematic staging.

Christopher Innes*: We'd like to begin with the beginning, which is how you became interested in theatre?*

Simon McBurney: Well, I had a teacher who would say to me, 'If an actor has forgotten what it's like to play as a child, they shouldn't be an actor.' But, perhaps, one reason that I was particularly interested was because my mother herself had wanted to be an actress. She used to write little plays for us when we were small children, which we performed at Christmas time. There would be a script, and she would write the music, and we would learn our lines, and make the props, and we would decide where it was going to be and what the stage effects were and so on.

So your first involvement with physical theatre came long before any formal training . . .

Those plays were little pantomimes, and I loved the pantomime that was performed every other year in Cambridge by an old music-hall lag called Cyril Fletcher, who was brilliant with children. His pantomimes were really quite old-fashioned in many ways – they had real physical routines in them, and they would even end with a Harlequinade: not the full-blown Harlequinade of the nineteenth century, but the last echo down the centuries of *commedia dell'arte*. I remember that particularly because the person who used to take us every year to the pantomime was a woman called Enid Wellsford, who wrote a wonderful book called *The Fool*[1] – which was an absolutely definitive account of the life of that theatrical figure. I used to sit next to her, and she was always incredibly disappointed in the Harlequinade because she said it wasn't like that of her childhood. Betty Astelle,

---

[1] Enid Wellsford, *The Fool, His Social and Literary History*, London: Faber and Faber, 1935.

who was Cyril Fletcher's partner and played the principal boy, in her fishnet tights, even aged fifty-five or whatever, would always perform in the Harlequinade. So it was vaguely Harlequin, and it was vaguely Pantalone – but it was more like a sort of five-minute ballet and not terribly well done.

But growing up in a university town like Cambridge, with a strong theatrical tradition, must have been a particularly rich context.

Yes. By the time I was thirteen, I had performed in *The Tempest*, in *Macbeth*, in *Julius Caesar, Much Ado about Nothing, As You Like It*, partly because I was a child in a university town where there were a lot of productions of these things going on and they would need page boys every now and again. And that continued at school, where there were school plays and house plays, and all sorts of things that we performed. One that particularly struck me was an Ionesco play on death, called *Jeux de massacre* in French, and translated as *Here Comes a Chopper*. And when I was sixteen, I directed one of the house plays, which was Max Frisch's *Andorra*. Then, when I was about seventeen, a bit of a turning point was that I performed in a school production at a national student drama festival and won the best actor award. In my mind, I just thought, well, I can do that. I know I can do that; so why don't I do that? Afterwards when I went to university in Cambridge, I performed in about nine productions a year – a huge number – some of which got to the Edinburgh Festival.

Of course, Cambridge had established a reputation for home-grown comic, physical theatre with the group centred round John Cleese. Were you part of the Footlights?

I did perform with Footlights, and I appeared on television with Peter Cook, although I didn't really have very much in common with that kind of, um, elitist club. That wasn't really my spiritual and political home, which was Socialist, and more along the lines of a rather different experience: as a result of one particular performance at the Edinburgh Festival, somebody said, 'I'm opening a club in London called The Comedy Store,' and would I perform at the opening night. So then, aged nineteen or twenty, I performed at the opening night of The Comedy Store.

Simon McBurney (b. 1957)

You singled out Ionesco when talking about performing at school; and Continental European influences have clearly been a major factor in the theatrical style you developed. But Cambridge sounds rather insulated.

It was this kind of slightly split world that I lived in, where I participated in Footlights but also did quite a lot of experimental theatre; and I went to see theatre in London, particularly the things from Eastern Europe, like Tadeusz Kantor, that were going on at the Riverside. I remember seeing Suji Teriyama from Japan, and companies from India, and an extraordinary Belgian group called *Radéus*, which means radish. And I became fascinated . . . there was another world out there, quite different from the world where people went from Cambridge into the RSC, and then gradually into television . . .

Was this how you came into contact with Lecoq, who is always cited as a major influence on your work? And was he really as significant for you?

My father died, and a love affair collapsed. I wanted to escape, and so I went to live in Paris where I lived for four years. I spent two years studying with Lecoq, but in the evenings I also studied with Philippe Gaulier, who is still working in Paris. And then we'd go and see all of Brook's shows because Brook had quite a close relationship with Lecoq, and he would invite us to his dress rehearsals. At the same time I watched things coming out of the *Schaubühne*, the work of Peter Stein, and so on.

It sounds a quite eclectic mix.

Yes. I went to see a lot of theatre, and I felt, very often, that I didn't see the kind of theatre that I wanted to see.

Was that just the boulevard theatre you found unsatisfying, or does that also include Brook, Stein . . .

Some of Brook and Stein and the others, the work I saw, was inspiring – really wonderful. But none of it was the kind of theatre that I wanted to do. And I was determined that if I didn't find it, then I would make the kind of theatre that I wanted to see. At the same time, I performed a lot on the street in order to make money in order to go to the theatre school, and I felt quite strongly that I didn't want to hang around waiting for somebody to ask me to do something. I wanted to be doing, not waiting.

So how did you make that first step?

After Lecoq I started to work with a man called Jerome Deschamps, who was trained by the Comédie-Française and nothing to do with the Lecoq system at all. I did a couple of shows with him, as well as making a short film. And, I started the company while working with Jerome.

I put together an entirely fake tour. I put together some fake publicity with a friend, and we sent it off – in those days you could just send them off to Arts Centres and say, 'Are you interested?' Then we just rang them afterwards and said, 'Have you got our information? When can we come?' And, you know we didn't have a show. We just made claim to having a show; then once we had a little tour, we said, 'Well, now we have to have a show.' So we made a show.

And which show was that?

That was called *Put it on Your Head* (1983). It had the simplest possible setting: on the beach with deckchairs. People liked it, so we applied for a grant from the Arts Council. They gave us £1,000, which we used to make the next show: a piece called *A Minute too Late* (1985), which was partly about my father's death. And then, after five years of making devised shows, and making a film for television, and doing education projects all over the place, and touring all over the world – all the way through South America and the Far East and in Europe – we came back to London.

What brought you and the company back to England?

I had a friend in London, Pierre Audi . . . [2] When I was in Paris he was just starting out at the Almeida, which he took over as a kind of a toy store where somebody had been murdered, and turned into a little theatre. It was very, very rough in those days, but he was always looking for things which were new and challenging. And Pierre Audi gave us fifteen weeks at the Almeida, where we did thirteen shows – both us, and our friends. We gave an opportunity to a little new

[2] Artistic Director of the Holland Opera for fifteen years, now head of the Holland Festival.

company called 'The Right Size' to do some work, Hamish McColl and John Foley, who then went on to make things like *The Play what I Wrote*.[3] During that season, Annabel Arden and I decided that we needed a central piece, and decided to tackle Dürrenmatt's *The Visit* (1989), which was a turning point because we took it apart. We treated it in the same way as we would treat our own material.

To return to an earlier point: is there a way that you could describe for us the kind of theatre that you wanted to see?

In Paris in those years there were the dance companies coming through; and the relationship between dance and theatre fascinated me very much. But there's always the notion that, really, theatre could have a more profound impact, be of greater consequence to the people who were watching it – and initially I was interested in meaning and effect: how what you did affected the audience, how the audience was a part of the whole performance. In a sense, the easiest way for me to do that was making people laugh, because you had an absolutely immediate response whereby you could gauge whether what you were doing was captivating the audience or not. And, of course, I was very fascinated by improvisation.

When you are devising on a theme, a subject, what do you start with? Do you start with an image? Or do you start with a story? An object?

Yes, it varies, but it has to be the right sort of image or object. And one of the most beautiful objects, because it contains . . . the space of the human body, is a door frame; and doors imply movement, as well, even a sort of movement that expresses the culture. [*Takes out a folder of photographs*] You can see, here, this is a Neolithic house on the edge of Papa Westray in the Orkney Islands. In Neolithic times, this would have been sand and the sea would have been probably further up. So, this doorway is incredibly poignant because it says something about the nature of the protection that they had to create against the elements and for defence, too, because there are no windows in this house. The door is the only source of light and you have to crouch to come in.

---

[3] A musical farce about Morecambe and Wise, directed by Kenneth Branagh, which won an Olivier award in 2002.

Do you collect images, like these doors, that feed into your productions?

Sometimes, yes. Perhaps even more moving is the fact that the houses that came afterwards, which are these [*Points to other photos*], are pretty much the same and these are still lived in today. I find that very touching because there is a sense of continuity of ten thousand years, whatever.

This sense of history is, of course, what you got into in Mnemonic *(1999).*

Mnemonic, yes. But, it's something that's always interested me because my father was an archaeologist. And so, coming full circle back to the question of what theatre I wanted to see: when you do comedy and when you make people laugh, then you feel a kind of necessity in what you're doing for people. There is this simple engagement, where you are involved virtually in creating a kind of party, which is absolutely visceral, but where the audience doesn't feel they have to learn something from what you're doing.

And so, to answer this question about what was necessary in theatre, we need to think in terms of what is absolutely necessary. Can you make theatre where you say, 'Oh, I need that.' As a human being, I need to eat my bread, and I need to drink my water, and I need to have children, and I need to shit. Yet we know that there is part of the *homo sapiens* brain which is dedicated to the analysis and the reconstruction of music; and there is no part of the brain which is not there for some necessary reason at its origin. So music must be necessary, in some way, to human existence. In other words, we would not be able to exist without music. A life without music is impossible.

So, for you, the basis of theatre could be seen as music and dance.

I tend to think more like Meyerhold than Stanislavsky, because rather than thinking of actors as being sort of determined by a whole set of psychological circumstances, what interests me are the actions that these thoughts give rise to. Aristotle called theatre an act and an action; and in many of those acts, the act is committed and then comes the thought. Or what otherwise might be called the consequence is only known afterwards. Sometimes people know the consequence even before they commit the act, and yet they continue to commit the act even though their thought tells them that they shouldn't commit it: the act comes almost by itself. Of course, I'm thinking of Greek tragedy here. But, by and large, in drama most stories are about people doing something, and then what happens as a result of it.

There seems to be a big gap between the ritual qualities of Greek theatre and contemporary drama, but of course they both share a sense that the inner spiritual state has more value than the external person or context.

For me, as a young man particularly, the expression of what we felt . . . how you express a situation, and what you feel it ought to be, was exciting. When I saw forms of expression that seemed to most accurately convey internal sensations, I seemed to be returned to childhood, where we understand because we don't have access to certain sorts of vocabulary. So we feel it as a sensation, something beyond words.

Have you seen works that represented this non-verbal aspect? Who influenced you along these lines?

The way Tadeusz Kantor tried to deal with history as a kind of dream or fantasy, the way that Pina Bausch would try to deal with the nature of theatre and talk about the experience of the audience and the stage, by making her dancers jump off the front of the stage and run and shake everybody's hand. both were important for me.

The work of these directors makes for extremely vibrant theatre. Yet there seems to be a quality of despair in your pieces.

What was enormously important to me was feeling that the majority of our lives were totally banal. And that behind the banality of sitting down and having a cup of tea, was . . . I always felt, oceans of despair and disaster in stories. So, very often, in early shows, what interested me was the idea that the action revolves around a single moment. And that the whole show is only about a single moment, one tiny moment in time, in which everything is present and you sense what people are thinking. So rather than being a long story, it's a very short story which is then expanded over an hour and a quarter or an hour and a half. I would look at people around me in different situations in London, or wherever I was, and I would think: What is the story of that man and that woman walking down the pavement, sitting on that train? So I would constantly come back to the same thing. To a certain extent that's remained with me. Most of the devised pieces have a constant sense of repetition of image and place; and I'm very interested in the circular story, not just the linear storyline.

You talk about circularity and repetition. Thinking about your devised pieces, that seems to carry through beyond the individual pieces to your career as a whole. For example, A Minute too Late *gets revised in 2005, almost as a kind of classic piece of Complicite theatre. I don't know what you think about being thought of as a classic in your own lifetime, but how do you keep a devised piece so that it remains the same? Or was it the same as the original production?*

No it was not the same. It's never the same; it's different every time you bring it out because you start to change it. We've been asked to do that piece again, and I would quite like to change it further, to try and do something completely more with it and new with it, if we could.

To come back to the technical aspect of the devising process: how do you work with these actors to develop something out of nothing? Because it's nothing until it's realised in concrete terms, is it?

It's sort of chaos, and you work very often out of mess of one sort or another. You go in and you do whatever takes your fancy, really.

Who decides what works and what doesn't? And how do you put the show together?

By and large, I put the shows together. So, what you end up with is a huge number of fragments. The way that I make devised theatre varies an enormous amount, and I feel much more comfortable when it comes to stories or storytelling now than I ever used to in the past. *Mnemonic* was a very, very complicated process because the philosophical concerns had to be worked out. And one of the things that I did was to write a story to work from.

For example, in developing John Berger's work for performance, I wrote a story and then I put it to him, and then he wrote some words, and I wrote some words, and they started to coincide, and we used to take little cards and try and write the story in a set of one-liners. So

I would have that in my mind when I came to the rehearsal room. I already had a story mapped out in one way or another, which required a *mise en scène* to make it work. But then it remained in fragments among all sorts of other fragments while we were in rehearsal. Eventually, you have these fragments all over the floor and all over the walls and on bits of video; and you just simply start at the beginning, and you try and put them together.

And at what stage do you bring in material from other sources? For example, in Mnemonic *in 1999, where you used narrative from Conrad Spindler or Rebecca West?*[4]

Early, very early. The Rebecca West material came in largely because my mother had been Rebecca West's secretary, so I knew Rebecca West as child. And I had quite a close relationship with Sarajevo through a Bosnian friend of mine who'd been in the company doing *The Caucasian Chalk Circle* (1997), who invited me to go to Sarajevo just literally after the war finished. It was an absolutely staggering experience. So I started to meditate a lot about the fragmentation of Europe and what lay at the heart of that . . . and I became interested in the relationship between memory and culture, because, you know, we can't have consciousness without memory. But our consciousness is a cultural phenomenon; and our sense of culture is also based on another form of history, which is our collective history or what is commonly known as collective memory.

Your work tends to alternate between physical theatre without words, and theatre that uses all sorts of multimedia. Do you choose to shift these means of expression depending on the material?

If I have something to say, I use any means possible to say it. So that if I think that the best way of expressing this is through a moving image, which happens to be a video image, then I will do so. I also think that these are just tools. For me, video is an utterly human event. [*Holding up a stone axe head*] This is what my father called

---

[4] Conrad Spindler, *The Man in the Ice*, London: Weidenfeld and Nicholson, 1994; Rebecca West, *Black Lamb and Grey Falcon: A journey through Yugoslavia*, London: Macmillan, 1955. Both books formed part of the material used in *Mnemonic*.

technology; now [*Holding up a cell phone*], today people call this technology. But they are in fact the same thing; just slightly different forms of technology: there is an electrical charge within this piece of rock, and even though the electrical charge is not quite the same as the one in the phone, at a fundamental level the electricity is exactly the same in terms of the relationship between the molecules. There isn't a chip in this stone, but there is another sort of memory.

Even so there's a difference in the response to actors on a bare stage, versus actors surrounded by video screens. What makes you bring in video screens or work with a video artist like Frances Laporte?

When people talk about technology with a play, they tend to talk about it as if it's something exceptional. But my guess is that this perception will die out just as the chat died out about certain sorts of sets in the nineteenth century, which were all the rage back then – like the stage-machinery at Drury Lane: you know, there are still the original rollers that the horses used to run on so that they could gallop across the stage. How thrilling must that have been at first! Yet, at a certain point, people are no longer fazed; there is nothing new about it. So, when I use video, it's just simply another form of impression which can bring a piece of theatre alive and help you say what you want to say; help you get the story across and help you to imply certain things and create the dimension that you want to create. Moving images are so much a part of our everyday lives.

Did you see any television yesterday at all?

I saw a little bit of Wimbledon.

But whether you actually turned on a television set or might have listened to the radio, or not, probably in the street you would have seen something subliminally on screens in windows, you will have heard some sort of recorded music. And, almost certainly, being in London, you will have been filmed. All that is just simply part of the means of communication, which involve every part of our lives. So when I make a piece, then, as far as I'm concerned, video is part of the grammar of the show, just as it is the syntax of the way we live our lives. I don't really make a separation. What I can say is that every time I make a show, I use whatever means are appropriate to the material.

Simon McBurney (b. 1957)

But with Measure for Measure, *at one point while touring India in 2005, you did a performance with the video screens in one theatre and then without them in another. Can you comment on the experience of doing that?*

Well, material circumstances. When we planned it, I thought, 'Well, fuck it, I'm not going to sort of patronise our Indian audience by saying, "We can't have what we did in London." So let's take the whole thing and see if we can make the whole show as we did it originally.' But then, if we were going to do a tour at all, we couldn't take all that technical stuff along with us everywhere, simply because of the sheer cost of it. So we said, 'Well, that shouldn't preclude us doing the show. Let's just do the show anyway, and I'll restage it; because we know the words so well; they're totally in our bodies, so that we can do it in any other circumstance.' And I used the same thought when I filmed *Measure for Measure*, which I did at the end of playing it in London.

Were you still playing it when you recorded the production?

Yeah, playing it the same time I filmed it. That was meant partly as an exploration into the way that theatre and film co-exist.

The second time you did Measure for Measure, *in 2006, you not only directed it, but also acted the Duke, which is a very central role indeed. How do you find that alters the way you approach the play when you are actually the central focus of what you're directing?*

It makes it very difficult for everybody else. But it's something that I've always done. I'm an actor first and foremost. And I'm a director by chance rather than design. Rather than director, I would say I'm a theatre-maker. I think of a director as a kind of fake job in any case.

There's a wonderful man, a music critic called Hans Keller. I don't know if you remember him?

How is he relevant?

He wrote a book in which he took a knife to his own profession, saying, 'There is no such thing as a music critic'; and he went on to list various other musical professions as jobs without real function, among them the conductor; and I would say a theatre director is quite similar.[5]

5 Hans Keller, *Criticism*. London: Faber and Faber, 1987. (An émigré from Vienna who later became a charismatic figure at the BBC and a trenchant commentator

I don't have any problem with that because I think theatre is a charlatan's profession; and the charlatan has a very honourable tradition. But I'm a performer. That's where I started and that's how I make things. I can feel when something is right. I have a sense of what the whole thing looks like.

You mean, a physical sense?

Yes, when I'm in it. Also, when I'm acting in a piece, I tend to hear the architecture of the whole thing, not just what I'm doing. I'm not making an exceptional claim for myself in saying this. I think a lot of people could do that. All actors do, at least to some extent. They feel something about the whole piece, even if they have to sit out in the wings or in their dressing rooms. I always want to participate in the whole experience.

So that, as a director, you work from inside a production . . .

To go back to what I said earlier, and what I feel very strongly about, the experience of theatre – is that theatre doesn't really exist. A play is not theatre, we know that; but what the actors act on stage is not theatre. Theatre is created in the minds of the audience. It's an imaginative act. It's this act of collective imagination which is so critical to theatre and why, if you like, there is something necessary in theatre, because it tells us something about the nature of what it means to be human. Part of the nature of what it means to be human is to imagine together.

But Simon, you're going to be imagining differently according to the elements that are being offered for you to imagine with.

Yes, of course. But the key thing is not the elements that are offered to you, but the act, which the audience undergoes, and whether they all see the same thing at the same moment.

Well, they won't though, will they, either literally in terms of sightlines, or in terms of how their personal backgrounds condition their perception?

Of course they won't see exactly the same thing. But when you're doing comedy, you can get different degrees of laugh, and the

on a host of issues – including football – Keller was a leader in musical psychology.)

laugh that you really want is the one where you feel that 99 per cent of the audience go 'Ha', together. Then you know that that is . . . and you can feel it and it goes up in musical waves. It goes, 'Ha ha ha; ha ha ha ha; hahaha; ha ha – bang.' And it's the one that will often get a round of applause. At that point, you know that the audience is all hearing and imagining the same thing at the same time. Now it doesn't have to be comedy. It can be a silence in the audience. It can be weeping, It can be an in-breath. It can be something as simple as your awareness of the way that an audience is paying attention.

Can you talk about Genoa 01(2002) *in terms of this unifying connection to the audience? How did that piece come about?*

Well, when I was asked to do something to take to Genoa, there were various people from the festival at the Royal Court, and I was handed this little script. I was fascinated because it was an account of what happened in that particular G7 summit from the point of view of the protest; and I was interested in this sequence of voices. What tickled me was that I hadn't read anything which was so straightforward in its account of protest or resistance since the sort of agitprop stuff I had seen at the end of the 1970s. And I was just fascinated to see what would happen by putting it out there.

So in this case political passions became the unifying force for the audience, rather than the laughter of comedy.

Unfortunately, it only had two showings, which meant that I didn't really get a chance to adjust the nuances of what I wanted to do, and so, in a sense, it wasn't quite fair on the piece. The piece was very exposed on the first night, very bold. But by the second night, it had already started to take a shape from giving a musicality to the words in the way that I wanted the words spoken, which was extremely neutral. The difficulty was that, like most actors, the actors all got very involved, and they gave it a lot of emotion. I kept saying, 'You know, we take away the emotion from this and we allow these events to speak for themselves.' Well, we never quite achieved that, but I was fascinated whether it would be possible to make that material work in another way.

In other words, you were consciously working against the material, which as a script struck me as very documentary.

What I didn't want was that people should go, 'Oh, we've heard that before; we don't want to be told anything; we don't want to listen to a piece of didactic information.' I didn't feel it was didactic in any case, although it could come across like that.

In fact the whole piece seemed very different from your usual work.

In terms of the kind of work that I do, I'm constantly interested in what I haven't done before. In terms of *Genoa 01*, what interested me was the subject: in other words, the resistance and the politics of it, and to remind people of what actually had happened and to remind that there is resistance of some sort.

Not just the subject, but also the form of presentation – because it was a stage reading.

Because it was kind of a stage reading, yes, and because it's very bold in its politics, and also because it's not obviously a piece that has an imaginative construct at its centre. So it was very challenging to try and make it work. But I like taking on things that people think are not necessarily possible to do. That's why I loved doing *The Street of Crocodiles* (1992), because nobody could see how that could possibly be dramatic, or work theatrically. Lots of people came out at the beginning saying, 'Yes, but where's the story?' But by the time we finished the run, people were absolutely transported by it. They were made aware that drama exists as something other than the idea of the well-made play. Conflict and dramatic situations can occur in so many different ways, particularly when you're talking about the nature of the imagination or, indeed, as we were talking about earlier, the nature of memory.

When you talk about the nature of the imagination, the object I've been most conscious of is all the chairs that appear in your pieces.

The chair, for me, is a far more common thread in my work because what I'm very moved by is the space of the human body when the human body isn't there – the implication of the human body – which is implied by the chair in the same way as a door frame is the space that a human body occupies. I am very interested in the body itself and its presence because it seems to me that is fundamental to all theatre – the presence of the body, what it does and how it acts and reacts, underlies every theatrical act.

Simon McBurney (b 1957)

Even when you are, perhaps, performing the most verbal kind of theatre: Shakespeare's plays, as you have several times for the National Theatre?

But I would say that Shakespeare was the most physically present – you have to be so physically present in Shakespeare for it to function. All those actors that people tend to allude to when they think of a literary tradition are in fact extraordinarily physical. Think of people like Richardson and Gielgud and Olivier: the thing that Gielgud did with physical presence was very particular. I mean, it was registered in his voice.

In parts of *Measure for Measure*, I wanted people to stand stock still. The way I rehearsed it at the beginning was I wouldn't allow anybody to do anything. I just wanted them to speak the words directly out to the audience ... what I think is difficult in Shakespeare is not the fact that people are verbal from the neck up, it's the fact that they're all trying to act. Don't act in Shakespeare. Find the music. Find the musical rhythm of it, first and foremost. If you can find the musical rhythm, then you can find the shape, the dramatic shape and the emotion at the heart of it, because Shakespeare gives you clues as to why something happens, in the words themselves.

So would you suggest that the phrase often used to describe your work as physical theatre is actually nonsense?

All theatre is physical. It so happens that I have a facility to move – so I am interested in the physical expression of an emotion. I'm interested when someone can do a backward somersault, that you can have a feeling of joy as a result. And this response to movement could be the purest expression of joy. You don't have to smile or make a series of clichéd signs. You can find a more original way and a more exciting way to express that moment. That's what you want to do: to pull the audience along in the forms of expression that you find for that moment in the drama.

And do you find when you're doing a back flip, or any athletic movement, that as well as expressing joy to the audience, it makes you feel joyful?

It can do. It can make you feel joyful, but the key is that the audience should be taken by surprise. The physical act should have an intensely powerful effect on the audience. So in Elizabethan times, the effect must have been extraordinary to see the king's body brought in and laid on the stage in a coffin, at the end of Shakespeare's *Richard II*, that physical effect must have had a shocking resonance.

In your view, then, it is the cultural and intellectual context that makes the physicality of theatre powerful?

Yes. And the shocking resonances of these physical acts are critical to our understanding and our engagement with the audience.

So for you, the actor doesn't have to feel the emotion that is being expressed?

Yes. I mean they're welcome to feel it. But the most important thing is conveying the feeling, because, as I said before, the theatre takes place in the minds of the audience; and it is the audience who must feel, not the actors. However, if in getting the audience to feel, the actor doesn't understand what it is they should be feeling, then, of course, it will become very superficial – as, for example, towards the end of the nineteenth century because of the conventional nature of acting. Then at the beginning of the twentieth century, you've got the revolt against that, with everyone going back and saying, 'Yes, but what do we feel? And if we play what we feel, maybe, the audience will recognise the truth of what we're doing, then they will feel it too.'

Are you referring to Stanislavsky's concept of actors searching inside themselves for emotional truth, or to the Expressionist's attempts to find physical techniques for expressing emotion directly?

It's a certain sort of realism that's important. Actors start to try and really feel an emotion; and that becomes very shocking. The audience go, 'My goodness, there are people really crying. They're really feeling it!' But then, of course, that becomes a cliché as well, because everyone's seen it a hundred times on stage, on film – someone crying. Then they go, 'Well, that's not such a big deal, I see it every day when I go and watch the latest soap opera.'

So you have to continually change your approach in order to find new forms or emotional realism that would be equally shocking?

You know, we live in a time in a society where we are surrounded by more fiction than any other time in history, and so we are anaesthetised to a certain extent to what goes on around us. Therefore, as artists, when we are trying to express these things, we have to reveal them as being true. In order to reveal them as being true, they have to have the shock of revelation because most of the time, as spectators, we don't quite believe the truth of what we see because we've become more and more aware of fiction. At the same time, the more we don't believe, the more people become fascinated by what is supposed to be true. So, in terms of television, in the beginning you get the sort of stories that are shocking, but that soon stops being real. Then it's game shows, which are supposed to be real people in real situations, and eventually, it ends up with just watching people sitting in a room where they don't know they're being watched, or they forget about it. So you get the situation of *Human Zoo* and *Big Brother*, or any other kind of so-called reality television. By now, we're so inured to reality television that we're inured to reality.

To take this from a slightly different perspective, is that partly why you have tried performing in untraditional places, as with Mnemonic, *or together with live music – as in* The Noise of Time *(2000) – and in that millennial production, is there a particular reason for choosing the music of Shostakovich?*

Shostakovich because, of all artists of the twentieth century – almost more than any other artist – he managed to describe the horrendous and ambiguous relationship between personal action and public declaration, which accompanied all the different forms of tyranny that were at the centre of the twentieth century. And we, of course, are still enormously affected by these tyrannies, living in the consequences of their actions. Growing up at the end of the twentieth century, I was fascinated by him. Somehow, through the music, he was so able to make you feel the . . . moral dilemma of the twentieth century. You feel the light and the dark; you feel the humour and the tragedy; you feel the violence and the sensuality, very often within a single piece.

But when you are staging a piece to accompany this music, you are injecting physical movement. How do you determine the relationship of movement to music in that piece?

One of the things it seems to me is that frequently you have to shape an image in people's minds before they can see what's going on. You have to find a way of ushering people through a door . . . into a new space: partly because of this sense of numbness that people have, but also because we separate out the nature of our theatre – the nature of theatre in our lives – that's to say we go to a theatre and we think of that as theatre; and very often we don't think of Sunday lunch as theatre. But that is also theatre in its own way.

Shostakovich is theatre. The symphonies are enormously dramatically structured.

Of that, there is no doubt. And so my feeling was that if you listen to the Fifteenth Quartet on its own – and it's a very difficult quartet to listen to – so you couldn't imagine that you're going to listen to *Death and the Maiden*, then a piece of Brahms, then Shostakovich's Fifteenth. There has to be a story that leads up to it. By and large, when Shostakovich's Fifteenth is performed, it's played with Twelve, Thirteen and Fourteen before it, and then you hear Fifteen. So in playing Thirteen and Fourteen, what are you doing before you arrive at Fifteen? Well, essentially, you're telling a story of how Fifteen is arrived at because you hear the relation to the earlier pieces. So what you're actually hearing is also a dramatic and biographical story.

In a sense what I wanted to do with the Fifteenth, is to make people think about all different sorts of aspects. To restructure people's minds in the same way as when they watch *On the Money*. In playing a trick on them, [leading them to think] that they were simply going to listen, they felt they were within a concert. But then they were not within a concert. Then they were made to think about the radio, and they were made to think about listening. I played them different sounds and different thoughts and different ideas to make them listen in a new way. So that when the notes finally started, you have a story out of which it emerges. So that just as an artist will try and make us look at something they see, and we see it from a different perspective – just as sometimes we go to the same place which is a favourite viewpoint, and the view we see looks different – I wanted people to come to this piece and feel that they were listening to it with new ears; that they were discovering things within it that they hadn't thought about.

But that also had to do, surely, with the fact that you were moving in counterpoint to the music.

Certainly. But whether what we did before they played made any difference, or whether the orchestra played it differently because of what we did, I know that most people, when they came out of the experience, felt that they had heard this piece in a new way.

Would it be true to say that this was the closest that you have come to being a choreographer?

No, I mean, there's choreography in *A Minute too Late*. Indeed, there's a whole formal dance. I love working with movement, and I love the consequence of movement. I like to play with movement always, and I find music absolutely inspiring. But I would very much like to make a piece which is only movement, which perhaps has no formal narrative – stories talk.

When you speak about opening up completely new spaces, no form of narrative and so on, does this relate to the work funded by what you call your accomplices, which you describe in one place as 'the creation of new mischievous and deviant and disruptive work'?

Experiment, experiment: it's a purpose in itself. In order to achieve work at this level, I need to be constantly trying new things out, and I've done a lot of different exploratory and experimental work . . .

Do you mean through your workshops?

Workshops – yes. And, as it were, I've started work on pieces, but I don't know when they're going to appear. So, yes, that's part of where the accomplices come in because they help fund those experiments and those experiments give rise to pieces, and they merge eventually. They merge later down the line.

So your workshop is kind of internal exploration that may, eventually, result in new pieces. Or may not.

One piece of exploration might lead into another piece of exploration, so that the new piece I'm working on, which is about mathematics, also will probably involve certain bits of work that I've done on physics which is interesting. Some of which connects back also into earlier pieces. I mean, I did quite a lot of exploratory work on memory and the biochemistry of memory to make *Mnemonic*.

There's clearly an internal consistency to your career, both thematically and stylistically. As a closing comment, is there any particular vision that motivates your work?

These things are a little bit like saying, 'So they'd already had an experience. Their brains were thinking in a completely different way.' Of course, inevitably, you lose some people because some people would reject the whole experience out of hand and, therefore, reject anything that happened afterwards. But, by and large, most people went through it. So what is the most sunflower part of the sunflower? You know, it's impossible to say what it is. I mean it appears to be one thing, but that is dependent on another, and once you start taking the sunflower apart, then you can't see the whole. I can't really see the whole of what I do, or the reasons for what I do.

I can sort of make things up; and when I give interviews I tell what I consider to be a large number of rather delightful lies. I'm aware that I repeat a lot of stories, and sometimes I try not to repeat those stories, but I'm gradually trying to write some of these things down myself, and to find forms in which I can write them down.

Chronology of selected productions

1983   *Put it on Your Head*, devised by Theatre de Complicite. Almeida Theatre, London

1985   *A Minute too Late*, devised by Theatre de Complicite. Institute of Contemporary Arts (ICA) Theatre, London

1986   *Foodstuff*, devised by Theatre de Complicite. The Albany Empire, London

1987   *Anything for a Quiet Life*, devised by Theatre de Complicite. Almeida Theatre, London

1989   *Anything for a Quiet Life*. Film version
(Co-director with Annabel Arden) *The Visit* by Friedrich Dürrenmatt, adapted by Maurice Valency. Almeida Theatre, London

1992   *The Street of Crocodiles*, adapted by Simon McBurney and Mark Wheatley from the stories of Bruno Schulz. Royal National Theatre, London (NT)

1994   *Out of a House Walked a Man*, adapted by Jos Houben, Simon McBurney and Mark Wheatley from the writings of Daniil Kharms. NT, London

Simon McBurney (b. 1957)

The Three Lives of Lucie Cabrol, adapted by Simon McBurney and Mark Wheatley from the story by John Berger. Theatre de Complicite, Manchester City of Drama Festival

1997 (Co-director with Juliet Stevenson) *The Caucasian Chalk Circle* by Bertolt Brecht, trans. Frank McGuiness. NT, London
To The Wedding, adapted by Simon McBurney, John Berger and Mark Wheatley from the novel by John Berger. Radio production on BBC Radio 3
The Chairs by Eugene Ionesco, trans. Martin Crimp. Theatre de Complicite, Royal Court Theatre, London

1999 *Mnemonic*, conceived and directed by Simon McBurney, devised by Theatre de Complicite. Lawrence Batley Theatre, Huddersfield
The Vertical Line by John Berger with Sandra Voe. A site-specific production for the disused Aldwych tube station, London

2000 *Light*, adapted by Simon McBurney and Matthew Broughton from the novel by Torgny Lindgren. Theatre de Complicite, Lawrence Batley Theatre, Huddersfield
The Noise of Time, based on the life of Dmitri Shostakovich. Theatre de Complicite with The Emerson String Quartet, Lincoln Center at the John Jay College Theatre, New York

2002 *Genoa 01* by Fausto Paravidino, trans. Gillian Hanna. Royal Court Theatre, London

2003 *The Elephant Vanishes* by Haruki Murakami. Setagaya Public Theatre, Tokyo

2004 *Strange Poetry* by Simon McBurney with Gerard McBurney. Walt Disney Concert Hall, Los Angeles

2004 *Measure for Measure* by William Shakespeare. NT with Theatre de Complicite, London

2007 *A Disappearing Number* by Simon McBurney. Theatre de Complicite, Barbican Centre, London

Selected bibliography

Fleischer, Mary (2005), 'The Elephant Vanishes', *Theatre Journal* 57: 1, 115–17

Halliburton, Rachel (2005), 'The World's a Stage', *New Statesman* 18: 841, 41–2

Hopkins, D. J. and Shelley Orr (2005), 'Measure for Measure', *Theatre Journal* 57: 1, 97–100

McBurney, Simon (2007), interviewed by John Tusa, 'Transcript of the John Tusa Interview with Simon McBurney', BBC Radio 3, 21 November 2007 www.bbc.co.uk/radio3/johntusainterview/mcburney_transcript.shtml

(1999), 'Simon McBurney' in *On Directing: Interviews with Directors*, ed. Gabriella Giannachi and Mary Luckhurst, London: Faber and Faber, pp. 67–77

Medlock, Tim (2007), 'In a Thicket Asian', *Theatre Journal: ATJ* 24: 1, 287–90

Mendus, Clive in conversation with Maria Shevtsova (2006), 'Competitive Co-operation: Playing with Theatre de Complicité', *New Theatre Quarterly* 22: 3, 257–67

Williams, David (2005), 'Simon McBurney' in *Fifty Key Theatre Directors*, ed. Shomit Mitter and Maria Shevtsova, London: Routledge, pp. 247–52

7　Katie Mitchell (b. 1964)

A graduate of Oxford University, where she performed, directed and was President of the Oxford University Dramatic Society, Katie Mitchell moved quickly into the ranks of the Royal Shakespeare Company, the Royal Court and the Royal National Theatre (NT) where she is an Associate Director and where, by the end of 2007, she had staged twelve productions. She reaped awards along the way, the first a Time Out Award in 1991 for *Women of Troy*, which, in a new production in 2007 from Don Taylor's translation, won her the notoriety she had already begun to attract with *A Dream Play* (2005). This was largely due both to the production's very stylised, hallucinatory quality and the fact that it was based on a heavily edited adaptation of Strindberg by playwright Caryl Churchill, to which Mitchell and her actors had added their own material. Probably no director in Britain today divides critical, and at times public, opinion as much as Mitchell.

However, the challenge to Mitchell as a director has come not from institutions or critics – her early works were unanimously praised – but from texts, which she treats meticulously – 'precisely' and 'accurately', she would say – in order to seize but supersede the words on the page. She analyses texts in great detail and probes into their sociocultural and historical contexts with admirable scholarship; and the honour she thus pays them covers both the classical repertoire, in which the Greek tragedies rub against Chekhov, Ibsen, Strindberg or Beckett, as well as her contemporaries, Martin Crimp foremost among them. Crimp, with whom she has established strong collaborative ties in his capacity both as playwright and translator, provided her with a translation/adaptation of *The Seagull* (2006) whose excisions (asides, soliloquies, expositional dialogue) and colloquialisms (for instance, Masha tells her husband Medvedenko to 'piss off') caused widespread debate. Yet his intention to make the play 'fully connect with contemporary audiences' (quoted in the *Evening Standard*, 28 June 2006) accords with Mitchell's desire to make classics speak in the language of the times. Hence her affinity with Churchill's rendition of Strindberg and with Taylor's vernacular 'update' of Euripides, including *Iphigenia at Aulis*, which she directed in 2004.

Mitchell may have come as much under fire as Crimp for her jagged, Modernist *mise-en-scène*, its nervous play and twentieth-century anachronisms (gramophone, microphone and tango, among them). But none of it was merely 'director's theatre at its most indulgent', as the *Guardian* critic, Michael Billington, had asserted (28 September 2006). Its purpose was to extrapolate from Chekhov's play rather than offer a to-the-letter interpretation of it – Mitchell's means of getting to the core ideas of the work, of extracting the marrow that invigorates the skeleton made up of words. In this she is not altogether different from Stanislavsky, who sought the life behind the words, the substance within surface appearances and the clear, focused energy that allowed actors to incarnate what they were saying, feeling and doing. Her extrapolatory approach is, in fact, part of her preoccupation-tussle with texts: a way of working closely with them, thereby acknowledging their potency, but also of making them flesh without making them literal; thus a way of *not* making texts sacrosanct.

Frequently, in her productions, extrapolation takes the form of dance so that dance serves as a metaphor for the relations between people in a particular situation and the emotions criss-crossing between them. The tango in *The Seagull* was not a metaphor eloquent enough in that production's oddly disconnected scenic world to make its point. By contrast, the quickstep in the 2007 *Women of Troy* to the blast of big-band swing succeeded in metaphorically articulating the confident authority of the war machine, its ruler–victim dynamics and its devastating impact on the body and soul, individual and collective.

Mitchell had already explored the metaphor of dance for a war situation in *Iphigenia at Aulis*, the prelude to the Trojan War of which

Trojan Women is the aftermath; and both are redolent with memories of Pina Bausch, Mitchell's fierce admiration for the choreographer having become increasingly palpable in her work over time. In *Trojan Women*, she resolves the problem of how to tell a tale of unspeakable horror by showing it in a surreal environment. A cacophonous soundscape that ends in a deafening bomb blast in a nice middle-class London theatre – the National Theatre, to boot – is an integral part of this surrealism: the reality at issue is so monstrous that, to be grasped at all, it can only be seen and heard as surreal, as something beyond normal apprehension. By adopting this stratagem, she clinches the recurrent themes of her work – war, violence (in various guises), the family – through which, in the past five years, she has foregrounded the moral, social and political collapse inherent in the spin-doctoring on the war in Iraq. This war and its 'collateral damage', the supreme euphemism of current 'spin', is evoked both metaphorically *and* subliminally rather than in explicitly analogous terms. The mechanisms of spin are, in another, more generalised social context, largely the subject of Crimp's *Attempts on Her Life* of 1997, which Mitchell reviewed ten years later in 2007 with a dose of caustic humour in a production whose fully deployed technology, visible in every moment to the audience, is both the media and the message of the slippage between fabrication and truth.

Yet, although her work has a political edge, it is not consistently openly sharpened by a political viewpoint, as is the case of Peter Sellars, for example, who figures in this volume. Mitchell's emphasis is on what she calls 'behaviour' which, too, undergirds her attitude to texts. In her words:

> The question is whether you think theatre is performing words, or whether you think it's representing human behaviour . . .
> My interest is in being thorough about representing behaviour and emotion. I love words, but I am not interested in doing live literary criticism.
>
> (*Guardian*, 24 November 2007)

Behaviour on the stage, for Mitchell, is not a matter of behaviouristic, knee-jerk reaction on the part of actors, but of their appropriate externalisation, kinetically, of the emotions of their characters. She grounds her investigations in the research of neuro-scientists, for example, of Antonio Damasio, to whom she refers in her conversation with the author to follow. (Damasio's books include *The Feeling of what Happens: Body and Emotion in the Making of Consciousness*, 1999 and *Descartes' Error: Emotion, Reason and the Human Brain*, 2000.) Here Mitchell proves to be in relay with Stanislavsky, attempting to develop by the scientific means available at the beginning of the twenty-first century the research he had carried out at the beginning of the twentieth, inspired by the physiologists and psychologists of his period. It is important to repeat that his initial research via science into the corporeal impulses of emotions and their corporeal manifestation was for the purposes of finding the principles of acting. The drawbacks of Stanislavsky's scientific project apply also to Mitchell, but, in her own way, she shares his passion for trying to make the actor's art and craft knowable in order to extend the actor, together with the art and the craft.

To this end, Mitchell's work with actors entails collective dis-covery, which is acknowledged in the programme for *Waves* (2006) as 'devised by Katie Mitchell and the Company' from the novel *The Waves* by Virginia Woolf. Similarly, the programme for *Attempts on Her Life* notes that 'Katie Mitchell and the Company' had directed the production. Much of the work in rehearsals is improvisation through which actors and director evolve a shared way of doing and under-standing. And it is precisely her need for a shared 'language' that drives Mitchell to work as much as possible with the same actors again and again so as to construct ensemble-like conditions when such condi-tions are lacking in Britain. She works essentially with the same production team as she moves from theatre to theatre – sound and costume designers, choreographer, and so on – with the same sense of ensemble in mind.

With *Waves* and *Attempts on Her Life*, Mitchell explores bodily impulses from another angle: how they are activated in the making of sounds and images by all sort of makeshift as well as technologically advanced means. *Waves*, for instance, operates like radio drama – paper is rustled, floors are scraped, water falls to simulate the sound of rain – except that the actions producing the sounds are reproduced by video and computer images. *Attempts on Her Life* is a much more ambitious variation on the play of sonic and visual effects, which the actors make while, simultaneously, they record and film what they are making. Film cameras, cables, headphones, small images, enlarged images and screen images that dwarf the human beings configuring them – all this speaks about spin, identity, conspicuous consumption, celebrity mania and the mechanisms of making television, movies and theatre. However, from an actorly point of view, crucial to Mitchell, it obliges the actors to act and react quickly, on the spot. This is not altogether unlike the principle of spontaneity for keeping actors alert and alive as they go 'live' that is familiar from LeCompte and The Wooster Group, even though it comes from a very different vision and method, and gives quite different results. Mitchell's use of technology is, fundamentally, a variation on her goal of 'representing behaviour and emotion' as she rejects 'live literary criticism'.

Maria Shevtsova: *You went on a grant from the Winston Churchill Memorial Trust to research director training in Russia, Poland, Georgia and Lithuania. Why did you go there rather than anywhere else?*

Katie Mitchell: I had always wanted to see how theatre was made in these countries. I started my own little company when I was at school, which I took up to the Edinburgh Fringe in the mid-1980s. While there, I saw some work from Poland, which made a very powerful impression on me. There was a female director, whose name I cannot remember, who tried to do *The Maids* in a really weird place, a performance by Tadeusz Kantor and Theatre of the Eighth Day. Later I saw work in London by directors like Lev Dodin, Anatoly Vasilyev and the Polish company Gardzienice. I decided to go to Eastern Europe because I was looking for a different type of theatre to what I saw in Britain. There was something – and I couldn't put my finger on what it was – that was absent, if you like, here. And I had a hunch that I would find it in Eastern Europe. This hunch was based on what I'd seen of theatre from those countries, particularly the work of Gardzienice with whom I spent a lot of time subsequently. Going to observe the work of Wlodzimierz Staniewski [founder of Gardzienice] was probably the nearest you could get to a practical understanding of the physical and vocal work that Grotowski had written about in *Towards a Poor Theatre*.

Before I went to Poland I went to Moscow and Leningrad, as it still was in 1989. I had already been to Leningrad in 1988 on an architecture tour. I really wanted to see the work of Lev Dodin and saw *Stars in the Morning Sky*. Dodin's wife, Tatyana Shestakova, whom I had already seen in Klimov's film *Come and See*, was just remarkable in it. Indeed, the whole production was extraordinary because it was fully imagined by the actors. It wasn't a discreet, mediated, modified version of human behaviour. It was a fully imagined version of it, probably closer to how we are with all our bumps and rough edges and ugliness and cruelty. There were no theatrical clichés in the acting. It was just fully and accurately imagined. If you were in that situation, you could understand perfectly why you might behave like that. It seemed to be very, very logical.

Russian and Polish films and books had made a deep impression on me. For example, I was introduced to the films of Tarkovsky at university, and the combination of subtle acting with poetic images in films like *Mirror* and *Nostalgia* had a lasting impact on me. As did Klimov's *Come and See* and his wife Laura Sheptiko's film, *The Ascent*. *Come and See* remains my favourite film of all time. Then there is Solzhenitsyn and Tolstoy. I read a lot of Russian literature as an adolescent, so I was very immersed in nineteenth-century Russian culture.

Why Tarkovsky, Solzhenitsyn and Tolstoy?

I love the wilfulness of these artists. Tarkovsky manages to get out precisely what is in his head, frame by frame: accurately, precisely, it obeys his own logic. His work is immaculate and he is a constant master of his medium. And, he's interested in very big and hard ideas in terms of human experience. Tolstoy: I just loved *War and Peace*. His humanity reminds me of Homer. They are right about war, and they judge no one. They have a very big prevailing idea, which is, finally, that they are pacifists. Tolstoy's exquisite drawing of human detail. The way the gunshot hits Andrey, and how everything goes slow and he falls back, onto the ground. Ah, I've opened Tolstoy, and guess who's walked through? Dostoyevsky, of course! Well, now, I'm going to *The Idiot*, which is my favorite Dostoyevsky novel. Solzhenitsyn? I was quite interested in him politically, in what he had suffered. *The Gulag Archipelago* was my first entry into his writing. I realised that he had done in *August 1914* what Tolstoy had done in *War and Peace*: it was exactly the same novel, the same form, the same idea – only much later on. Again, it is just so thorough and precise, and looks at human beings without mercy, forensically, as much as it is possible to do this.

What is striking about everything you have just said is the recurrent motif of war. Is your concern with war behind your decision to turn to the Greek tragedies, starting with Trojan Women *(Women of Troy for your production) in 1991? And you have come back with a new production of* Women of Troy *in 2007.*

Those productions were responses to very specific wars going on at the time. *Women of Troy* was a response to the first war in the Middle East and the Russian invasion of Lithuania; *The Phoenician Women* (1995) and *The Oresteia* (1999) were responses to the Bosnian war; *Iphigenia at Aulis* was a response to the 2004 war in Iraq. I revisited *Women of Troy* in 2007 because it was the most perfect play about the aftermath of a war. I hoped that the production would therefore speak to the situation in Iraq now. Obviously there is not a direct parallel between the play and Iraq, but the text does raise questions about the behaviour of victims and victors alike in a post-war environment.

The production has no resemblance to the one I directed in 1991. It is a different translation – Don Taylor's. Nearly half the text has been cut and the use of sound, music and dance creates another personality for the chorus.

Which of the five did you find the most challenging?

The Oresteia. I was in charge of the first play, *Agamemnon*, which is relatively straightforward. I struggled with the second, *The Libation Bearers*, and I didn't have a strong idea for the third. I realise in retrospect that you can only direct *The Oresteia* if you have a very clear picture of what you want to do with the *Eumenides* because it's the climax of the whole work. What happened in my production, and I imagine this happens in other people's, is that the climax comes with *Agamemnon* and then, after that, it's a matter of diminishing returns.

Of course the big climax happens when Athena comes down to earth.

It should be, but we didn't have a strong enough idea for that arrival to work dramatically.

I was very struck by the fantastic sense of flow in your Iphigenia, *by its dynamics, energy, rhythm and pace. You kept up the momentum, and all your actors kept it up. How did you work with them to achieve this?*

It is very difficult to talk about it without going through all of the steps of the rehearsal process, which create the layers of what you see in the final production. All the actors are working with several very specific, concrete tasks all the time. Most of them have three or four very difficult tasks, and these tasks are supported by changes in light, sound and design.

Also, there were sections of free improvisation in *Iphigenia*, which required a certain type of focus. For me, everything is in the planning before you get to the rehearsals. So, you analyse the material very carefully, not its surface detail, but the deeper structure underneath the text. You look for the turning points in the text, which I call 'events', and then you look for what people are playing in between these 'events'. You are looking for the structure of ideas in the play. What is it actually about? I think the themes of *Iphigenia* are war, violence, political expediency, the family. It is hard to talk about process because it involves so many simple, concrete tasks.

Maybe you could give me an idea of how you do it by breaking it down a little, step by step?

There is the pre-rehearsal analysis, where, as I said, I analyse the events and intentions and the idea structure of the play. Also, I analyse the characters' histories, from when they were born up until the beginning of the action of the play. I work alongside the designer to make choices about the environment that will help the actors play the text. Not just any environment, but the one that will actually help them play the text as I have analysed it. Then, obviously, there is research. One needs to know who Euripides was, why he wrote the play, and what was happening in his country at the time. In the case of this script, I needed to do a lot of tiring textual-genesis research because Euripides died before he had completed his text. He had written all the Chorus lines and about 60 per cent of the scenes in total. His son or nephew then did some additional rewrites before it was performed. Then, a hundred years later, someone called 'the reviser' – frightening name – changed what was there and added other material. So, even trying to find your way through that to try and work out what play Euripides wanted to write is quite a job. That is the bulk of the preparation.

Once in rehearsals, the first thing we do is read the play. No one reads their own part. We read it in a circle with each actor saying a line at a time. They are encouraged to read it for the sense only. Then we list the facts. This is the information in the text which is non-negotiable. For instance, it is Greece; Iphigenia is the daughter of Clytemnestra and Agamemnon; Helen is in Troy with Paris; there is a town called Aulis, and so on. Then we list the aspects of the material which are less clear. These aspects are put in the form of questions: When did Paris take Helen to Troy? When did Agamemnon and Clytemnestra get married? How old is Iphigenia? Where is Aulis? We keep to very simple facts and questions all the time. And, then, different actors will be set different tasks so that we can begin to answer some of the questions. For example, the actor playing Agamemnon will research the number of ships in the Greek fleet; the actor playing Clytemnestra will find out about the walled city of Argos where the family lived; the actors in the Chorus will start to do research into where Aulis and Calchis are. Wherever possible, these research tasks are tailor-made to fit individual actors so that they only research what they actually need to know in order to play the scenes in the play.

The first thing to emerge from this work is a sense of place. Very soon the actors will have drawn a map of the area. In this case it included Greece and Troy (part of modern-day Turkey). They would also have a more detailed plan of the cities of Aulis and Calchis. Each actor would then build a plan of the house where they lived, room by room, and the immediate environment.

Every actor then has to organise the facts about their character's history in linear order and look for the gaps, which, over time, will have to be filled in. In order to pin down the precise years in which events took place the actors have to start to work together with those actors playing characters with whom they share a history. A consensus is reached by reading the text, talking about the impressions it gives, and historical research. Then we do improvisations of the main events in all the characters' biographies. We start as far back as we need to and then do the improvisations in the order in which they occurred. As far as I remember, the first improvisation we did was about the death of the father of Menelaus and Agamemnon, the loss of the kingdom and the war the two sons had to fight to regain the throne, which happened about thirty years before the action of the play began.

Sometimes the actors also have about twenty minutes a day to work on their own character. They can work on whatever aspect of the character they choose.

How do they do that?

They have to choose a specific time, a specific place and a specific activity or idea to investigate. The only caveat is that the character has to be on his or her own. For example, one of the women from Calchis, which is where the Chorus comes from (Calchis is opposite Aulis), could decide that she wants to investigate the theme of war and how she talks to the gods. She would decide to be in her prayer room, she would choose a specific god to pray to and she would ask that god to stop her husband going to war. It would be 11am, her son would be at school and the servants would be out shopping.

Does the action necessarily have to be verbal? Could it be mime, or purely movement?

It just has to be the behaviour of the character in a specific time and place. In some situations people don't talk, they just think. In other situations they might talk to themselves or just do a banal activity, like cleaning their boots. The actors' task here is simply to enact a slice of their characters' life. All the actors do the exercises simultaneously in the rehearsal room. That way they feel less scrutinised by me and their peers and can get on with filling any gaps they have in the picture of their character.

Alongside this, we do practical work on the themes of the play. I would ask the actors to think of a situation from their own lives which relates to any one of the play's three or four themes. These slices of life are re-enacted in front of the group and help us see the actual meaning of the intellectual ideas behind the play. So, for instance, we measure the idea of violence against a very practical exercise where someone enacts something violent that happened in their real life. For example, one actor had been going out with someone from Belfast and they were stopped by the police. We look at what really happens to human beings, physically, mentally and psychologically when they are in life-threatening situations.

Recently I did some research into the biology of emotions and this work was also fed into our rehearsals of *Iphigenia*. Science defines six primary emotions: anger, fear, surprise, disgust, happiness and sadness. We studied the negative range because those are the ones that dominated in the play: anger, fear, sadness and surprise. For scientists, the definition of an emotion is a change in the body, internally and externally. So, as we did improvisations based on specific emotions, we looked at what happened physically to the body when these emotions occurred. At the end of each improvisation, I would ask the actors, 'What did you notice?' and encourage them not to project psychological readings of these situations, but simply to notice what happened physically. How did the person clean their shoes, fast or slow? How were they breathing? Was their head to the side or not? What about their hands? Were they twitching?

As well as primary emotions there are also social emotions, like jealousy, envy, and background emotions. Background emotions are physical changes taking place at a low level, like when you feel 'a bit under the weather' or 'a bit low'. Later, when we came to work on the scenes themselves, we would often decide on the primary emotion generated by a turning point in the action and ensure that it was played precisely physically. The Chorus, in particular, did a lot of work on physicalising emotions accurately. This work might well have contributed to what you called the 'energy' and 'momentum' in the performance.

Every day the actors also do movement work to prepare for acting and, in the case of *Iphigenia*, they danced the foxtrot daily because it was a big ingredient in the production. I try to break the day into a balanced diet between movement, dance, improvisations (like the ones I have described), research and text work.

After about two weeks of this diet we return to the text to analyse the events or turning points in the machinery of the play. We then give names to the events and the sections in between the events. Next I start to ask the actors what their characters play in between the events. There are lots of different words to describe this, like objective, intention, task. I tend to avoid these terms as much as possible and instead ask, 'What do you want to make the other people do?' The answers to these questions are then noted down. When we first do the first scene rehearsal we concentrate on the events and tasks. These are the deeper structures that run beneath the surface of the words. In that first rehearsal the actor practises these structures. It does not matter if the actors do not remember the precise words of the text. They only need say what they remember of the text or invent other words to make other people do what they want them to. This way of working is incredibly useful for actors because they play the play at its deeper level. They do not play the surface of words, which, as we know, is such a small part of what actually happens between people. This is a Stanislavskian way of doing the first scene rehearsal, and I think Dodin works in the same way, too.

He does. How did you come to this approach?

Much mainstream theatre here is very preoccupied with words and hearing them spoken clearly. There is less interest in representing human behaviour accurately, where words take more of a back seat. Expressions of human behaviour in theatre tend to be either exaggerated or too discreet or made up of self-conscious and artificial gestures and sounds. This type of theatre does not interest me. When I went to Eastern Europe in 1989, I started to see another type of theatre that was not interested only in speaking words clearly or characters behaving artificially. I was lucky enough to watch Lev Dodin and Anatoly Vasilyev training young directors. I spoke to the Lithuanian director, Euimentas Nekrosius, and watched three of his productions. I met the Georgian director, Georgi Tumanishvili, and watched him teach students for a couple of afternoons. These are very extraordinary practitioners, all of whom, I discovered, practise a different version of

Stanislavsky. Since then, I have tried to understand, practically, how to make that type of theatre.

Many people have helped me on this journey, some taking a lot of time to teach me different aspects of Stanislavsky's system at different points in my career. Tatyana Olear, who trained as an actor with Dodin and then performed in his *Cherry Orchard* and *Claustrophobia*, came twice to the UK to do two two-week workshops with British actors and myself. The director James Macdonald and I were watching, and then she would set us directing tasks, many of which we found very difficult. It was rather wonderful. There we were, in our forties, and unable to set up an improvisation efficiently or diagnose the idea of Chekhov's *The Seagull*. Those four weeks were a tremendous influence in my working practice. Tatyana also saw productions over a period of two years, giving very useful notes on the work.

At around the same time, in 1999, I met the director Elen Bowman who had trained at the School of the Science of Acting set up by Sam Cogan. Cogan had combined a training in Stanislavsky at GITIS, the prestigious drama school in Moscow [now known as the Russian Academy of Theatre Arts], with work as a psychiatric nurse before coming to the UK in the 1970s. His very rigorous director's training reflected both fields of interest and entailed a high level of psychological self-scrutiny. I trained with Elen over two-and-a-half years in one-on-one sessions or together with the actor Robbie Bowman. It was incredibly useful because, as Elen said, in order to get better at directing, you have to study yourself in life. This helps you analyse a character and makes you learn how to help an actor to get into the skin of a character.

I had a three-year Fellowship (2001–4) from The National Endowment of Science and the Arts (NESTA) and studied neuroscience through the books of Antonio Damasio, a Portuguese–American neuroscientist, with the help of the neuroscientist Mark Lythgoe.

Did your NESTA research have to do with body functions?

No, it did not start out like that. James Macdonald and I were invited to apply for the grant and in our application we put down different disciplines related to the theatre which we wanted to research: dance, visual arts, architecture, psychology and music. Our aim was to see whether the investigation of any of these disciplines would enhance our ability to direct. I found most of the disciplines relatively easy to investigate, but psychology foxed me. I stumbled across biology by chance at a dinner party. Somebody said, 'If you are having problems with psychology why don't you step back and look at biology? Neuroscientists today, having neglected the biology of the emotions for years, are coming around to it because they think it is the gateway to consciousness.' So I started to read in the area and found it enormously useful. It is the removal of the skin, if you like, of psychological reading and getting down to the nuts and bolts of brain scans and what the body does. But, this came right at the tail end of the research.

How did the actors, when working on Iphigenia, *find this research useful?*

I have to go back one step, and then I will give you an example. Antonio Damasio defines an emotion as a change in the body, which is legible to someone looking at you. Of course, there is also change inside the body which accompanies the external change, but that is pretty invisible. When you receive a stimulus, which triggers a strong primary emotion, there is a half-second delay between the stimulus and your becoming conscious of it. There are bodily reactions to the stimulus in that half-second. If it is a very life-threatening thing, like a bear, you could jump back five metres. But, because we are not conscious in this half-second, we do not always remember it. So, sometimes, in our acting, we edit it out. This means that the audience cannot read what is happening.

In *Iphigenia*, for example, Achilles, the young hero, prepared his whole life to go to Troy and fight in the war. He is not interested in women or in getting married. In fact, he is sick of them because all the mothers in Greece keep throwing their daughters at him. He is then told, out of the blue, that he is about to get married. In our production, the actor took the risk of taking a three-metre leap backwards in surprise at the news. The leap filled that critical half-second and everyone in the audience knew that the emotion the character was experiencing was surprise. Throughout the performance we tried to add all these extra physical frames in: the frames of what happens physically in that half-second between stimulus and becoming conscious of the emotion. These are involuntary bodily reactions. They are like the reaction that happens when you blush.

There is a lot of surprise in the play and you have noticed that the Chorus often physically jumped to mark that surprise. This was something they had to practise. We studied the emotion of surprise quite a lot and how it affected us physically. Of course, we were working outside in and inside out, both at the same time, and both methods were feeding the process. All the work on the physicality of emotions was designed so that the emotion targeted would occur in the audience. Sometimes, for the emotion to occur, you just have to replicate the physical responses accurately and not try to repeat an inner emotional state.

It is astonishing to think about it in these terms. I think the audience was totally gutted.

The actors were all working to unsettle you, and they were primarily doing that physically. So, none of the characters were ever allowed to settle physically. The background emotion, as the scientists call it, which we were aiming for was anxiety. (A background emotion is a low level of bodily change, like when you say 'I feel a bit low.') You'll notice how in life you are always shifting, moving, fiddling if you are anxious. There was no stillness until the little girl, Iphigenia, arrived. To enhance the stillness we had all the action go into slow motion for her arrival.

This may account for my sensation, as I watched the production, of its perpetual motion.

Yes. It was constructed, of course. The actors all knew the event which surprised them, so everyone was going to jump, to a greater or lesser extent, depending on the impact of the event on their character. When you are watching this occur, the effect that you immediately get is change. Then there is another event, and another change. What creates the sensation of motion that you refer to is probably due to this and due also to the very strong emphasis on time and place in the production. The actors had to play the time pressures for real. In some cases the characters could barely communicate what they needed to communicate because they were under so much time pressure. They

191

Fig 7 *Iphigenia at Aulis* (2004). Directed by Katie Mitchell. Photograph by Ivan Kyncl

also played place. They really imaged the place they were in and really imagined that there was an army of thousands stationed through the door of the building where they were standing. These are really simple ingredients. I am not saying anything new at all, but, sadly, these very simple concrete tasks, like time and place, which are demanding to play, are often omitted from pieces of work and the result is that nothing happens in real time or in a real place. Instead, we get a mixture of everyday behaviour from real life, where time and place affect our actions, and behaviour derived from stage conventions. When the two types of behaviour get mixed up in a production, which is often the case, it is very hard for the audience to read what is going on because the two types of information come at them – one artificial and one life-like.

How did you sensitise your actors to playing time? Did you have time exercises?

Oh, it is very straightforward. If I said, 'Maria, you have only got five minutes to do this interview with me' – this would completely determine how we speak to each other. As a director, you set different time tasks depending on the effect you want. And you set different tasks about the place. You make them imagine different things about the place.

How about the production's rhythm? Did you have the actors pace around or do something off stage so that they could come back in with great momentum?

Oh, yes. The actors never stopped acting, whether they were on stage or not. They had booths off stage in which they could improvise and, in some cases, the booths had microphones in them so that their offstage improvisations could be relayed onto the stage to interact with the action in the scene. Clytemnestra and Iphigenia, for example, would go through a backstage door into a booth which had furniture, objects and a table – it was the room in which they were staying in the hotel. They continued the actions that they would have done – getting changed, nattering to each other or whatever – and these improvisations were relayed through microphones back into the room for the Chorus to react to. Even before they both arrived in the hotel before their first scene, Clytemnestra and Iphigenia had a separate booth, which represented the carriage that was taking them to Aulis. They started improvising the journey in the carriage at the beginning of the show, but did not come on stage for their first 'scene' for about twenty minutes. Then they arrived, did one scene, went off and kept improvising in the booth until they came back on. They never stopped acting, even though we did not see every bit of their acting. Similarly, Agamemnon, the Chorus and everybody else had booths or places off stage where they could either prepare for their first scene or continue the action in between scenes. It was all structured backstage like that so that the actor could keep acting because then the audience gets a higher quality of work.

You can see the war motif in the costumes: these are women of the 1940s. What inspired you to have the Chorus – all women – dance the foxtrot?

We wanted to bring the production as close to our time as possible. However, we could not bring the action any further forwards than 1940 because the arguments made by a woman (Clytemnestra) to save a child include womanly virtues, like good housekeeping, which are an anathema now. The 1940s was the latest we could set it. The gender politics in the play would not be credible if we set it after the 1940s.

Why not?

Because they would be making arguments in modern-day clothing that we would find extraordinarily stupid. Because, now, we would make different arguments to political leaders in order to stop children from being killed. I mean, obviously there are some basic arguments like, 'She's a child', 'She's our daughter', that make sense to us. But, there are other ones like, 'I keep my house so well', or, 'Everyone who comes to my house for dinner parties has such a wonderful time', or, 'Your palace is always clean', that would, I think, make people laugh.

Foxtrot? In the ancient Greek productions it is said that the performance moved from the sung or spoken word to dancing, especially in the choruses. We wanted to find a way of being faithful to these formal switches in the original, without donning masks and doing strange arm movements from old vases. One of the big ideas in the play is power and we were keen to find a way of investigating this in the choruses. In the scenes we worked on the idea of these women's powerlessness in the face of latent male violence. We continued to do this in the choruses, but using the form of dance. The women were, if you like, dancing at gun-point in front of a faceless male audience. The change of form into dance stimulated and surprised the audience and kept them more engaged in the ideas of the production. Originally, I thought it should be waltzing, but my movement director said, 'No, women of that type and class are more likely to foxtrot than waltz', and he was right. We also needed a form of social dance that would feel inappropriate in the circumstances.

Then there was the influence of Pina Bausch working on our thinking. She often uses social dance to provide a structure to movement which is repeated, or breaks down, or is inappropriately executed.

I also particularly liked your sound score, with sound coming in and out, giving different perspectives of sound.

That's Klimov! But Gareth Fry was a fantastic sound designer. We have worked for many years together and realised, over time, that you can use sound as powerfully as visual information or acting. It is another tool to work with on creating emotion in the audience and, therefore, communicating the idea of the play. Obviously, in this play, we wanted to unsettle and disturb. Sound working on a subliminal level can really do that. Much of the sound was played at quite low levels. And it supported the physical work the actors were doing on anxiety. When there was an event in the scene, the sound would change with the event. The sound designer followed the map of events and intentions that the actors were playing. He was working hand in glove with the actors, deepening and supporting their work. He was also in rehearsals for a few weeks before we did technical rehearsals in the theatre so the actors had an opportunity to work with the sound.

You have placed a great deal of emphasis on structure. How much freedom do the actors have to make individual choices in the structure? I am sure that you do not say, 'You do this, you do that.' You are not a mechanistic director, but how much leeway do they have for their own fantasy?

Well, an actor's fantasy is very dangerous! I call their fantasies affinities. This is a word which Elen Bowman taught me. If, for example, there are four themes in a play, a director will have an affinity with one theme, possibly with two. If you just direct one or two of the four themes, you will be directing only 50 per cent of the play. It is the same with the characters. The actor reads the character and turns it round like a three-dimensional object, and, unconsciously, is drawn to the side that he or she likes or has the greatest affinity with. For example, the actor playing Clytemnestra might notice several sides of the character – mother, queen, wife of an army general – but most likely she will be drawn to mother more than the other two aspects of the character. If she were only to play the mother, which is the easiest to reach and probably chimes personally with her the most, then she would neglect the rest of the character and her performance would be unbalanced.

The worst thing that can happen is that the actor sees some side of the character to play which isn't even there. So, for me, the fantasies of actors – or directors – are not always useful if they manifest themselves in affinities. When affinities get in the way of the actor I tend to draw them back to the writer. The writer becomes the mediator. I say: 'It is very interesting that you, as the actor, have this thought about your character, but what does the playwright mean when he or she says x' and I refer them to a bit of the text. I could say: 'I know you might find it distressing, but, unfortunately you are going to have to absorb what is there in the play.' A lot of it is making actors see the three-dimensional structure of the play and the character so that they play everything, not just one little muscle of it. However, I do not tell them where to stand, or, if I do, I do it much later on in the process. Mostly, as long as they are acting logically in the situation, I do not mind where or how they do it.

Well, that is freedom of a limited kind.

What they have to play is their intention, time, place, the events, all the facets of their character and all the relationships their character has. You know the actor who is in a room of ten people and only plays one relationship, as opposed to ten. You have to play ten. It is more stimulating.

How have your productions affected your sense of your work as a director?

I'm not sure directors think like that. If you stand on the outside, you can think like that and put it together. If you are on the inside, you do not make measurements. Or, the measurements you make are so fine, and about a specific aspect of the working process. You never come up above your work and look down upon it as if it were a map of a city and go, 'Oh, I see now how that happens.' There are, however the odd moments of insight. I once realised that I only directed plays about war or family. That dawned on me when I was updating my CV one day. But, that was a chance occurrence. I'm pretty sure that directors do not try and create meaning in that way for themselves.

Let me try to put it this way. You know how, in everyday life, with time, we slowly become more and more conscious of ourselves and see patterns emerging in what we do. And, slowly, we can articulate something about ourselves. Call it self-consciousness, or self-awareness, or introspection. Does a director slowly build awareness of how he or she works?

That definitely happens. You can have this wonderful moment when you do not have as much time as you need to prepare but you know you are prepared because you know exactly what tasks the actors need to focus on in order to do the play.

And you know how to pose the question correctly and communicate it accordingly?

Yes. It is not that you are without fear, but you have the right amount of fear.

You have four Chekhov productions behind you. Is it true that directors feel they should tackle Chekhov at some point in their life?

I suppose every director wants to direct Chekhov. He is difficult because he is not a playwright.

Oh? Go on.

Sometimes he is a playwright and sometimes he is a prose writer. Therefore, sometimes his plays are relatively straightforward to do and, at other times, they are near impossible. Normally, the impossibility comes in the more lyrical fourth Acts – in *Uncle Vanya* (1998) and *Three Sisters* (2003), for example. Chekhov's writing seems in transition from one genre to another in *The Seagull* (2006). There are bog-standard farcical scenes, like Arkadina persuading Trigorin to come back to her in Act Three, mixed with exquisite symbolism, like the blast of wind in Act One or the flapping curtains of the discarded stage in Act Four. We tried to draw up the more poetic muscle of the play but kept running aground on the other material. I have a love–hate relationship with Chekhov. If I was just reading the material as literature and did not have to put life in front of an audience on stage, I wouldn't mind at all because he is so accurate about human behaviour and has a forensic, merciless eye. But he is not always formally accurate. He starts writing a play and it slides into a novel and then back into a play. It might just be my taste, but I really find some of his lines a bit crude for theatre, especially when people say things that they would only think. So I think it's a good idea to have your scissors to hand when you're about to direct Chekhov.

What did you scissor in Three Sisters?

Not as much as I would do now. Often, you only know what to cut after you have done a piece. Cutting a text can also be a perilous business. By mistake you can cut through major arteries! I understand now that it takes hours of work to analyse Chekhov in order to direct it because you cannot see the deeper structure easily. You look and look, and think, 'Where is the event?' 'Where is the turning point?' 'What intention could possibly link all the words the character is saying in that unit together?' It is terribly hard. *Three Sisters* was a labour of love, of analysing line by line. Even so, there are sections of Act Three, which I think are weak. I do not know what some of the characters are playing. I have no idea why Irina has incredibly long speeches in that room, at that time, to those people. Sections of Act Four feel expositional. I think it is really challenging and, if you do not get the deeper structure, it is like walking through a snowstorm. You cannot see anything.

Speaking of the difficulty of seeing – what about A Dream Play *(2005)?*

We spent most of our time looking at dreams. People brought in their dreams, and we tried to re-enact them. We studied how dreams operate and tried to apply those rules to the text, which was fascinating. We devised material as well as working on Strindberg's text.

Katie Mitchell (b. 1964)

Do you mean 'devising' for this in the sense in which you meant the term earlier?

No, it is bolder. In *Iphigenia*, the text goes along and then there might be a two-minute improvisation within an agreed intention and purpose. The actors go off the text into improvisation and then back onto the text, whereas with *Dream Play* we went off the text for much longer into devised material and also cut substantial swathes of the play. The overall map of Strindberg's play was there, with its big themes and ideas, but we added material from our dreams to it.

We also book-ended the story with two scenes about the person having the dream in the waking world before he falls asleep because there is nothing worse than not knowing whose dream it is. I am sorry I am so literal, but I need to know who the dreamer is. It could be one of three people. Some people argue that it is three people dreaming simultaneously, but I think there would be a credibility issue for the audience because of it. So we added two new scenes taking place in the waking world. We see the character who is about to have a dream, and what his life is like, and why he had the dream. We understand why he had the dream and then we wander inside his psyche.

It appears from the production's dance sequences that you pay homage to Pina Bausch. Has she influenced your thinking about staging, and how?

I first saw Bausch's *Nelken* in Paris when I was twenty-three: it was breathtaking. The influence was originally to do with costumes, psychology and her articulation of male–female communication (or non-communication). Later I studied her work on video and noticed the attention she pays to design, space and light. These observations subsequently influenced my work with designer Vicki Mortimer. And, yes, the dance sequences were a quiet homage to her.

How different is Caryl Churchill's rendition of Strindberg's text? Did she consult you or work in collaboration with you as she was writing?

We used about 40 per cent of Strindberg's text in Caryl's version. The rest was devised material from different sources, mainly the actors' dreams, Jung's book on dreams and Freud's *The Interpretation of Dreams*. At the point that I asked Caryl to do the version

I had no idea that I would only use such a small proportion of the original text. However, I had a hunch that I might chop some of the text and add new material. I told Caryl this. When Caryl was working on the version, we had several meetings where we went through her version together. So it was a collaborative process at that point. Afterwards, Caryl came to several rehearsals and, when she wasn't able to, we kept her abreast of all the changes and cuts we were making.

Did her version pose any particular questions or problems for you from a directorial point of view?

No. She was very true to Strindberg's original material so the problems that we faced were those inherited from Strindberg. If anything, Caryl made our job easier by finding a more compressed form of words that mirrored the Swedish better and by using anachronisms that communicated the original ideas more effectively to a British audience today.

Waves (2006) and *Attempts on Her Life* (2007) are very different stylistically from your preceding work. Do they indicate a change of direction?

The multimedia work on *Waves* was something I had been dreaming of doing for many years. It's probably the production I most wanted to make since starting out in the 1980s – but a production I could not work out how to achieve until now. I have struggled with the linear narrative and language obsessions of the mainstream theatre for most of my career. I have never been convinced that it is the most efficient way of articulating how we experience the world. It is certainly not how I experience the world. My experience is more fragmented. I remember a book by Paul Broks about two theories of self [*Into the Silent Land: Travels in Neuropsychology*, 2004]. One is the Ego Theory: we are driven along by a homunculus that sits in our head, like a driver in a car. This self does not change from when we pop out of the womb until we die. The other is the Bundle Theory: we are a constantly changing bundle of people, always reconfiguring ourselves in response to external stimuli. Many scientists think this is how the brain functions. The Bundle Theory suits me. And Woolf's writing gets very close to that. Her book liberated me from the constraints of narrative, and the video allowed me to use image instead of words to capture behaviour. Yes, it does mark a departure for me. And there is more multimedia work on the horizon. I will tackle Dostoevsky's *The Idiot* using the same tools, Schubert's song cycle *Die Wintereise*, a project on Glenn Gould and Asperger's Syndrome, and an opera by Luigi Nono.

You have staged operas, but did Handel's oratorio Jephtha *(2003) – a different form from opera – pose any staging difficulties?*

When we were working on *Jephtha*, the main problem was finding a style for the acting and motivating the choruses so that they were credible psychologically. In the end, we opted for realism, a strange solution given the formality of the music. The Chorus of forty were given individual characters, backhistories and clear functions in each scene where they appeared. This was a challenge which the Welsh National Opera Chorus rose to with gusto and, in many ways, it was their absolute commitment to the characters they were given, the world we were making and the issues at stake that made the production work. In many ways, it is about a community as much as it is about individuals.

As far as the protagonists were concerned, we worked, except for a few things, as I would have worked with actors on character, relationships, time, place and so on. The rehearsal periods are much shorter in opera – five weeks compared to theatre's eight weeks – and much of the time can be taken up with musical concerns. We therefore did less work on areas like backhistory, improvisation and textual analysis. After about three days of working on these things, we moved on to the scenes themselves. So much depends on the conductor's contribution and it is impossible to measure the nature of that contribution unless the singers are actually doing the scene. We ended up working more on the hoof, but always insisting that the actors adhere to the values of fourth-wall realism.

The overriding challenge was to present the story, characters and events so that an audience would believe that they were happening in real time to real people. It was made in the run-up to the invasion of Iraq and we wanted the production to have a conversation with that situation.

What was different in your staging of Jephtha – and also of opera – from your staging of plays?

If you have a Chorus of forty people you simply can't ask them to improvise on a nightly basis. You have to fix what they are doing. Neither can the singers improvise very much since they need what they are doing physically to be pretty fixed so that they don't worry about how to sing and move at the same time. Therefore, what happens on stage tends to be more planned when I work on operas than when I work in the theatre. For example, when working on the design of a play, I will concentrate on making a world and leave the minute details of how that world is used until very late in the rehearsal process. The use of space evolves with the actors. In opera, I tend to have worked through the use of the space in much more detail. The operas will always be more choreographed by myself and the movement director than the plays.

This is an abridged version, also updated for the purposes of this book, of Katie Mitchell and Maria Shevtsova's conversation in *New Theatre Quarterly* (2006) 22: 1, 3–18.

Chronology of selected productions

1989   *Stars in the Morning Sky* by Aleksandr Galin. Royal Shakespeare Company Fringe Festival, Stratford-upon-Avon

1990   *Arden of Faversham* (anon.). Classics on a Shoestring, Old Red Lion, London
Vasya Zheleznova by Maxim Gorky. Classics on a Shoestring, The Gate Theatre, London

1991   *Women of Troy* by Euripides. Classics on a Shoestring, The Gate Theatre, London
A Woman Killed with Kindness by Thomas Heywood. Royal Shakespeare Company (RSC), The Other Place, Stratford-upon-Avon

1992   *The Dybbuk* by S. Ansky, trans. by Mira Rafalowicz. RSC, Barbican Centre, London

1993   *The Last Ones* by Maxim Gorky. Abbey Theatre, Dublin

Katie Mitchell (b. 1964)

Ghosts by Henrik Ibsen. RSC, The Other Place, Stratford-upon-Avon

Live Like Pigs by John Arden. Classics on a Shoestring, Royal Court Theatre, London

1994   *Rutherford and Son* by Githa Sowerby. Royal National Theatre (NT), London

Henry VI: The Battle for the Throne by William Shakespeare. RSC, The Other Place, Stratford-upon-Avon

1995   *Easter* by August Strindberg. RSC, Barbican Centre, London

The Phoenician Women by Euripides. RSC, The Other Place, Stratford-upon-Avon

The Machine Wreckers by Ernst Toller, in a new version by Ashley Dukes. NT, London

1996   *Endgame* by Samuel Beckett, Donmar Warehouse, London

1997   *The Mysteries* (anon.), in a new version by Edward Kemp. RSC, The Other Place, Stratford-upon-Avon

Beckett Shorts by Samuel Beckett. RSC, The Other Place, Stratford-upon-Avon

1998   *Uncle Vanya* by Anton Chekhov, in a new version by David Lan. RSC, Young Vic, London

1999   *The Oresteia* by Aeschylus, in a new version by Ted Hughes *1. The Home Guard 2. The Daughters of Darkness*. NT, London

The Maids by Jean Genet, trans. by Martin Crimp. Young Vic, London

2000   *The Country* by Martin Crimp. Royal Court Theatre, London

2001   *Katya Kabanova* by Leoš Janáček. Welsh National Opera, Cardiff

Mountain Language/Ashes to Ashes by Harold Pinter. Royal Court Theatre, London

Iphigenia at Aulis by Euripides, trans. by Don Taylor. Abbey Theatre, Dublin

Rough for Theatre II. Film for *Beckett on Film Project*, Blue Angel Films/Tyrone Productions for Radio Telefís Éireann and Channel 4

2002   *Nightsongs* by Jon Fosse. Royal Court Theatre, London

Face to the Wall by Martin Crimp. Royal Court Theatre, London

Ivanov by Anton Chekhov, in a new version by David Harrower. NT, London

2003 *Three Sisters* by Anton Chekhov, in a new version by Nicholas Wright. NT, London

Jephtha by George Friedrich Handel. Welsh National Opera, Cardiff

2004 *Iphigenia at Aulis* by Euripides, trans. by Don Taylor. NT, London

Krapp's Last Tape by Samuel Beckett. Dramaten, Stockholm

Forty Winks by Kevin Elyot. Royal Court Theatre, London

2005 *A Dream Play* by August Strindberg, adapted by Caryl Churchill. NT, London

The House of Bernarda Alba by Federico García Lorca, in a new version by David Hare. NT, London

2006 *Not I* by Samuel Beckett. Radio play for Beckett on BBC, Radio 3

The Seagull by Anton Chekhov, NT, London in a new version by Martin Crimp.

Waves, devised from *The Waves* by Virginia Woolf. NT, London

2007 *Attempts on Her Life* by Martin Crimp. NT, London

The Jewish Wife by Bertolt Brecht, trans. by Martin Crimp. Young Vic, London

St Matthew Passion by Johann Sebastian Bach. Glyndebourne Festival Opera

The Sacrifice by James MacMillan. Welsh National Opera, Cardiff

Women of Troy by Euripides, in a new version by Don Taylor. NT, London

2008 *The City* by Martin Crimp. Royal Court Theatre, London

Selected bibliography

Giannachi, Gabriella and Mary Luckhurst (eds.) (1999), 'Katie Mitchell' in *On Directing: Interviews with Directors*, London: Faber and Faber, pp. 95–102

Katie Mitchell (b. 1964)

Kemp, Edward (1997), 'Introduction' in *The Mysteries, Part I: The Creation*, a new version for the RSC production by Katie Mitchell, London: Nick Hern Books, pp. v–xviii

    (1997), 'Introduction' in *The Mysteries, Part II: The Passion*, a new version for the RSC production by Katie Mitchell, London: Nick Hern Books, pp. v–xvii

Mitchell, Katie (1994), interviewed by David Tushingham, 'Keep Working. Keep Open. Keep Learning. Keep Looking' in *Live 1 Food for the Soul: A New Generation of British Theatremakers*, ed. David Tushingham, London: Methuen Drama, pp. 81–91

Mitchell, Katie (2005), interviewed in *Pinter in the Theatre* by Ian Smith. London: Nick Hern Books, pp. 191–8

    (2008), *The Director's Craft: a Handbook for the Theatre*, London: Routledge

Normington, Katie (1998), 'Little Acts of Faith: Katie Mitchell's *The Mysteries*', *New Theatre Quarterly*, 14: 2, 99–110

Shevtsova, Maria (2006), 'On Directing: a Conversation with Katie Mitchell', *New Theatre Quarterly* 22: 1, 3–18

8   Peter Sellars (b. 1957)

As a student at Harvard, Peter Sellars had already achieved notoriety in 1981 as America's *enfant terrible* through his updating to Cape Canaveral with space rockets of the Renaissance sword-and-sorcery epic *Orlando Furioso*, in Handel's eighteenth-century operatic version. And the label continues to fit with his trademark bristling hairstyle, provocative productions and overtly challenging approach to both his work and the public, even though Sellars (after high-profile artistic appointments, now in his fifties and with a track-record of transcontinental work), today counts as one of the more established figures in North American theatre. Working in his formative period with LaMaMa, as well as with The Wooster Group and Elizabeth LeCompte, Sellars has roots in the modern American avant-garde. There are points of similarity to Robert Wilson as well, although the influence goes both ways: Wilson was to produce a version of *Alcestis* with rockets, also at the American Repertory Theater (ART), just five years later. But Sellars's updatings of eighteenth-century operas all had specific political reference, as with his 1986 *Così fan Tutte*, set in a stereotypical New England diner, where at one point its metal walls glowed red: American suburbia as Hell.

This political edge, sharpened by his tenure during the Reagan years, from 1984 to 1986, as Artistic Director at the American National Theatre (ANT) in Washington D.C. led Sellars to develop works like *Nixon in China* (1987) – the first of his many collaborations with the composer John Adams – or, more recently, Euripides' *The Children of Herakles* (2003) set in the context of contemporary refugees, and a 2006 presentation of Mozart's unfinished opera, *Zaide*, explicitly focused on modern slavery. From his early visit to China, where he adopted Madame Mao's ideological propaganda pieces, Sellars has been deeply critical of American society and its political development. But unlike Wilson, Sellars has never withdrawn from the American scene, even if at one point he publicly refused to work in New York in protest against the crass commercialism of Broadway; and he teaches at the University of Southern California, Los Angeles (UCLA): not – significantly – limited to Theatre, but as Professor of World Arts and Culture.

The style Sellars imposes on his productions is no less provocative and extreme. While he recouped a magic–realist type of naturalism in one of his earliest student productions, using exactly the same setting of live birch trees covering the stage for Chekhov's *Three Sisters* as Peter Stein had, barely five years earlier, for Gorky's *Summerfolk* (1974 – a text Sellars himself was to adapt a decade later in 1984), in general Sellars's use of naturalism is a form of social commentary, being openly incongruous or deceptive. The extremely naturalistic 1998 production of *The Marriage of Figaro*, set in the New York Trump Tower, the latest spectacular of excess at the time, is one example; another is the 1985 ANT production of *The Seagull* where, as Sellars describes here, the naturalistic interiors were undermined by the lighting. By contrast his 1999 staging of Stravinsky's *The Story of a Soldier* demonstrates his eclecticism, combining contemporary US uniforms and weapons with giant folk-art cut-out figures and rococo cartoon-clouds, backgrounded by cave-art graffiti reminiscent of Paul Klee (Stravinsky's contemporary, whose art formed the basis for 'Seven Studies' by Stravinsky). Similarly, in the 2005 *Doctor Atomic*, Sellars's explicitly documentary libretto is presented through Brechtian bareness and counterpointed by ritualistic Pueblo Indian corn-dances.

The combination of these complementary forms of provocation has frequently caused critical outrage, particularly in American reviewers and audiences. This did not prevent a successful tenure as Director of the 1990 Los Angeles Festival – a post he was appointed to again in 1993. Even right at the beginning of his career, Sellars had filled a major administrative and artistic role as director of the Boston Shakespeare Company (1983–5). Yet it is hardly surprising that as

Fig 8 *The Story of a Soldier* (1999). Directed by Peter Sellars.
Photograph by Kevin Higa.

Director of the 2002 Adelaide Festival, Sellars's approach caused
clashes with the funders of the festival and Australian politicians,
which led to his acrimonious departure. On becoming involved with
the Adelaide Festival in 1999, Sellars asked, 'How is it that in the good
[economic] times just about once a week there is a massacre in an

208

American city? Just about once a week now. Your kids are trying to kill each other . . . you have no official enemies left who can tell you to stop except your own kids, except the person next door who takes out a sawn-off shotgun. A culture of violence, it is so deep.' And he commented: 'The question is how can we now put back at the centre of our artistic practice what has formed the power of artistic practice through history but has been missing hugely in the last generation, which is very simply social justice.'[1] This approach is programmatic for his vision of theatre.

However diverse in style, Sellars's work is immediately recognisable through the way he foregrounds coherent, yet complex images. His directorial approach is informed by the minimalism of Japanese Noh theatre, and by the stylised movement developed by Robert Wilson, but it is also characterised by the merging of dance or movement and song or speech, which had impressed Sellars in Chinese Kunshu theatre. In concept this means words or musical notes being paralleled by gesture and movement, yet in practice – as observed in *Doctor Atomic*, where choruses were composed by a front rank of dancers, who displayed the moves, while singers half-hidden behind supplied the voice – it may be more the impression of unity in motion and vocalisation that is achieved. At the same time, his productions are striking for their high degree of precision, texturing and intellectual depth, achieved through the extremely long rehearsal times that Sellars has managed to gain through his extensive use of co-development between companies in the United States and in Europe. So, for instance, after six years of script and musical development, his production of *Doctor Atomic* started off at the San Francisco Opera in 2005 (timed to coincide with the fiftieth anniversary of the Hiroshima bomb, was developed with De Nederlandse Opera (spring 2007) returning to the USA for a production in Chicago (December 2007), with rehearsals in each venue and many of the same performers reappearing throughout. Indeed, already in 1998 Sellars was awarded the prestigious Erasmus Prize for his work in combining

---

[1] Peter Sellars, 'Cultural Activism in the New Century', ABC TV, 19 August 1999: www.abc.net.au/arts/sellars/text.htm.

European with American opera and theatre cultural traditions, and in 2006 he organised the New Crowned Hope Festival in Vienna, as its Artistic Director.

In fact if there is any single category into which Sellars might fit, it would be as a postmodern theatre director. One of the more openly intellectual of the figures in contemporary theatre, he is known for doing all the dramaturgical work for his productions, making his own extensive literature search for context, and a surprising amount of his work is based in theory. His updatings of classical or eighteenth-century pieces count in many ways as a form of quotation, as well as taking on elements of pastiche. His open combination of widely divergent theatrical traditions, together with (on a more individual scale) the artifice and stylisation of paralleling word and gesture, introduce a metatheatrical artistic self-consciousness. His fore-grounding of style, cross-cultural focus, and even his eclecticism can equally be seen as postmodern aspects. At the same time, his search for political immediacy and effectiveness, together with his socialism, links Sellars to the earlier twentieth-century tradition of Piscator and Brecht, whose work was also a recurring theme in Sellars's early productions.

Christopher Innes: *You are known for your eclecticism, and I want to start by asking about the influences on your work . . . When you were much younger, you spent some time in Japan. How much did it influence your work?*

Peter Sellars: Well, I was very fortunate to have had exposure to Japanese culture as a teenager, first at the Loveliest Marionettes, where they did a very beautiful production of *Beauty and the Beast* using classical Japanese puppets. Margot Lovelace had been to Osaka and studied Bunraku there and it was astonishing to be taught Bunraku at the age of twelve in Pittsburgh, Pennsylvania. That was part of my theatrical world. Then, when I was at Harvard, I had a Kabuki *sensai*, and when I left Harvard, my mother moved to Kobe, Japan, for five years. So I had a real base there in the Kansai area and my *sensai* hooked me up with members of his theatrical dynasty in the Grand Kabuki in Tokyo.

Peter Sellars (b. 1957)

But my real reason for going to Japan was that I was obsessed
with Noh drama. The things I love: Wagner and Symbolist theatre and
all the theatre that I like to imagine from the 1890s to about 1910: that
strange, eerie, nocturnal, Symbolist theatre; and the early works of Bob
Wilson, which I grew up with – this beautiful sense of time, of space, of
care of walking, care of a small gesture, in fact, holding a large secret.
All of that can be seen in Noh – and I was particularly interested in the
temple performances – in the performances that were part of a larger
ritual. And so I would travel always on festival days to attend Noh
plays, not in the indoor theatres in Kyoto, but in the Shrine-Inara, or
the Itsukushima Shrine in Miyajima across from Hiroshima.

You also went to China, I believe.

Going to China was very important for me artistically, though
China, I didn't understand at all. I was wandering around Shanghai,
and I saw this theatre and all these people going into it, so I basically
followed them and walked into a Kunshu opera performance. I'd
always thought singers had to just sing. Dancers had to just dance. And
here were people who were both singers and dancers . . . and acrobats.
It was astonishing. I had no idea what I was seeing, but I saw these
women moving in this incredibly stylised way with parallel gestures
while they were singing. So, I went back to America and I thought,
'Well, singers should be dancers.'

At the same time, I was also working with the National Theatre
of the Deaf on a Kabuki Western and so I was with deaf actors and
working all day with people whose act of communication was with
their body, which was very, very powerful. And I came from the
combination of the Kunshu in Shanghai and the National Theatre of
the Deaf to working on *Orlando* and *Così fan Tutte*. And *Così*, those
women singing in duet – 'Well', I said, 'let's choreograph this and let's
have those beautiful gestures which they share and pass back and
forth, the same way they pass back and forth musical phrases.'

*You've always had a political edge in your work – and in those
days, when Mao was still alive, the political scene in China was very
extreme.*

I was obsessed with communist Chinese culture, and with the
Cultural Revolution. I was very engaged with the Yan'an forum talks

of Mao as cultural questions, and I loved and wanted to direct the propaganda plays of Madam Mao. You know, those five plays that were the only plays that were allowed to be performed for all those years – I was very fond of them.

You wanted to perform them in America?

Yes. I was going to make my LaMaMa debut because, of course, everyone has to pass through LaMaMa, and I proposed one of the less well-known ideological plays from the Cultural Revolution. And people were horrified. They said: 'Oh my God, you know, people lost their lives, and you want to put this on?'

So it was never produced?

Well, eventually it became the Red Detachment of Women in the second Act of *Nixon in China*. That was the only way I could finally stage one of those ideological ballets.

I want to go into more detail about your connections to Elizabeth LeCompte, because she is one of the other people we're interviewing.

For me, my training was always through apprenticeship – my approach was very, very traditional, which is, people you admire, you work with them – Elizabeth is the director I most admire in America and probably the world for her moral intensity and her rigour in creating a set of structures, which actually pierce into this profound spiritual realm where she invites the actors to go to a place that is both embodied and then disembodied. And the kind of vivid way in which she just peels the surface of American life, exactly by concentrating on that which is most superficial. In the process of concentrating on these superficialities, of course, they crumble and dissolve in the intensity of her regard; and suddenly all the atoms are released for some kind of amazing set of free associations.

In any case, I invited [The Wooster Group] to the Kennedy Center in Washington when I was running the American National Theatre (1984–6), for a series of very long residencies in which we made the first steps of *The Temptation of St Antony* of Flaubert, which was a text I brought to the company, and I always wanted to do. I worked with the group quite a lot in those months choreographing, you know, the 'Peter Sellars School of Dance' type of theory – fairly

Peter Sellars (b. 1957)

silly things to the ballet music from Gounod's *Faust* – and, of course, Liz just absolutely shredded everything I had done. So it was not in any way perceivable in the finished show. What she does is, obviously, she atomises everything so that things recombine and tiny fragments become part of a new texture. But it let me be around the group for a couple of years and those years were really formative for me. I was able to absorb some of her strategies. But at the end of the day, Liz is so contrary. You know . . . no one can be her. She is the only person who can begin to do what she does. And it's why the imitators of The Wooster Group are a sorry spectacle because they have created a language that is theirs alone.

Even before you had met her, you had done your updatings of Mozart – the Cape Cod diner Così fan Tutte *in 1986 – and it strikes me those productions overlap to some extent with the kind of work she was doing.*

Yes. I think probably her work had the effect on me that my work probably had on many other people, which is to say, fury! When I first saw *Route 1 & 9*, I was so disturbed and so upset – just as I was when I first saw Patrice Chéreau's work when I was eighteen years old. I felt cheated because the work refused to flatter my preconceptions and my desires, and I was furious, like when I first experienced the work of [Jean-Luc] Goddard. And those are all for me good signs. You realise when something really stirs you, you're forced to re-examine everything.

And is this the same effect you aim for in your own productions?

No, not at all! I'm always convinced that everything I'm doing is transparent, available, and presented to the audience with the greatest possible sense of generosity and clarity and availability – it's just so available. And then I'm stunned when people are extremely upset and feel that crucial things are missing and how could I do something that was, you know, so aggressive against the material.

But isn't it true that you do quite deliberately go 'against the grain' in the way you treat well-known texts?

You know, for me that question of going against the material, 'against the grain', is very, very, very important in order to recognise

213

the grain. Dialogue is the heart of theatre, which is ... a conversation. It's not just a one-sided action, and, therefore, there has to be something that provokes the dialogue. This is what going 'against the grain' does. It tests the material, gives the sense that this is not yet finished, that we have to keep on talking about this.

Much of your early work dealt with comedic material; and I've always wondered whether comedy allows more freedom for experimentation.

The only thing that, actually, is able to overturn those hierarchies and create the possibility of an imagination of justice in the midst of massive injustice is humour. And humour is so alive and so dangerous and so ungovernable, and I love that. So a lot of those early pieces had humour very deeply woven throughout. At the same time, I have to say, that that's also Handel, Mozart: that's the eighteenth century. In the eighteenth century the smartest people expressed themselves through humour rather than through outrage. Or, the outrage, if you were Jonathan Swift, came through humour, and that, to me, was very potent when I was young. And, obviously, when you are young, you're outraged about a large number of things.

Of course, it was also Liz's wonderful gift – this tremendous shocking irreverence – and then, suddenly, you're putting the world on notice.

Yet with LeCompte it was The Temptation of St Antony, *which you wanted to adapt – and it seems that, alongside the comedy, there's a strong religious element in your work.*

Always. For me, art is creating a sacred space, particularly in the American television culture that is relentlessly materialistic and where our lives are constantly defined in material terms rather than anything else. One of the things that art does is create more of a balance when the world is imbalanced. And so, I think in our generation, it has become incumbent upon us to make some space for spiritual life as artists. Art always offers a place that goes beyond doctrine – whether it's in Buddhism, whether it's in Islam, whether it's in Christianity, whether it's in the Hebrew tradition, there's this other space that's opened up through poetry, through the visual arts, or through dance and theatre, that is spiritually charged, but is not a litmus test for true believers.

Peter Sellars (b. 1957)

Presenting sacred material in a secular society seems to pro-duce a similar duality, disjunction to some of your updatings of classical works – Così in a Cape Cod diner, Orlando *and the space programme.*

The question is to what extent is there a shared language and to what extent is there something that does not translate. That's always an important question in my work. I feel a little guilty because a lot of my early shows were updatings of things – and then that became such a fad. But I was never really just updating them. I was always delib-erately leaving dislocations as well as locations. I was always trying to say, 'Well this fits, but also this doesn't, and I'm not lopping it off; I'm calling attention to that fact.' I'm interested in the contradictions as well as the consonances. In our television culture, you're always told what to think. And that's one reason why people who are formed by that culture can become frustrated in my shows, because I really am not telling people what to think, but trying to create a space in which thinking is possible.

Yet your work tends to be greeted with emotionally violent, even visceral reaction, which doesn't leave a lot of space for the sort of objective thought you're describing.

My productions do tend to have a very, very strong effect; and, frequently, 70 per cent of the audience leaves every night during the performance. But in *Merchant of Venice,* in *The Persians,* in *The Children of Herakles,* people stuck around.

The most powerful thing about theatre is not what people are thinking about during the show. I never worry about that – whether they applaud or don't applaud at the end, it doesn't matter to me. They can leave; I don't want to know what they think. For me, theatre begins the next morning when somebody calls somebody who they care about, and they say, 'I saw the most incredible thing last night. It was horrible,' or, 'it was great' – doesn't matter – it's them describing to somebody who was not there, what they saw. That person becomes the creator, the artist, as they describe something they saw, but, of course, no one else in the room saw that – they saw it.

I'm really interested that you say your most highly politicised productions, where you would expect the strongest emotional reaction, the audiences did not walk out. Can you take us through the way this worked?

It really challenged the American Repertory Theatre to produce *The Children of Herakles*. They had a special grant from The Carr Foundation and so we were able to have refugees come to speak and refugee children on the stage and had meals and transportation every night – really a huge operation and lots of community work. And then the range of speakers that came every night were from the highest echelons of Homeland Security, to immigration judges, to detention-centre workers: the whole gamut of people involved in immigration, all came to speak during those performances.

Were these participants the people the performance was really aimed at – rather than for the regular audience?

Theatre is about creating the occasion for conversation that is missing to occur. That is, of course, the basis on which Sophocles and Euripides wrote their plays. Usually the most important things that happen in your own personal life happen at dinner; and in *The Children of Herakles* the performances were framed by dinner. Every night before the performance, there were two private dinners. Something you learn in any kind of community work is, that people need to be fed; and you can sustain a community project if you make food available for kids. So one was for the children who were going to appear on stage. Then the politicians who were going to appear on that night and the refugees who were going to speak with them would also have a private dinner – as with our opening night in Vienna, where we had the [Austrian] Interior Minister and three Nigerian refugees who were living on the street.

What was the format for the public part of the performance?

The evening began for the public with an hour of conversation that gives the context and lets each of these different participants in the process of immigration speak from their reality and compare notes on their realities. Every night with *The Children of Herakles*, we had a moderated panel; in this case, the minister and these three immigrants. And, in each case, we tried to get a very visible media figure to welcome the audience and to moderate the talk beforehand. So there was somebody trusted [by the audience], whose presence would also make sure that what we were doing got into the media. That was very constructive. Then there's an intermission, and then we come back and perform this play from 2,500 years ago, *The Children of Herakles* by Euripides.

How did this drama from the distant past merge with the present-day realities?

What was quite amazing was how many lines suddenly jump out of the play at you as contemporary. I deliberately used a translation from 1947 just to show that I wasn't updating anything, and because of the first hour, the audience was attuned to the argument, so suddenly something that would have just gone by jumped out because the audience was already listening differently. And so the resonance of the lines was very vividly in relief. You suddenly got a silence – an intensity of people really grasping what was at stake, and that the Athenians had been actually struggling the same way.

And in Vienna, those performances were in the Austrian Parliament with its statues of Greek figures, there were these refugees. It was the first time a Muslim woman has spoken in the Austrian Parliament – ever – and to have those children seeking refuge at an altar, inside the parliament chamber, was quite a strong image.

During the performance, another group of the refugees were across the street, cooking. And we invited the entire audience and the kids and the refugees and the politicians to dinner at the end of the performance. And everybody went across the street and ate food prepared by the refugees. And you were sitting at a table with the African kids you had seen on stage, talking. The politicians were there, everybody was there, and that final breakthrough comes from welcoming somebody by breaking bread together, because actually sharing food is where people finally become human. So, the total arc of *The Children of Herakles* was from the private dinner before, to the public shared meal at the end; and the arc of transformation it was tracing could only be made possible by art.

Could you expand on that?

We could make a space for people to say something they could never otherwise say, and explore something very dangerous; because art makes the space to propose and explore and ask questions, not just to give a snappy answer. The nightmare is the rush to judgement that is on every news programme. This was a space where nobody had to come up with an answer; and what I asked the public officials who appeared and the immigrants, refugees and people without papers, over and over again, was 'What are you thinking about when you're lying awake at 3 and 4 o'clock in the morning?'

Have you seen any change in policy following the performances of this piece?

Well, I think that, you know, sometimes one always has to be modest, and you know the thing about art is it's not advertising. You know, it's not like tomorrow everyone changes their toothpaste, whereas in advertising that is what you're hoping for and then you can measure it. For me, art is about the things that are immeasurable, that cannot be quantified and that happen across a generation.

More recently (2006) you staged Zaide *at the Lincoln Center; and again included pre-performance discussions about contemporary slavery and ways of abolishing it; and you've done the same pre-performance sessions with the productions of* Doctor Atomic . . .

Doctor Atomic makes the case for abolishing nuclear weapons now. In San Francisco [leading up to the premiere at the War Memorial Opera House] we had an astonishing series of programmes with Richard Rhodes. Here [at De Nederlandse Opera in Amsterdam, May 2007] there's a whole programme in the week of the opening with leading Dutch activists. Jonathan Schell will be in Chicago [for the December 2007 staging], we'll do a programme with him.[2] We will do a series of programmes in Chicago because, of course, that's where the scientists who signed the letter to Truman are from – it was the Chicago scientists who founded the *Bulletin of Atomic Scientists*, which keeps the atomic clock. That is still being published in Chicago. So we'll work with the *Bulletin of Atomic Scientists* people and really make this series of programmes about eliminating all nuclear weapons now.

[2] Richard Rhodes, Pulitzer Prize-winning author of *The Making of the Atomic Bomb*, Simon & Schuster, 1986, and of *Arsenals of Folly: The Making of the Nuclear Arms Race*, Knopf, 2007; Jonathan Schell, author of *The Seventh Decade: The New Shape of Nuclear Danger*, Metropolitan Books, 2007.

Peter Sellars (b. 1957)

Watching your rehearsal, it's the contemporary resonances that come across most strongly, although all the material in Doctor Atomic *seems strictly historical.*

To look back to the beginning of the Cold War – and the anti-communist stuff going on at that time – was a way in which John and I could speak about America today, about government lies, about secret things going on, about everybody knowing better but doing something else. And it was a way that we could deal with the Bush administration, with post-9/11, with this kind of apocalyptic scenario in America at war with the world, and the consequences of your own image of yourself as a citizen. And so *Doctor Atomic* has all of that as a subtext, and it's very provocative. The opera is an uncomfortable piece. You watch the entire collusion at every step of the way.

Yet on the surface with John Adams's powerful and surprisingly melodic music, those long sweeping dances, even the Japanese voice-over saying, 'Water, please. For the children', instead of the explosion of an atom bomb, it's also an oddly pleasurable experience.

Ostensibly it's a friendly subject, but that's of course part of the strategy with a lot of John's pieces. *Nixon in China* is ostensibly a friendly topic and then once you get into it, you realise the waters are deep. You thought it was just a wading pool and it turns out it's deep out there and the water's in over our head. *Nixon in China* goes to very dark and very deep places, while announcing itself as a harmless comedy. *Nixon in China* followed a very specific Molière strategy. Working at the Kennedy Center [as Artistic Director of the American National Theatre], I was the court entertainment for the second Reagan administration, and when you're that close to the workings of the government, and the level of injustice is so flagrant, you will get nowhere shaking your fist at it. You have to create that Molière structure . . .

The setting of Doctor Atomic *is so austere, it's almost Japanese.*

You've put your finger on it – the opera ends before the bombing of Hiroshima, but of course, it's to place Hiroshima there. I think when most Americans come to an opera about the atomic bomb, they expect some kind of Steven Spielberg, George Lucas giant spectacle. We're living in the society of spectacle; and so what theatre can do is actually remind everyone of human presence. In America when we

219

premiered *Doctor Atomic*, some people were shocked at the austerity of it, but it was also an attempt to echo and point to a moment when American artists made a new language for theatre – Martha Graham, Noguchi – a single gesture in a void, and one of the reasons I wanted to work with Lucinda [Childs] on this is because Lucinda was part of a generation of artists with Bob Wilson, Phil Glass and other American artists who made a new language in the 1970s. I wanted somebody who had created an iconic dance language that you could immediately recognise as no one else's.

You speak of new languages, yet there are elements in the staging that are strikingly ritualistic, seeming to hark back to the origins of theatre.

I'm genuinely interested in the voices of our ancestors. I'm genuinely interested that people of other generations and previous eras are speaking through us; that we can inhabit their bodies and they inhabit our bodies. And so, to me, that is a very powerful part of drama and it's what drama is in ancient cultures all over the world. And what the meaning of the Passover ritual is. For me it's such a very deep question of ritual of what it means when you allow your ancestors to enter your body.

So in Doctor Atomic, *that's why you bring in the Pueblo Corn Dancers in the middle of the scene where the scientists are arguing?*

Absolutely. What I'm interested in is the presence of simultaneous cosmologies. [In *Doctor Atomic*] you have this cosmology of nuclear physics, and you have a cosmology of weather that is coming from people who do a rain dance and are talking to ancestors and rain gods. And so, for me, the simultaneity of those cosmological systems and the rituals of each of them are very, very potent. Whereas before, science was actually held as something that was against indigenous culture, now in the twenty-first century we're beginning to realise that these different knowledges, different languages actually have profound points of intersection, and there is beginning to be a new kind of dialogue opened up. And so, for me, I'm always trying to test the limits and the possibilities of these different languages.

You clearly believe in the theatre and democratisation, yet you have devoted a significant amount of your energy to opera – which has the reputation of an elitist art.

Peter Sellars (b. 1957)

Well, one thing that's terrific about working with John Adams and about being able to make a new body of work is when you announce something called *Doctor Atomic* [Chicago premiere, 2005] or *Nixon in China* (1987) all kinds of people show up. You don't just get the usual little coterie of opera fanatics. Though those are also the decision-makers and the opinion-makers; and the other thing for me about opera is that you are speaking to the power structure and that's an important group of people to talk to.

On the other hand, that's the other reason why I also take the ability to televise these things very seriously because you have no idea who is watching, thank God! And people who are casually flipping, see something that isn't like everything else and, maybe, stop.

Is that partly why you set Don Giovanni *in Spanish Harlem . . .*

Well, it makes good television. But . . . one thing people didn't quite understand was that I was deliberately using television images and filtering Mozart through them; and, at a certain point, they can no longer hear the strain and they explode. I love that. I love taking these images that we're surrounded by and really testing them and pushing them to an extreme where we realise these images aren't capacious enough for everything we're feeling, everything we're thinking, everything we're hoping for. And they need to be exploded, and we have to go beyond that. That's the hope.

Recently, I rewatched a video of your Così *set in the Cape Cod diner, and it struck me that there's this hugely realistic setting and these extremely artificial, no artificial is the wrong word, extremely stylised movements. And I see some of the same sort of thing in the new opera you are working on right now,* Dr Atomic.

Absolutely. I mean, in the second Act, that little diner turns into Dante, when all of that aluminum turns red hot and molten, you know, and you're in hell itself. What I always love is taking something that's 'realistic' and, after a while, it turns into an image and then it goes beyond that and turns into a world that is uninhabitable. And so the diner becomes this oven in one of Dante's circles. To me, this tension is always between realism and poetry.

This symbolic level beneath a realistic surface seems to be something constant in your work.

You're always trying to create a language of gesture that has poetic possibilities because people are singing – and I don't just mean in opera, because when I do theatre most of the plays that I do are written by poets: Gertrude Stein, or Aeschylus or Shakespeare. And, to me, realism is not just realism. What I love, like a Rothko painting where you can't tell when one thing becomes the other, is that you're finding a poetry in the real world, and you're finding very real things in the world of poetry. And everything is underpainted, so there are layers underneath that keep showing through or, at least, implied. One of my favourite things is to stage things that people can't see, but you feel. Just the way Rothko will underpaint a colour that you can no longer see. But that colour is in there, vibrating.

I see what you mean on a general level, but can you give me an example of staging something people can't see?

Well, I will have one character in a place that is not visible to the audience and is not lit – but I'll give them a very specific thing to do that has a very intense emotion. Just the same way when you walk into a room, and you can feel emotion there, so the audience feel something: they just don't know where it's coming from. To me, those vibrations of real emotion in a room are the most powerful thing in theatre. We're from such a culture based on reading what's in front of our eyes and, to me, one of the deepest things is most emotion doesn't present itself to our eyes. Most emotion . . . everybody's trying to hide it, and you have to sense all the questions that nobody's asking. Rarely are people communicating what they're thinking with what they're saying. So I deliberately try and build whole emotional states that arrive and break invisibly.

That sounds like one of Stanislavsky's principles. But clearly your way of working is not just naturalistic.

Sometimes you support [these emotional states] with the lighting; sometimes you support it with the sound: I'm always interested in the synaesthetic, the overlap of the senses, where one sense is provoking another, and how emotion works in that context. As in Jim Ingalls's amazing lighting in *The Seagull* [Washington, 1985], where George Tsypin's set had all these underpainted colours, and was lit frequently from behind. Colour was being poured into the set from behind, so you couldn't see it, but there was this strange internal glow that would build across twenty-minute arcs, so it was imperceptible. You couldn't literally see a light cue, but the room was being invaded by some strange purple and then, at the end of every act of *The Seagull*, as you know, Chekhov has a little word, just a tiny little line, where suddenly the whole illusion shatters. It's all been a dream. And so after pumping purple into a green set, or green into a purple set, we suddenly took all that light out. And you saw big spots in front of your eyes, and you couldn't recognise the colour of the set you were looking at any more. That snapping out of a dream, that sense you actually didn't know what you were seeing when, suddenly, it evaporates in front of your eyes. Those kinds of strategies I love because it's working with the visible world in a way that lets the invisible forces have their presence.

That's a striking example – but it also shows a deep symbolic level in your productions for even the most realistic material, which reminds me that since you did Nixon *in China, you've actually developed a trajectory that moves increasingly towards lyric theatre, and you've done more of that. Is that accurate?*

What I'm always interested in is collaboration – the intersection of different art forms; the intersection of different cultures; the intersection of different life experiences – and I'm interested in opera as a collaborative space. But also because theatre is hard to do in America because most actors are involved in television and in film. So it's very hard to keep a cast; and the way I like to work in theatre is across months, and professionally that's unheard of. It rarely happens, unless they have a Broadway run – and even then they leave for television in a second. In New York, there's no way to put together theatre that has this kind of timeline and resources. Making a show, you can never get a Meyerhold rehearsal time, or a Stanislavsky rehearsal period. The only way you do it is to do it in five cities, and then we really are spending six months on one text. So I have to do it with the support of European festivals, usually, which means making the work in America, bringing it to Europe, and then, finally, taking it back and showing it in America. So my long answer to your question is: I don't intend to work more in lyric theatre than spoken theatre. It's just that organisationally, if you do opera, everybody knows you're going to need all of these resources.

To me, what theatre's about is the place where people meet, where art forms meet, where cultures meet, and where conversation takes place – which is impossible to handicap in advance, where you really don't know where this will go. Opera is most self-evidently a world where I can rally those forces. But I'm overdue to go back to theatre right now. I feel it very strongly. So in the next couple of years, there's going to be a couple of theatre productions coming up.

What kind of plays have you selected?

One is a project that I've had with Toni Morrison. I've always thought *Othello* was a terrible play. One day I told her that, and she spent the next five hours telling me how wrong I was. This began a very long conversation which resulted in my proposing that she write a play called *Desdemona*, which would be a feminist view of *Othello*, letting this young woman speak more for her generation and letting all the out-takes in Shakespeare finally come forward.

You can no longer say in the twenty-first century that a mixed marriage has to result in catastrophe for everyone. That's just not acceptable. It's one of the key images in Western culture – and I say we do not have to hand this on to the next generation uncritiqued. So in inviting Toni to create an alternate of images, I'm setting up a dialogue with Shakespeare that we can really respond to.

With a piece where you yourself are creating the script, as with Doctor Atomic, *how do you approach the work?*

The libretto came from classified documents, but also from culture. Baudelaire, of course, which is what Oppenheimer was carrying around and reading: he and his wife would communicate to each other in a secret code from Baudelaire ... then, of course, also the *Bhagavad Gita* that Oppenheimer had in Sanskrit in his coat pocket wherever he went. And, for the women, the great feminist poet, Muriel Rukeyser, who is just being discovered again in America now. She's before Sylvia Plath and Anne Sexton. She would go down to Tennessee to the hearings about the black lung disease and write incredible epic poems about the miners. In the 1940s, she wrote a lot about science. In the 1950s she was under investigation by the McCarthy committee. And in the 1970s, shortly before she died, she was arrested over the Vietnam War protests. She's a tremendous protean figure; her poetry is magnificent; so I use her words for what an intelligent American woman would be thinking in the 1940s.

When you are actually developing a new show, how do you operate? How do you create a production?

You have to immerse yourself deeply in the material, and there's always a stack of books about everything that I'm involved with, and I love research. I've never worked with assistants. I love imagining things. I love somehow touching the texture of things.

Can you give me an example of how that works to create a text for performing?

In *Count of Monte Cristo* I had done such a job on the text. The stagecraft was quite spectacular and, as you probably know, the text that we used was Eugene O'Neill's father's text, which was a real dreadful penny-melodrama. James O'Neill had really boiled it down . . . I mean you could really see the baldness; it was grim. And I really wanted to prepare for Eugene O'Neill, who is the author I really want to stage and I've never done O'Neill yet. But that was a way of preparing. I needed really great language.

So I revised it extensively with very generous licence of Byron and the King James Bible, particularly Ecclesiastes, Jeremiah and the Psalms.

Melodrama of course is music drama. What sort of music did you use?

The music was Schnittke, but also speech. The Bible and Byron gave me that Shakespearean dimension where the words had this weight and this tremendous moral echo. Words come to you from across time, you know, and, so I could insert an entire psalm about releasing the prisoners, feeding the hungry. You know nineteenth-century melodrama was about all of that; great language and the libertarian struggles. So Byron was right there, and I could put the entire poem of darkness in and just stage that as what the Count of Monte Cristo said in prison. And so I was able to give such a lot more meat on the bone and give it the intensity and weight of nineteenth-century melodrama but with a lot more vitamins.

You start with a text that you frequently redo yourself; you appoint actors who come from different traditions; where do you go from there? Do you create a director's book with moves, gestures . . .

Well, there are different processes. For example, *The Merchant of Venice* (1994) was coming off of the uprising in Los Angeles, and so I set Venice in California, and was dealing with the economic history of racism, which is racism in its primary economic function . . . that's why Shakespeare calls this play about racism *The **Merchant** of Venice*. It's about doing business; it's about slave labour; it's about setting up ghettos; and the history of the ghetto – it's no different now than it was several hundred years ago. At all events, the Jews are played by African-Americans, Portia and her friends are wealthy Asians living in Bel Air and all the Venetians are Latino. And there are only two white people on stage: the judge and, of course, the famous racist Launcelot Gobbo.

We had a large cast of primarily people of colour who were never cast in Shakespeare before. Some pimp in a movie, or a cop, or a drug dealer: those were the roles that were available for people of colour, over and over again. And so what was really interesting was the range of actors – with their rhythms [of speech] from Jamaica, Mexico – and this whole idea of what Shakespeare needs to sound like. What happens if you bring people with other rhythms to these words? Can we discover another set of rhythms in this material from cultures actually that are based on rhythm and where would that go? So the first rehearsal period had two main features. One was gathering all the cast around a single table, going through the play line by line across a week; stopping with every line and going around the table, having everybody say what that line meant to them and relate a personal experience that line evoked. By the time we were done, you realise that there is no one reading of that line. You realise that what you think you're saying, someone else is hearing very differently. And we also ended up with this astonishing library of shared experience, and you realise that is being sparked by this text, from very different cultural histories.

Then I gave them Manning Marable's *How Capitalism Underdeveloped Black America*, and Noam Chomsky on *Free Trade Agreements in Latin America*, and Eduardo Galeano's *Open Veins in Latin America*: economic texts that were about the way this exploitation that's described in the play actually worked. You know, Shakespeare wrote this play in 1602, the date of the founding of the Dutch East India

Company, which was the beginning of a certain way to do business. And it's no accident that the play's endlessly about gold and silver and lead. It's about the mines in Latin America; it's about where all this stuff came from that built Europe. So we traced all of that, and we did both the sixteenth- and seventeenth-century histories and the contemporary results with the state of trade with Africa and the bauxite mines in West Africa, in Guinea, where none of these things have shifted. Then we did the Bible, the *Bhagavad Gita*, the *Tao Te Ching* and the Koran.

And you created a performance text out of this?

Yes. We interspersed readings from all these books with Shakespeare so that you actually can't tell the difference. People were wondering, 'Now, was that Shakespeare?' And it turns out, no: that's Noam Chomsky. Or it turns out that's the Koran. Put Shakespeare's lines up against lines from all these sources, and you begin to hear Shakespeare in a different way.

The BBC made a film of the process for a television show . . .

We made a film with the BBC the second week, which was of these actors reading the lines from the play the second time. Then the other thing that I could do was show what happens when we rehearse. One of my favourite parts of that film is just Paul Butler, who played Shylock, saying two words beginning his speech to Antonio with 'Fair Sir . . . ', and it took ten minutes of pulsing those words over and over again. I said, 'Now Paul, let's be fair; you want him to be fair; you want to be fair; what would it mean to be fair? What does fair mean with skin colour . . . ? Just to be able to say 'Fair Sir' until we actually got what was at stake for this play – to say those two words to somebody who was trying to destroy him – it's a half-hour rehearsal. The audience has no idea that we would spend part of a day just trying to say two words. And so the film has a lot of repeating lines over and over and over again with a whole range of meanings, because the audience is never aware that in rehearsal we're weighing all of these possibilities. Should that line be horrifying? Should that line be ironic? Should that line be heartfelt and sincere? A lot of my favourite things in Shakespeare are like Chekhov – they're lines of one-syllable words. Very simple and endlessly, endlessly profound and challenging.

At the same time, you have a set design that imposes certain decisions and frequently, as with the rehearsals for Doctor Atomic, *you have choreography that is very specific . . .*

Most of the sets I work with are radically open. They don't limit the meaning, they extend it, and the spaces themselves are open and subject to constant transformation.

Choreography is very important because I like structure. I want the audience to perceive structure. At the same time, for me, what the choreography does is that it leaves the performer psychologically and spiritually open, because I'm not telling him how to interpret meanings. The move is just a move. It could be executed with any emotion. It's just a gesture and the gesture doesn't limit the meaning, just focuses it. I've not imposed upon the actor anything except a structure, but within that structure what that gesture means could be subject to an incredible range of interpretation and change. So actually what I'm doing is keeping the performance wide open for a whole series of random shifting and developing possibilities, while giving it a structure that grounds everybody and a set of relationships that insists that people have got to deal with each other. For me, the beauty of the choreography is always that it's an empty vessel. It just holds something . . .

Opera – like Doctor Atomic, *where there's a great deal of choreography that goes with the music – lends itself to dance more than straight theatre. Is there a difference in the way you approach the two forms?*

There are two different strategies for me – one for theatre and one for opera. Opera is very basic because every night at bar 312, at beat 3, you have to sing C *sharp*. It's not some nights you feel like C *sharp* and some nights you don't. You have to sing it. So, I give a rigorous physical structure to the singers that matches the score. So that the C *sharp* is dependable, and they know where they'll be, what their body is doing, so everything can arrive on schedule. And so, in an opera, choreography is about creating a schedule – what's free and open are all the emotional and interpretative things.

In theatre, it's the opposite. You do not want the same thing to happen two nights in a row, ever. So you're actually setting up structures that insist upon something random, where every night the performers are in the midst of discovering something they never knew before. Because what theatre does is privilege the moment of discovery where we and the actors are all discovering something new at the same time. And if somebody's telling you something that they already know, and we already know, it's not interesting.

Do you have specific techniques for doing that?

You have to build in rehearsal that this moment is going to be a deep well that the actor can draw on infinitely and every night come up with something different. And so you're not setting up predictable things and certain expectations. You're setting up the absence of pre-dictability, so that every night the actor actually feels vulnerable rather than have a predigested, predetermined outcome. The result is every night the play ends in a way we've never seen it end, because we arrive at a different place every night, because the act of discovery involves us in zones that we can't anticipate, and we can't handicap.

And how much input do the actors have with this? How do you work with your team?

Well, the way I work is so collaborative that I'm already involved with multiple voices, and trying to create a process that is about listening – all of us, and isn't, you know, me as the director as the last word but, I think, the opposite. And so, I don't feel like that traditional structure where there is this final eye of the director and somebody for the director to talk to. But, in fact, we're all talking every day and it's always up for grabs . . .

Does this translate into the multiple viewpoints, which you've mentioned before?

I deliberately have too many things happening at once – so unlike television or film where you're always told where to look, there's always at least four other things going on. To me, what's satisfying is no two people looking at the same place, and so no two people see the same thing. It's one of my very favourite things about theatre – we all saw the same movie, but we didn't all see the same show in the theatre. And the diversity of the audience's experience is why in my shows it's very rare that the whole audience laughs at the same time. I very much encourage this wide open space, which insists upon a lot of responses – not a single unified response. Obviously, there are moments in certain plays where, yes, there's a fairly unified response but even then, usually, there are things in motion that usually prohibit that, or something else that's more edgy and strange. Again, I'm very fond of making things that none of us know how to describe because, to me, theatre is about experience and experience is beyond words, which is, I do recognise, why, frequently, I don't fare very well with critics because they have got to sum it up in a few paragraphs. And with my shows you can't just sum it up and put your finger on it; it's going to take a long time to digest.

Chronology of selected productions

1979   *Bedbug* by Vladimir Mayakovsky. Loeb Drama Center, Cambridge, Massachusetts
Much Ado about Nothing by William Shakespeare. Loeb Summer Season, Cambridge, Massachusetts
Lulu by Frank Wedekind. Loeb Summer Season, Cambridge, Massachusetts
The Inspector General by Nikolai Gogol, trans. Sam Guckenheimer. American Repertory Theatre, Boston, Massachusetts

1980   *Don Giovanni* by Wolfgang Amadeus Mozart. Monadnock Music Festival, New Hampshire, Massachusetts
A Day in the Life of the Czar / I Too Have Lived in Arcadi by Frank O'Hara and V. R. Lang. LaMaMa Experimental Theatre Company, New York
Santur Opera by Ivan Tcherepnin. Festival d'Automne, Paris

1981   *Orlando* by George Friedrich Handel, American Repertory Theatre, Cambridge, Massachusetts
Saul by George Friedrich Handel. Emmanuel Music, Boston, Massachusetts
Armida by George Friedrich Handel. Emmanuel Music, Boston, Massachusetts

1982   *Mahogany Songspiel* by Bertolt Brecht and Kurt Weill. Agassiz Theater, Cambridge, Massachusetts

1983   *The Lighthouse* by Peter Maxwell Davies. Boston Shakespeare Company, Boston, Massachusetts

Peter Sellars (b. 1957)

Pericles by William Shakespeare. Boston Shakespeare Company, Boston, Massachusetts

The Mikado by Arthur Sullivan and W.S. Gilbert. Lyric Opera of Chicago, Chicago

The Visions of Simone Marchard by Bertolt Brecht. LaJolla Playhouse, LaJolla, California

1984　*Hang on to Me*, adapted from *Summerfolk* by Maxim Gorky. The Guthrie Theater, Minneapolis

1985　*The Count of Monte Cristo* by Alexandre Dumas. American National Theater, Washington, D.C.

Giulio Cesare by George Friedrich Handel. PepsiCo Summerfare, Purchase, New York

The Seagull by Anton Chekhov. American National Theatre, Washington, D.C.

1986　*Così fan Tutte* by Wolfgang Amadeus Mozart. Castle Hill Festival, Ipswich, Massachusetts

(Co-director with Elizabeth LeCompte) *Temptation of St Antony* by The Wooster Group, inspired by *La Tentation de Saint Antoine* by Gustave Flaubert. American National Theater, Washington, D.C.

Idiot's Delight by Robert E. Sherwood. American National Theatre, Washington, D.C.

Ajax by Sophocles. American National Theatre, Washington, D.C.

Zangezi: A Supersaga in 20 Planes by Velimir Khlebnikov. Radio programme for 'Territory of Art' series, The Museum of Contemporary Art, Los Angeles, California

1987　*Nixon in China*, an opera composed by John Adams with libretto by Alice Goodman. Brooklyn Academy of Music, Brooklyn, New York

The Electrification of the Soviet Union by Nigel Osborne. Glyndebourne Festival Opera, Glyndebourne

Zangezi: A Supersaga in 20 Planes by Velimir Khlebnikov. The Museum of Contemporary Art, Los Angeles. (In Russian.)

1988　*Nixon in China* by John Adams with libretto by Alice Goodman. Television film version, Great Performances, PBS

Le Nozze di Figaro by Wolfgang Amadeus Mozart. PepsiCo Summerfare, Purchase, New York

Tannhäuser by Richard Wagner. Lyric Opera of Chicago, Chicago

1990   *Giulio Cesare in Egitto (Julius Caesar in Egypt)* by George Friedrich Handel. Television film version, the Decca Record Company and Polygram Video

Don Giovanni by Wolfgang Amadeus Mozart. Television film version, the Decca Record Company and Polygram Video

The Magic Flute by Wolfgang Amadeus Mozart. Glyndebourne Festival Opera, Glyndebourne

Così fan Tutte by Wolfgang Amadeus Mozart. Television film version, the Decca Record Company and Polygram Video

Le Nozze di Figaro (The Marriage of Figaro or the Day of Madness) by Wolfgang Amadeus Mozart. Television film version, the Decca Record Company and Polygram Video

1991   *The Cabinet of Dr Ramirez* by Peter Sellars, Mikhail Baryshnikov, Joan Cusack, Peter Gallagher and Ron Vawter. Film, Mediascope, New York

The Death of Klinghoffer by John Adams with libretto by Alice Goodman. Théâtre Royal de la Monnaie, Brussels, Belgium

Los Angeles Festival Documentary Project, documentary video programmes of 1990 Los Angeles Festival. Los Angeles Festival Film and Video Project

1992   *St François d'Assise* by Olivier Messiaen. Salzburg Festival

L'Histoire du soldat (The Story of a Soldier) by Igor Stravinsky. Ojai Festival, Ojai, California

Short Ride in a Fast Machine, educational video piece about *Short Ride in a Fast Machine* by John Adams. Los Angeles Festival Film and Video Project

1993   *Pelléas et Mélisande* by Claude Debussy. De Nederlandse Opera, Amsterdam, the Netherlands

The Persians by Aeschylus. Salzburg Festival, Salzburg

The Seven Deadly Sins by Kurt Weill and Bertolt Brecht. Opera de Lyon, Paris

The Seven Deadly Sins by Kurt Weill and Bertolt Brecht. Television film version, Decca Ltd, London

Peter Sellars (b. 1957)

1994 *Oedipus Rex* and *Symphony of Psalms* by Igor Stravinsky. Salzburg Festival, Salzburg
The Merchant of Venice by William Shakespeare. Goodman Theatre, Chicago. *It Is Now Our Time*, adapted from *The Merchant of Venice* by William Shakespeare. Goodman Theatre, Chicago

1995 *Mathis der Maler* by Paul Hindemith. Royal Opera House, Covent Garden, London
I Was Looking at the Ceiling and then I Saw the Sky by John Adams and June Jordan. Zellerbach Playhouse, UC Berkeley, California

1996 *The Rake's Progress* by Igor Stravinsky. Théâtre du Châtelet, Paris
Theodora by George Friedrich Handel. Glyndebourne Festival Opera, Glyndebourne

1997 *Theodora* by George Friedrich Handel. Television film version, NVC Arts and Warner Music Vision
Le Grand Macabre by György Ligeti. Salzburg Festival, Salzburg

1998 *Peony Pavilion* by Tan Dun. Wiener Festwochen, Vienna
Los Biombos, adapted from *Les Paravents* by Jean Genet. Cornerstone Theater Company, East Los Angeles Skill Center, Los Angeles, California

1999 *The Story of a Soldier* by Igor Stravinsky. Los Angeles Philharmonic, Los Angeles, California

2000 *El Niño* by John Adams. Théâtre du Châtelet, Paris
L'Amour de loin by Kaija Saariaho, with libretto by Amin Maalouf. Salzburg Festival, Salzburg

2001 *Bach Cantatas* by Johann Sebastian Bach. Cité de la Musique, Paris

2003 *For an End to the Judgment of God/Kissing God Goodbye* by Antonin Artaud/June Jordan. Tate Modern Museum, London
The Children of Herakles by Euripides, trans. Ralph Gladstone. American Repertory Theatre, Cambridge, Massachusetts

2005 *Doctor Atomic*, an opera composed by John Adams, with libretto by Peter Sellars. San Francisco Opera, San Francisco, California

233

2006 *Zaide* by Wolfgang Amadeus Mozart. Lincoln Center for the Performing Arts, New York

A Flowering Tree, an opera composed by John Adams, with libretto by Adams and Peter Sellars. New Crowned Hope Festival, Vienna

Selected bibliography

Berry, Ralph (2004), 'Shakespeare and Integrated Casting', *Contemporary Review* 285: 1662, 35–9

Cousins, Mark (2007), 'Beyond the Horizon', *Sight and Sound* 17: 7, 34–7

Gener, Randy (2002), 'Who Will Speak for the Children?', *American Theatre* 19: 10, 26–31

Littlejohn, David (1990), 'Reflections on Peter Sellars's Mozart', *Opera Quarterly* 7: 2, 6

MacDonald, Heather (1991), 'On Peter Sellars', *Partisan Review* 58: 14, 708–12

Mangan, Timothy (2005), 'The San Francisco Project', *Opera News* 70: 2, 22–5

Maurin, Frédéric (ed.) (2003), *Peter Sellars: Les Voies de la Création Théâtrale*, Paris: CNRS Éditions

Mikotowicz, Tom (1991), 'Director Peter Sellars: Bridging the Modern and Postmodern Theatre', *Theatre Topics* 1: 1, 87–98

Said, Edward W. (1997), '*Cosi Fan Tutte* at the Limits', *Grand Street* 16: 2, 93–106

(1989), 'Music: Peter Sellars's Mozart', *Nation* 249: 8, 289–91

Sellars, Peter (1985), interviewed by Mark Bly, 'Lyubimov and the End of an Era: an Interview with Peter Sellars', *Theater* 16: 2, 6–17

(1992), interviewed by Bruce Deffie, 'Conversation Piece: Director Peter Sellars', *Opera Journal* 25: 2, 43–56

(1996), 'Peter Sellars' in *In Contact with the Gods? Directors Talk Theatre*, ed. Maria M. Delgado and Paul Heritage, Manchester University Press, pp. 220–38

(1998), interviewed by Mark Bates, 'Directing a National Consciousness: Interview with Peter Sellars', *Theater* 28: 2, 87–90

(2005), interviewed by Bonnie Marranca, 'Performance and Ethics: Questions for the 21st Century', *PAJ: A Journal of Performance and Art* 27: 1, 36–54

Shevtsova, Maria (2005), 'Peter Sellars' in *Fifty Key Theatre Directors*, ed. Shomit Mitter and Maria Shevtsova, London and New York: Routledge, pp. 252–7

Shewey, Don (1991), 'Not either/or but and: Fragmentation and Consolidation in the Post-Modern Theatre of Peter Sellars' in *Contemporary American Theatre*, ed. Bruce King, New York: St Martin's Press, pp. 263–82

Smith, Terry Donovan (1996), 'Shifting through Space–Time: a Chronotopic Analysis of Peter Sellars's *Don Giovanni*', *Modern Drama* 39: 4, 668–79

Swatek, Catherine (2002), 'Boundary Crossings: Peter Sellars's Production of *Peony Pavilion*', *Asian Theatre Journal* 19: 1, 147–58

Trousdell, Richard (1991), 'Peter Sellars Rehearses Figaro', *The Drama Review: A Journal of Performance Studies* 35: 1, 66–79

9   Max Stafford-Clark (b. 1941)

Throughout his long career, Max Stafford-Clark has done more to develop the work of new playwrights than any other director, at least in Britain. Where others impose their own style on material developed communally by their companies, such as Elizabeth LeCompte; devise performance pieces with a long-term group of actors based on images, or on loosely interpreted non-dramatic literature, whether it eventually produces a script (as with Robert Lepage) or remains wordless mime (as with Simon McBurney's early pieces); or focus on staging new work by a single writer, as Peter Sellars has done over twenty years with the composer John Adams; Stafford-Clark's productions, with only very few exceptions, always start with a writer's script. In privileging the text, he might seem similar to a mainstream director such as Peter Hall. Yet while the traditional director may work on new plays, these are generally by well-established authors. In sharp contrast, the majority of Stafford-Clark's work has been with untried, or, at least at the time, unknown writers. And while he has also directed Shakespeare or particularly Restoration drama, even working at the Royal Shakespeare Company for a period in the early 1990s, these productions of classics have also been associated with the development of new works: so, for instance, while developing Timberlake Wertenbaker's first play to be produced, *Our Country's Good* (1988), he paired it with Farquhar's classic 1706 satiric comedy, *The Recruiting Officer*, which Wertenbaker's historical drama plays off, in order to immerse his actors in the period.

To some degree this emphasis on the development of new scripts derives from the organisations Stafford-Clark was associated with: in particular the Traverse Theatre in Edinburgh, which he joined in 1966 straight from graduating at Trinity College Dublin, and where he became Artistic Director in 1968; and the Royal Court Theatre in London, where his first production was David Hare's very early play, *Slag* (1971), and where he became the longest-serving Artistic Director from 1979 to 1993. Some distance, psychologically as well as geographically, from the West End, the Royal Court has always been associated with new writing since the famous Granville-Barker–Vedrenne seasons from 1909 to 1915, which introduced the plays of John Galsworthy and Harley Granville-Barker himself, as well as establishing Bernard Shaw's reputation. And when George Devine took over as the first Artistic Director of the English Stage Company in 1955, his mandate to develop new work by English dramatists specifically harked back to the era at the beginning of the twentieth century, when the Royal Court had been proposed as a National Theatre. His first season brought John Osborne's *Look Back in Anger* (1956), launching a renaissance in new British drama, very much based on the playwright. Similarly, the Traverse Theatre was founded in 1963 in response to a nascent Scottish nationalism, and, from the beginning, with an exclusive dedication to the performance of new writing. This found its first voice in Stanley Eveling, whose *The Balachites* (1963) was the very first new play produced by the Traverse as well as the first play by a writer based in Scotland. And it was Stafford-Clark who established Stanley Eveling as one of the most influential Scottish dramatists, directing no less than six of his plays between 1968 and 1974, and making him the Traverse's leading playwright.

On leaving the Traverse Theatre, in 1974 Stafford-Clark founded the Joint Stock Theatre Company, together with William Gaskill (then the Artistic Director of the Royal Court), David Hare and David Aukin, which developed working methods specifically designed to incubate new work. Stafford-Clark used research by the company of actors as the basis for workshops to inspire writing or flesh out scripts by the young playwrights who were also part of the group, such as David Hare, Howard Brenton and Caryl Churchill. This distinctive style of working with writers, labelled The Joint Stock Method, signally produced such influential plays as Hare's *Fanshen* (1975),

Brenton's *Epsom Downs* (1977) and, most famously, Churchill's *Cloud Nine* (1979). Although Joint Stock disbanded in 1989, its methodology was continued in the touring company Out of Joint, founded by Stafford-Clark in 1993 and still going strong. It was from the Royal Court too that Stafford-Clark adopted a particular approach to staging, which has also served to emphasise the writer. From his first 1956 season, Devine had included Brecht, producing the British premiere of *The Good Woman of Setzuan* (1956), and, under William Gaskill, who took over from Devine, the Brechtian bare stage and emotionally cool acting had become the established style of the Royal Court (in the index to a history of the English Stage Company, from the beginnings to 1980, there are twelve references to Brecht and, for example, only nine to Brenton).[1]

At the same time, Stafford-Clark defined what he derived from Gaskill as a working method that focused on attention to detail: 'The first lesson I learnt from the Court [was] that the "standard" of the "work" was the important criterion and that this led to the meticulous examination of every detail of the production ... I think this attention to detail derives partly from the rigorous demands made by the Royal Court's proscenium and size [just 400 seats]. The Court is a fine instrument – a microscope that examines and presents the detail of the work placed upon it and exposes the flaws.'[2] The best account of his directorial methods can be found in his detailed account of the rehearsal process he undertook for his 1989 production of George Farquhar's *The Recruiting Officer: Letters to George: The Account of a Rehearsal*.

At the Royal Court he continued to develop Churchill's drama, directing her next four plays – including *Top Girls* (1982) and *Serious Money* (1987) – and helped nurture a new group of emerging playwrights such as Andrea Dunbar (producing her first play, written at the age of fifteen, in his initial season as Artistic Director), Hanif Kureishi, Sarah Daniels and Jim Cartwright. During his tenure, seminal

---

[1] *At the Royal Court: 25 Years of the English Stage Company*, ed. Richard Findlater, Derbyshire: Amber Lane Press 1981.
[2] Stafford-Clark, in *At the Royal Court*, pp. 197–8.

productions presented by the theatre included *Insignificance* (1982) by Terry Johnson, *Victory* (1983) by Howard Barker, and *Rat in the Skull* (1985) by Ron Hutchinson, as well as *Our Country's Good*, which launched the career of Timberlake Wertenbaker.

With Out of Joint, Stafford-Clark continued his championing not only of new writing, but fresh styles of theatre. He was instrumental in encouraging the 'In-Yer-Face' genre, emerging from the Royal Court, that dominated British theatre in the late 1990s – producing Mark Ravenhill's *Shopping and Fucking* (1996), and Sebastian Barry's *The Steward of Christendom* (1995) and *Our Lady of Sligo* (1998) – as well as in reintroducing an extreme style of documentary dramatisation or 'verbatim theatre' through working with David Hare on *The Permanent Way* (2003), and with Robin Soans on *A State Affair* (2000) and *Talking to Terrorists* (2005). As he remarks in the interview that follows, he has also been particularly influential in promoting the work of female writers – not only Caryl Churchill or Sarah Daniels, but also April De Angelis and Stella Feehily.

Christopher Innes: *Let's start with the beginning. How did you become a director? What was your training?*

Max Stafford-Clark: In Russia, the first question interviewers ask is what masters have you worked with, and you have to explain that we don't quite do it like that. But I suppose I did have something of the kind when I was at the University of Dublin. At that time the Gate Theatre was being run by Hilton Edwardes and Michael Macliammoir; and although I never worked with them and only met Hilton Edwardes once, it was the first time I saw that directing involved posing an aesthetic. In that case, it was the kind of high camp aesthetic from the Glasgow Citizens' school. That was the first time I really saw what a director did. The second influence was the phenomena of LaMaMa and the Open Theatre and the Living Theatre. That was when I was in Edinburgh at the Traverse. The third influence was certainly Bill Gaskill and a period at the Court and the early days with Joint Stock when I worked with Bill on David Hare's *Fanshen* (1975) and other plays.

Theatre is a social art form, isn't it? But directing can be quite isolating. If you're an actor you get an opportunity to see others act all the time. Many actors say, 'Oh, I learned in rehearsal by watching so and so.' In directing, you don't get that opportunity; you're the one who's instigating work. There's a story I tell about driving an actress, Susan Williamson, home every night. She had worked with Peter Brook and Theatre of Cruelty and so on. I had a car, and she didn't and so I drove her home every night, and she would give me a fifteen-minute seminar. She would say, 'If you want Heather to dominate that scene, don't have her sitting down; you must get her standing up.' The next day she would say, 'You know, now she's running that scene; what's she wearing? Is she going to wear the glasses or is somebody else?' Then, working with Bill at a time when I was relatively experienced for a young director enabled me to take things a stage further. That's where the Brechtian approach came from, because he was influenced by the Berliner Ensemble.

Of course at that time [in the 1960s and 1970s] introducing Brecht's epic techniques to British actors must have been difficult.

That's true. I remember when doing *Fanshen*, there was a scene where the peasants have overthrown the landlords and then dress up in the landlords' clothes, and they're bullying the landlords. What happens is that they create a new underclass in the second Act, and the ex-landlords have become a semi-criminal element because they're pushed into it. People were saying, 'Oh, I don't think my character would bully the landlords. He's far too timid.' Actors were doing what actors do, which is advancing reasons in a Stanislavskyish way – why their character would or wouldn't do what they thought. I said, 'No, that's not the point. The point is that everyone in the scene will have to commit to bullying the landlord because if you don't do that, then you don't create the situation that's true. You can't think about it in terms of Stanislavsky and what your character would always do; you've got to think about it in terms of the whole play and where the writer is going; and you've got to find a way for your character to mistreat the landlord, otherwise you don't create the underclass that promotes trouble.' So, yes, that was the first time I think I began to put into practice those ideas of the Berliner Ensemble.

Do you still work in that way – for example with Talking to Terrorists *(2005): the material sounds in some ways similar to* Fanshen?

Not really. Indeed, *Talking to Terrorists* was criticised by the Left – by what's left of the Left, as it were – because it doesn't give you a historical perspective, and it doesn't give you a historical analysis of why people become extremists. It gives you, instead, a psychological analysis, and that is more Stanislavskian. The other thing Stanislavsky teaches, doesn't he, is observing life – emotional recall. Certainly, you have to be dependent on both those things he talks about.

How have your rehearsal methods developed since the time when you were working with the Royal Court or Joint Stock? Do you approach the process in a different way?

I'm not conscious of being different, but you do hope that you respond to each play. Each play makes different demands on a director. The project I did before *Talking to Terrorists* was *Macbeth*. With a new play, you try and start without a concept and hope to find out the play as you go along. You're open to it. But there's no point in undertaking a classic unless you have some idea of why you are doing it. So, I think I have much more of a concept in *Macbeth*.

Do you work from a Director's Book – where actions, moves, staging details, emotional expression, sound and light cues, and so on, are all written down – and if so, at what point do you create this master-score?

Yes. I do. [*Picking up a large black-bound folder from the desk*] Choose a number between one and seventy-six.

Fifty-four.

Page 54. The England scene.

That scene is one of the more problematic in Macbeth ...

Yes, it is. [*Reading from the book at page 54*] So you've got 'Guides ... Urges ... Horrifies ...' Those are the actions. And then the intentions: 'Malcolm wants to test out Macduff ....'

Is this [Referring to the page] *an insert:* 'I've lost my hopes'?

Yes. It's lifted from another section of the play. But also you can see the initial idea. So, for example, it says [*Reading from the page*]: 'England: lots of Armani, deck chairs, gin and tonic. A warlord in exile, resplendent military uniform, decorations, newspapers.' So you understand, in part, why Malcolm addresses Macduff as he does. Not all of that was used.

Fig 9 *Macbeth* (2003). Directed by Max Stafford-Clark. Photograph by John Haynes

Max Stafford-Clark (b. 1941)

But all these were ideas that gave the living quality to the scene.

Yes. Then [*Reading from the page again*]: 'Malcolm is at Sandhurst' and 'Malcolm is twenty-one; Dad, Duncan is fifty-six. How many wives did Duncan have?' We used the African concept of marriage. There was a magazine called *Ovation*, which is the equivalent of *Hello!* magazine in Nigeria. There you see pictures of tribal chiefs with three wives – one perhaps their age, fifty-five, one in her early forties, one twenty-one – all dressed in exactly the same costume. Malcolm is twenty-one, wants to be picked up and wants to do something for the environment. What's his previous sexual experience? He's had an affair with Sally, a white librarian at Sandhurst. He's come back and sees what a state the country's in.

And Cawdor: the back-story of Cawdor is fascinating. There's only one line that refers to him. I think Macbeth is stunned at the beginning of the play that Cawdor has revolted against the king. At the beginning of *Macbeth*, there is a double invasion – Norway but also Macdonald with his kerns and gallowglasses, who comes from the Western Isles. Just from the geography of it, you can see that Duncan has got a double invasion on his hands. There are two battles going on – and we find him saying about Cawdor, 'There is no art to tell the mind's construction in the face / He was a gentleman on whom I built an absolute trust.' So Cawdor has been mixed. Once you set it in Africa, it all makes complete sense. For example, as soon as Yoweri Museveni got power in Uganda, all the generals who were in the National Resistance Army were wiped out over the next six or seven years. So not one of the people who led that revolt against Milton Obote with Museveni is now in power. In the same way, Cawdor has been top of the pecking order. Macbeth is a comparatively promising, middle-ranking officer, who takes the opportunity at the early beginning of the play to join his lot with Duncan. He could have gone with Cawdor.

Putting Macbeth in that context, of course, makes it clear. I notice when you were thumbing through the book that every now and again, you have blocking sketches. At what point do you do those in the production process?

Probably the day before I begin to move the scene. Or maybe the day after, if it hasn't gone quite right. The key thing about blocking is where you have the entrances and where the furniture is; and once you've fixed that, then the blocking goes from there. The designer often helps with that. In *Talking to Terrorists*, our young designer Jonathan Fensom saw an early run-through and said, 'Oh look, why don't you have her come on there, it would be much better', and you think how dare he be so impertinent. Then you think, no, actually, he's quite right. So those things often get fixed and then changed quite late.

Once you've got a design for the set, if it's complicated in any way, it's more difficult to change. So at what point do you bring the designer in?

Talking to Terrorists was a year's process; and it was pretty well two thirds of the way through. In *Macbeth* we had the set mainly fixed before the first day of rehearsal.

I'd like to go back to your point about the early influence of LaMaMa. What was it particularly about their working process that interested you? Was it because they were politically engaged in an explicit way?

LaMaMa and the Open Theatre were a huge influence. It was more the life and vigour and their kind of exuberant style. The work that influenced me most was actually from LaMaMa under Tom O' Horgan, who then went on to direct *Hair*. All the actors were musicians and I think they had absorbed, on a somewhat superficial level, some of Grotowski's exercises, so there was obviously a lot of physicality about their performance. By contrast we were quite text-based. That's always been the main thrust of my work with the Traverse Theatre, then with Out of Joint and then with the Royal Court. So it was a jolt to see the physicality in their work; and it was this that made them political. The Living Theatre – you know, when the actors [in order to symbolise the inhuman nature of government authority in *Paradise Now*, 1968] all stood up waving their passports in protest and shouting, 'I can't travel without a passport', and its kind of anarchy – never impinged on me quite so much. I only saw one of their performances. But LaMaMa and the Open Theatre were protest work, too. *Viet Rock* was making Megan Terry great acclaim at the time.

Back then Joe Chaikin, the director of the Open Theatre, talking about the way collective creation worked, said it was one of

*the problems of his company as well as one of its great strengths. Can
you comment on collective creation?*

Well, certainly we experimented with that in the genesis of
Joint Stock. With one of the first plays that Joint Stock did without
Bill Gaskill, *Epsom Downs* (1977), we agonised for days about where
we were going to play the play and decision-making became encum-
bered by endless meetings. We were split between whether it should
be a big epic show and go to the Round House or whether it should
be something more intimate and small and stay at the Young Vic, and
positions within the company became quite bitter. But what's interesting is which of the actors spoke up. Will Knightley, father of Keira,
was easily the most intelligent, coherent voice; the rest of us got stuck
in attitudes that we were passionately advocating and weren't open to
any sort of rational argument.

*What about the role of the playwright? In the Open Theatre,
Claude Van Itallie even launched a lawsuit, claiming his script had
been taken over by the actors, the acting exercises and so on.*

We never quite made that mistake. Bill came from the Royal
Court, and just as he was changing mine, Joint Stock was changing his
attitude. At the Court, we used to believe in the play – like people
believed in Presbyterianism or Socialism. There's one famous incident
when Bill was casting a Christopher Hampton play, when he came
down the stairs and said, 'I no longer believe in the play. I can't do it. I
must drop out.' You see, people like Edward Bond and Arnold Wesker
were brought up with the sanctity of that method: if you believed in
the play, you did it. Even if you had to cut it, or you had to change it –
you had to work with it. If you didn't believe in the play, you didn't
touch it. So Joint Stock's method of workshopping was a corrective
to that.

What do you mean by corrective?

I mean the script could be tampered with, could be changed in
performance. You could argue that this now happens too much; that
any play can be workshopped, or dramaturges come in and give their
opinion; and the sanctity of the playwright has been intruded on.
So Joint Stock started a process of intervention with the writer. But
with Joint Stock we always passed the material back to the writer so

that, say, with *Cloud Nine* (1979), we did a lot of investigation about sexuality, our own sex lives. But, at the end of the workshop, that material was absolutely handed to Caryl Churchill, and it was her idea and her initiative to carry on, entirely on her own – to set the first half in Victorian Africa and have a time lag between the first and second half, so the same characters were living seventy-five years later. All that was left to the writer. In the end, we deferred, as I hope Joint Stock and the Royal Court always would, to the writer's intention.

The Royal Court has always been seen as the hub of the development of the writer. You played a crucial role here in this period (1979–93) through which you made your mark: the way in which you nurtured writers. Can you say how that began? Who the first writers were? What the exchange was?

The first writer I, as it were, 'nurtured' was Stanley Eveling at the Traverse. Stanley, like Caryl Churchill is a top mind. He was the Professor of Philosophy at Edinburgh. When you're dealing with people that intelligent, they come from a different planet, so that was quite challenging. The play that we did was called *Our Sunday Times* and it was about the journey of Donald Cromer sailing solo around the world: remember how he disappeared, faking his log and his own suicide? That was an early experiment. When you work at the Royal Court, you're dealing with writers whom you want to produce, but you're not going to direct, and you're dealing with writers across the spectrum, so you're having to nurture senior writers like Caryl or Timberlake [Wertenbaker], who are there with their writing-in-progress, and you've probably got thirty-five writers who you have commissioned at one time; whereas here, at Out of Joint, it's probably five writers at one time – three immediately active. I've designed Out of Joint like Joint Stock, where you only do two plays a year. So, at any time, we usually only have three or four writers who are engaged. Right now, it's Stella Feehily, Mark Ravenhill, and Patrick Marber on the backburner.

Did you find a lot of resistance on the part of the writers when you began to create something more playable, checking whether a text was actually performance-wise enough? Did they take a strong position vis-à-vis the 'sacrosanct' text?

Max Stafford-Clark (b. 1941)

When you're interviewed by BA students or A-level students, they always expect that 'argument' is a bad word, so I always draw on the analogy of a marriage, where if there aren't any arguments, it leads to divorce. 'Argument' is a good word. Yes, I certainly have had arguments with writers, but they've not all been bad. And, of course, there are plays where you don't have to make any changes, plays like *Top Girls* (1982), which was really early, and was conceived entirely by Caryl.

At the other end, there were plays like *Our Country's Good*, which was developed completely through a workshop. That was my idea. I'd read Thomas Keneally's book, *The Playmaker*, and I was enjoying it so much that I went out and got a copy of [Farquhar's] *The Recruiting Officer* and read that before going back to the novel. This was when I was in America doing *Serious Money*. So when I came back, I had the idea of doing *The Recruiting Officer* and a play based on *The Playmaker* together. The idea was prompted by Keneally, and I presented the idea to Timberlake.

Research seems to be very much a basis of your productions. Can you talk about the role of research in play development?

I suppose in verbatim plays, you're flashing your research more nakedly, but research is an integral part of any play – a classic, or whatever. For example, in the production of *Macbeth*, we spent the first day of rehearsal talking to David Lan, a director at the Young Vic, who had spent two years studying witchcraft in Zimbabwe, and we talked about spiritualism and possession ceremonies, and so on. What he really defined for us was the social role of the witch or the witch doctor in rural society and how you had to approach a witch at a tangent and how powerful witches were and what status they had in the village. They were below a chief, but probably above a carpenter. That research was inspirational for *Macbeth*. And research has always played a crucial part, since the early days of Joint Stock. For example, there's a play in development at the moment that Stella Feehily, who wrote *Duck*, is doing. It's about the lack of a new journalism – as exemplified by Jon Snow – in this country; and in the course of writing, I prompted her to meet Jon Snow and talk to him, and through him she met other people.

As well as experts, or authors, you generally have the actors do their own research as a way of preparing for their roles. Perhaps the best-known example is Serious Money *(1998), where the actors interviewed people working in the City. How did this feed back into the production?*

Well, we sent the actors out to gather the raw material. They'd come back and re-enact the interviews they had done for Caryl Churchill, who then wrote the text. So, this was how one of the main characters in *Serious Money* came into being, like Zack, an actual guy, whom Caryl met when the play started running. That type of research may sound strictly documentary. But, by the time writers receive that research, it has already filtered through the actors' imagination. The actors spend a whole day on the floor of the stock market, watching and meeting stockbrokers; they come back the next day, three of them together; and they've got their notes in front of them, and the rest of the company come and interrogate them. They impersonate the stockbrokers they met – and with *Serious Money*, that often meant going into a kind of nonsense talk. They would play with 'Excuse me, I've got to take this call . . . two for three . . . if that goes wrong, then go for twenty-eight.' Now who knows what that means, but they reported it accurately. So in the play, Caryl had a scene at the end of the first half, which is on the floor of the Futures market. It seems to make sense when you work on it in detail and when you get someone from the Futures Exchange to come in, and they can kind of explain it to the actors. But it doesn't stay in your head, and anyway when it comes out on stage, they're chattering like bookies on a racetrack.

But have there been cases where the research has not so much provided the actual basis of the text for you, but allowed you, the director, to assess the accuracy of the dramatist's material?

Yes. *Epsom Downs* is a case in point. Howard [Brenton] approached Joint Stock with a text that he'd already written. Howard is always fascinating when he focuses on the role of the police, because his own father was a policeman, who later became a Methodist minister, and in several plays he has a corrupt father figure. But then, when we spent a very enjoyable time at Epsom Downs on Derby Day, it

248

became clear how Howard had biased his portrayal of the police. He had a scene in which the police were beating up gypsies under the stands, right? And after we got back from Derby Day, I said: 'Howard, the police were an extremely benign presence, you know. They were allowing the gypsies to do whatever they wanted. That just doesn't make sense, it's not accurate.' And he said: 'Yes, you're absolutely right', and wrote a different version.

During the day we were there, the company of nine were all doing different things, which was much the same sort of research as we did for *Serious Money*: some watching bookies, some watching gypsies, some watching in the area where the horses were all being saddled up, some watching the owners. You've got a team with twice as many as the *Sunday Times* Insight team and you've covered a huge aspect of the day. You then bring that experience back, and improvise it; and it provides Howard Brenton with a wealth of material and social detail – from the Aga Khan arriving, to gypsies on the downs. So the play is first formed in his mind, then tested and crafted by the research team, after which Howard puts it all together into the final version of the text.

You use the word 'improvise'. You were already improvising before Epsom Downs. *Has it been a consistent approach in your work with actors?*

Yes, in a word. But you use it for different things. For example, in *Macbeth*, there's a missing scene. Macbeth writes a letter to his wife clearly holding open the possibility that Duncan may be murdered. Macbeth comes in, she meets him, and he says as his last line: 'We will think further on it.' So he's prevaricating. The next scene, she says something like: 'I will be lily-livered ... if I had so sworn / As you have done to this.' So presumably there's a lost scene, where things get drastic enough so that he swears he will do it. But that scene doesn't exist, so it's important for the development of the characters to improvise that scene in some way. Of course, it's hilarious because they don't do it in Shakespeare's language. Instead, it's like 'Come on darling, I really think this is an opportunity we can't miss ... ' It becomes very bizarre.

So they do it in their own language.

Yes, but the actors have a memory of the scene that they have gone through. Then as a director, you've got to have the story in your head – some of it appears on stage and some of it doesn't.

In addition to this sort of background improvisation, do you ever improvise whole scenes that then get put on?

Certainly. In David Hare's *The Permanent Way* (2003), the actors came back having done an interview and tried to recreate that interview – but not as an improvisation. They're governed by what actually was said and try to reproduce it; but, as I often do in rehearsal, I would have two actors playing the one character. So in *The Permanent Way*, they might be rail-travel executives, and they both play that character simultaneously, which meant there were some answers that came out absolutely pat; and sometimes they were prompting each other. The effort of memory is not entirely on one actor; both of them can prompt each other – so that's a different form of improvisation. Then too with *Duck* (2003), the Stella Feehily play, we did a workshop and there were discussions about what scenes might be missing and what could take place in a scene, which preceded improvisation. There was a scene, for example, where a character was naked in a bath with her older boyfriend; there was a second scene where she was naked in a bath with her younger live-in lover; and then there was a third scene where she was fully clothed and talking to her girlfriend. In this play of eighteen short scenes, it was practically impossible for the actors to get dry and get dressed in that scene break. But we could improvise a scene in which she was actually getting dry, getting dressed and talking to her girlfriend. So we improvised that, which inspired the writer to go off and structure a scene around that activity.

I think the success of Joint Stock, like the Royal Court and, I hope, subsequently, Out of Joint has always been to pass the responsibility back to the writer. So it would be very unlikely that we would improvise a scene in order to prompt the writer to go off in a different direction. But, as in this example with *Duck*, where there is clearly a practical problem, there is an answer that could be discovered through a company activity. We try and get some sense of it – but then you pass it back to the writer. So I think we've gone to great lengths to

avoid what you described in the case of Chaikin about feeling that
the company was intruding on the writer.

Coming back to The Permanent Way, *did David Hare equip the
actors with a text that the actors then went and researched by
interviewing the various people involved? Or was the text made from
the actors' interviews?*

The play didn't start as anything more than a broad idea: just the
idea that the railways were privatised – that was the beginning of it;
and then four crashes – that was the endpoint. Was there any connection between the two? Obviously, we thought there was or we
wouldn't have undertaken the project, but what was it? We did two
weeks' research at the Royal National Theatre (NT) studio. And quite
quickly, at the end of five days, I think, David [Hare] found a story.
After that he selected the interviews that illustrated that story.

We worked very quickly and very confidently. So at the end of
the two-week workshop, David already had a rough draft that we read:
an outline based on the interviews, which was rewritten in the next
five weeks. And that became the first draft we went into rehearsal
with. But he was absolutely dependent on the actors to do the research.
Again, if you've got nine people you cover the ground nine times
quicker than one person might.

Even so, at the end of that two-week workshop, we found out
that there were holes in the research. We hadn't talked to a woman
who was a survivor in one of the crashes, and we hadn't talked to a
Permanent Way gangy. So that was additional research conducted
outside the workshops. In the same way, *Talking to Terrorists* really
took a year. During that year there were two periods of two weeks
when we had actors doing research. But interviews happened outside
that period, too. Again, the writer forms the story very late.

In Talking to Terrorists, *you interview people as you do for* The
Permanent Way. *It's a tricky business, isn't it? You have to in some
way prepare the people the actors talk to – the interviewees – for the
interviewing process. How do the actors go about it?*

Well, what you have on your side is that our society doesn't
provide people with sufficient opportunity to tell their stories. That's
why we pay so much for analysis. And what is analysis? It's just telling

your story. You go into a darkened room, and tell your story, or you tell the tribulations of your marriage to a counsellor, and then you sign a cheque at the end of it. We do exactly the same except we don't make people sign a cheque.

But the people you interview, they do know that their experiences are going to be taken and reworked and performed?

To the public, we do say that. But I don't think they ever quite believe it. For example, Terry Waite [the Archbishop of Canterbury's envoy, who was kidnapped by Hamas in Beirut]: we interviewed him for *Talking to Terrorists*. Now, he's a very charismatic, elder statesman, establishment figure. He came to us in the middle of winter, and he had an umbrella, coat, scarf and brief case. Getting him undressed in the room was a five-minute scene in itself – coats, scarves, discarded. He's a big man. He occupied a lot of space. So what you're doing is observing that; you're observing the interstices of social events, as well as what he says. I think we said, 'We're going to do this play and there may well be some of your words in it. There may well be a character based on you.' He accepted that, but I think he was still shocked when he saw the play. He laughed, but I think he hadn't quite anticipated that we'd go the whole way in reproducing it.

What about the effects on people who aren't public figures – people on housing estates? What about the people who aren't socially secure or 'acceptable'?

Well, when you have these post-show discussions, what always gets asked is, 'What do people think?' *A State Affair* (2000) shows a young man becoming a junkie, and the essence of the play is that the son took to drugs because his father's an alcoholic, with the need and addictive behaviour being all passed on. There was one performance late in the tour where the father himself was in the audience, and a few performances where some other kids from the hostel in the play were there as well. It's by no means a flattering picture of the father, but he was the man who, at the end of the play, led a standing ovation.

All you can say is that, although it is possible to offend people and get it wrong, people, on the whole, are very gratified to have their stories taken seriously – even if it's not a flattering picture.

Max Stafford-Clark (b. 1941)

In Talking to Terrorists, *did you have the opportunity of interviewing people in the Muslim community? And did they have the same openness?*

We talked to a group of young men in Luton. *The Daily Mail* had a whole series of articles about radical movements in Luton which supported Al Quaida, and so on. We went there and what we found was that at the mosque from which this one young bloke had come, they all hated him and thought he was a complete nuisance, and he'd been thrown out.

So what we have instead is a corrective, where they are saying, 'Because of the Sikhs I'm afraid to send my wife to the centre of town.' So much hatred is unbelievable. While we were doing an interview, a guy on the pavement yelled, 'Oy! f – Bin Laden!' An older man told us, 'We're not even 1 per cent fanatics, but they're listened to more than all the rest of us. We're all being lumped together, and we're a community that works well. But where's the news in that?'

Being with Muslims in Luton, you expected at least one of them to be a radical firebrand. But, in fact, they are the people who are saying what a pain in the arse the radical Muslims are.

Did you have any Muslim actors in the show? And did they get a different response in the interviewing process?

Yes. We had one, and he helped to gain our entry into the community. But what really made it possible was that there was an actor who was in *EastEnders* in the Workshop, although he didn't end up in the play. He gained entrance everywhere because they all watch *EastEnders*. He was, in fact, from Morocco – but nonetheless, it was the fact that he was in *EastEnders*, because they all watched it, that there was no difficulty getting them to talk. They want people to listen to their point of view.

How did the real terrorists feel about being made public?

They want their story told just as much. We talked to a man who used to be the leader of the Al Aqsa Martyrs' Brigade in Bethlehem. He talked about that with great clarity. But the present situation is that he's an exile in Dublin, and he's not seen his youngest son, who was born the day he landed in Ireland. His present state is one of misery, and so you have to capture that because that's the state he's talking to you from. He was part of the deal brokered by the Americans, where thirteen of them had to be exiled into Europe. I talked to another man who was a leader in the PKK, the Kurdish movement, and had been in prison for twenty-one years. And among the people in the IRA, we talked to the man who planted the Brighton bomb. Of course, most of them were retired terrorists.

Did you say who you were – a troupe of actors with a director who staged performances?

Yes.

And did they ask why you were interviewing them?

I don't remember anybody asking us why. But then, you're in an economic relationship, too. This was particularly so with the Brighton man. While in prison, he wrote a thesis on the inaccuracies of the way the conflict gets portrayed in popular fiction; and the IRA helped him when he came out. But he can't get work. If you say, 'We'll fly you to London and pay your expenses', he's the type of chap who might well say, 'Yes', as long as you're not going to pervert what he says. There's no reason why we should; and so he does it.

Do any of them actually demand to see the script before it's performed or after the interview? Do they want any kind of editorial control?

No. Nobody in *Terrorists* asked for that. But there's one example where we did change things. You remember reading about Craig Murray who was ambassador in Uzbekistan. He was fascinating when we talked to him, rather seedy in an Italian sweater and blue jeans – sandy hair, glasses – but he came with this extremely glamorous woman who looked like, well, she's a young belly dancer. As we talked to him, she was constantly mothering him, picking fluff off his sweater. Indeed, you find out that he's left his wife and been responsible for getting her a passport and getting her here, and they're living together. On the face of it, a man who is fifty-four with a belly dancer who is twenty-five is ludicrous, which we homed in on.

But then she came to see a run-through, and she clearly thought that we'd been frivolous about their relationship. We'd made her the source of a lot of comedy in *Talking to Terrorists* – she features in the second half – but actually it's a perfectly functional relationship. That was a corrective, so we corrected it without changing any of the lines. After that, the actress playing her and the actor playing Craig felt an increased responsibility to honour the relationship, showing it as clearly a functioning one.

But, in performance, which version do you think was better? The first one, the comic one or the ...

The second one. It was much better.

You mean the comic approach was the easy way out.

Yes. The easy answer was the first option and the second option was a complicated relationship, which is a working relationship, has its ups and downs, and is much more interesting.

Do you see part of your director's role as searching for that kind of complicated solution?

Yes, life is always more complicated. For example there's something fascinating about the head of the Al Aqsa Martyrs' Brigade. This section [of the script] is edited down from a two-to-three-hour interview, and his last speech goes like this: 'My wife is called Zainet. I have four children. Uday is nearly six years, Qusi is nearly five years, Alea is three-and-a-half, and my son is two-and-half years old; actually he was born on 22 May, the very day I landed in Dublin. I feel for my son more than anything in the world.' He kind of breaks down on stage, which is what he did in front of us in the interview.

What I now know, that I didn't know then, is he is in no hurry to go back. What we recorded was absolutely as it was when he talked to us. What I now know is that what we depict, and what the audience perceives as being a moving moment of somebody in exile, is complicated by the fact that actually he's not sure about going back to Bethlehem. Yes, he wants to meet his son, and he can't because he's still in exile, but the death of Yasser Arafat is a counter-pull.

Thinking about authenticity, do you make characters recognisable as real people? You described Terry Waite's costume. Did you copy that on stage, and how does this help the audience in visualising the character?

In *Talking to Terrorists* you've got a start with visual imagery because you've seen the original people and what they're wearing. And it can be very effective. Craig Murray, who, as you recall, stood in the

general election against Jack Straw in Blackburn, came to see a per
formance in Manchester. He was sitting in the audience, and he came
up on stage for the post-show discussion. In fact, it was fascinating
because he was actually wearing exactly the same sweater that
Jonathan Cullen, who was playing him, had worn during the performance. So you could see we'd got it right. Even his girlfriend was
wearing exactly the same things off stage as the actress who was
playing her. Both wore their hair in bunches with headscarves. One of
the victims we talked to is clearly identifiable as Norman Tebbit
[Minister in the Thatcher government, injured in the IRA Brighton
bombing of the 1984 Conservative Party conference in Brighton, where
his wife, Margaret, was permanently disabled], who is still a hate figure
to the Left. But he comes across as being very charismatic, which is
how we found him – so he's not the clearly identifiable hate figure
that left-wing audiences would like.

*If you're touring a play like this, with such recognisable figures,
do you see really radically different responses from audiences in different parts of the country?*

You really do find in England a north/south divide. I mean,
when you look at the political map of the last election, you see a sea of
blue over the country and there's only London and the north that were
Labour voters. So Manchester is a much more politicised audience
than say Salisbury or Bury St Edmunds. So, yes. The audience in
Manchester resented Norman Tebbit's presence in the play and
resented the fact that we were drawing sympathy towards him. They
wanted a political analysis, and wanted the comfort of hearing that
aggression leads to these people becoming terrorists.

*Right at the beginning of the interview you talked about a need
for any director to have an aesthetic that shapes the work. Can you
define your aesthetic – do you find you impose a specific style on what
you produce?*

Well, there has to be really, but I prefer not to think about it. I
suppose it's based on simplicity. What I've had to do is make a virtue
out of poverty. If you look back at the history of the Royal Court,
at one time they were doing plays with twenty-three characters like
A Changing Room, and could have twenty-three actors. But certainly,

by the time I was at Royal Court, that was impossible. *Top Girls* (1982) wasn't written to be performed by seven actors; originally it was written to be performed by eighteen actors. It was only when I said, 'We can't afford it this way', that Caryl said 'Oh, right. What you do is double these roles, and that would actually be fine.' So all aesthetics come from economics.

Also, all aesthetics and all acting is a response to architecture. I've been lucky in being able to do plays in a fairly intimate space – the Royal Court is the biggest small theatre you can have – and you can do a wide range of material, but don't need to fill space. A company like the RSC is much more dependent on pageantry and set design, whereas the Court is kitchen sink; performances there depend more on proximity and acting – about being much smaller and much less.

Your point about architecture being a determining factor is well taken. But on tour the architecture is never the same, so what happens if a production is designed to tour, like Talking to Terrorists?

You respond to the architecture you're in and what you find is the first performance each week is often the worst performance because what the actors are playing is a memory of the architecture of the last week. At the Royal Court, we always used to find when we transferred plays to New York where the theatre is much bigger, the performance became brasher, bolder and the characterisation simpler, in response. Then, when they came back to the Court, it seemed quite coarse.

What fascinates me is that back in the eighteenth century, Garrick was evolving an acting style for a 3,000-seat theatre. What the effect of that must have been is virtually what in the nineteenth century we came to call melodrama.

Elsewhere you have also talked about the way costumes can become a determinant for social behaviour. Your recent Macbeth, *setting the play in Africa, seems an extreme example of this. But, of course, there's also the theatrical history, since it's not the first black* Macbeth.

I knew that Bill Gaskill did a production at the Royal Court with Alec Guinness (1966) in which the witches were black, but I hadn't seen that. But *Macbeth* is an exception, because I came to visualise it quite late. I'd initially wanted to do a play about Africa, not to do *Macbeth*; they were independent ideas.

I talked to a number of black writers – Roy Williams was one – about doing a play set in Africa and using the story of Emma McCune, the white AIDS worker who married a Sudanese warlord. There's a book by a journalist called Deborah Scroggins called *Emma's War*. I wanted to use that story. And Roy Williams said, 'Well, I've never been to Africa. You know more about Africa than I do because I've not done as much reading. But I could write a play about Fulham' – which is where he comes from. So you think, 'Well, if you want a play about a failed state, Macbeth's Scotland is a collapsed state' – well, that's obviously true about a number of states in Africa. It's a play about the chaos and anarchy once one warlord displaces another. It's all here in *Macbeth*. So if you want to do a play about the state of Africa, it seems an easier choice to do *Macbeth* than it is to commission a writer to write a new play.

And, of course, it's about magic, too; and it's easy to accumulate a whole file of pictures from Africa relating to this. There's one extraordinary picture in the programme [of *Macbeth*]. There's a guy [*Pointing to a photo*]: he's fit, and he's got a tight T-shirt on, and he's got an AK47 balanced on one hip. But he's wearing a white veil and a fright wig. As we discovered, in Nigeria, particularly, what child-soldiers would do was to raid a wedding shop, and take the white gloves, the wedding veils, the wigs because they believed that, if you cross-dress and went into battle dressed as a woman, you'd be immune from bullets. So when Macbeth cries, 'Bring me my armour', what Seaton brings him is a long white wedding gown, and a fright wig. I always knew, of course, that this could be a source of giggles.

Did the audience actually respond to that as you anticipated?

No. By that time it was pretty scary. There were no laughs at all. [*Looking at photos*] Another child-soldier: and this one is actually wearing a Glengarry, a Scottish bonnet.

Some of these photos are horrific.

Yes. That's an image of Lady Macduff. It's a picture from the Internet of a young Rwandan Tutsi with her eyes burnt out. You see her eyeballs hanging out, and she's still alive – and you think: where would things like these happen? Only in Shakespeare.

There's also an image published in the *Independent* in February last year: a photo of rebels in Haiti; all very powerful blacks, and one's got a great cutlass in his hand. One of the others is carrying a pole, and on the top of the pole is what looks like a sort of black pennant – it's a penis, and, of course, that image comes from *Germinal*: there's a moment [in Zola's novel] where the miners have mutilated a foreman. It's all there.

One last question, you mentioned writers you were using in
Out of Joint.

Stella Feehily, Mark Ravenhill, and I mentioned Patrick Marber, but he's on a long-term project. Also there's Roy Williams, and Rebecca Lenkiewicz who wrote *The Night Season*, which was performed at the National.

Why did you select this particular group of writers?

I suppose when I started Out of Joint ten years ago, it seemed difficult to define the work. The first thing we did was *The Queen and I* from a popular novel by Sue Townsend. The second thing was *The Man of Mode* [by George Etherege] together with *The Libertine* by Stephen Jefferys. Then the third thing was *The Steward of Christendom* by Sebastian Barry. So you ask, what draws that work together: a new play on a Restoration classic, an adaptation of a popular novel, and an Irish lyrical drama? Well, the danger was that nothing drew them together.

But now that Out of Joint has an identity, that's no longer a problem. So, I suppose it's diversity we're looking for – established writers like Mark Ravenhill and Patrick Marber; and new writers like Stella Feehily and Rebecca Lenkiewicz. And we're also looking for ethnic diversity, which is one reason for including Roy Williams. Also, remarkably, in ten years the balance between women and men writing has been exactly even at Out of Joint. The output of productions by women had been 8 per cent in the years at the Royal Court leading up to 1979. From 1979–93 it was 38 per cent and at Out of Joint it's been 50 per cent.

That's remarkable.

Chronology of selected productions

1965 *Oh Gloria!* by Robert Shure. Traverse Theatre Company, Edinburgh, Scotland

1968 *The Lunatic, the Secret Sportsman, and the Woman Next Door* by Stanley Eveling. Traverse Theatre Company, Edinburgh

1969 *Dear Janet Rosenberg, Dear Mr Kooning* by Stanley Eveling. Traverse Theatre Company, Edinburgh

Sawney Bean by Robert Nye. Traverse Theatre Company, Edinburgh

Dracula by Stanley Eveling. Traverse Theatre Company, Edinburgh

1970 *Mother Earth* by Ian Brown. Traverse Theatre Workshop Company, Edinburgh

Our Sunday Times by Stanley Eveling. Traverse Theatre Workshop Company, Edinburgh

1971 *Sweet Alice* by Stanley Eveling. Traverse Theatre Workshop Company, Edinburgh

In the Heart of the British Museum by John Spurling. Traverse Theatre Workshop Company, Edinburgh

Slag by David Hare. Royal Court Theatre, London

1972 *Hitler Dances* by Howard Brenton. Traverse Theatre Workshop Company, Edinburgh

Amalfi by David Mowat. Traverse Theatre Workshop Company, Edinburgh

1973 *Magnificence* by Howard Brenton. Royal Court Theatre, London

1974 *Shivvers* by Stanley Eveling. Traverse Theatre Workshop Company, London

X by Barry Reckord. Traverse Theatre Workshop Company, London

(Co-director with William Gaskill) *The Speakers* by Heathcote Williams. Joint Stock Theatre Group, Birmingham Repertory Theatre, Birmingham

1975 (Co-director with William Gaskill) *Fanshen* by David Hare. Joint Stock Theatre Group, Institute of Contemporary Arts

(ICA) Terrace Theatre, London

1976   *Light Shining In Buckinghamshire* by Caryl Churchill. Joint Stock Theatre Group, Royal Court Theatre, London
(Co-director with William Gaskill) *Yesterday's News* by Jeremy Seabrook. Joint Stock Theatre Group, Aldershot, Hampshire

1977   *A Thought in Three Parts* by Wallace Shawn. Joint Stock Company, ICA, London
Epsom Downs by Howard Brenton. Joint Stock Theatre Group, Round House, London
(Co-director with William Gaskill) *A Mad World, My Masters* by Barrie Keefe. Joint Stock Theatre Group, Young Vic Theatre, London

1978   *Museum* by Tina Howe. New York Shakespeare Festival (NYSF), Public Theatre, New York City
The Glad Hand by Snoo Wilson. Royal Court Theatre, London
A Prayer for My Daughter by Thomas Babe. Royal Court Theatre, London
Wheelchair Willie by Alan Brown. Royal Court Theatre, London

1979   *Cloud Nine* by Caryl Churchill. The Joint Stock Theatre Company, Royal Court Theatre, London
Sergeant Ola and His Followers by David Lan, Royal Court Theatre, London

1980   *The Seagull* by Anton Chekhov. Royal Court Theatre, London
The Arbor by Andrea Dunbar. Royal Court Theatre, London

1981   *Borderline* by Hanif Kureishi. Joint Stock Theatre Group with Royal Court Theatre, London

1982   *Top Girls* by Caryl Churchill. Royal Court Theatre, London
Operation Bad Apple by G. F. Newman. Royal Court Theatre, London
Rita, Sue and Bob Too by Alan Clarke. Royal Court Theatre, London

1983   *Falkland Sound/Voces De Malvinas* by Louise Page. Royal Court Theatre, London
The Grass Widow by Snoo Wilson. Royal Court Theatre, London

1984 *Tom and Viv* by Michael Hastings. Royal Court Theatre, London

1985 *Rat in the Skull* by Ron Hutchinson. Royal Court Theatre, London

      Aunt Dan and Lemon by Wallace Shawn. Royal Court Theatre, London

1986 *A Colder Climate* by Karim Alrawi. Royal Court Theatre, London

      Prairie du chien by David Mamet. Royal Court Theatre, London

1987 *Serious Money* by Caryl Churchill. Royal Court Theatre, London

1988 *Our Country's Good* by Timberlake Wertenbaker. Royal Court Theatre, London

      The Recruiting Officer by George Farquhar. Royal Court Theatre, London

      Bloody Poetry by Howard Brenton. Royal Court Theatre, London

1989 *Ice-cream* by Caryl Churchill. Royal Court Theatre, London

1990 *My Heart's a Suitcase* by Clare McIntyre. Royal Court Theatre, London

      Accounting for the Future by David Jenkins. Royal Court Theatre, London

      How Now Green Cow by Julie Surchill. Royal Court Theatre, London

      Etta Jenks by Marlane Meyer. Royal Court Theatre, London

1991 *Three Birds Alighting on a Field* by Timberlake Wertenbaker. Royal Court Theatre, London

      All Things Nice by Sharman McDonald. Royal Court Theatre, London

1992 *Hush* by April De Angelis, Royal Court Theatre, London

1993 *King Lear* by William Shakespeare. Royal Court Theatre, London

      A Jovial Crew by Richard Brome. Royal Shakespeare Company (RSC), Swan Theatre, Stratford-upon-Avon

      The Country Wife by William Wycherley. RSC, Swan Theatre, Stratford-upon-Avon

1994 *The Wives' Excuse* by Thomas Southerne. RSC, Swan Theatre, Stratford-upon-Avon

The Queen and I by Sue Townsend. Out of Joint Theatre Company, Royal Court Theatre, London

Road by Jim Cartwright. Out of Joint Theatre Company, Royal Court Theatre, London

The Man of Mode by George Etherege. Out of Joint Theatre Company, Royal Court Theatre, London

The Libertine by Stephen Jeffreys. Out of Joint Theatre Company, Royal Court Theatre, London

1995   *The Steward of Christendom* by Sebastian Barry, Out of Joint Theatre Company, Royal Court Theatre, London

The Break of Day by Timberlake Wertenbaker. Out of Joint Theatre Company, Royal Court Theatre, London

Three Sisters by Anton Chekhov. Out of Joint Theatre Company, Royal Court Theatre, London

1996   *Shopping and Fucking* by Mark Ravenhill. Out of Joint Theatre Company, Royal Court Theatre, London

1997   *The Positive Hour* by April de Angelis. Out of Joint Theatre Company, Hampstead Theatre, London

Blue Heart by Caryl Churchill. Out of Joint Theatre Company, Royal Court Theatre, London

1998   *Our Lady of Sligo* by Sebastian Barry, Out of Joint Theatre Company, Royal National Theatre, London (NT)

Our Country's Good by Timberlake Wertenbaker, Out of Joint Theatre Company, Royal Court Theatre, London

1999   *Drummers* by Simon Bennett. Out of Joint Theatre Company, New Ambassadors Theatre, London

Some Explicit Polaroids by Mark Ravenhill. Out of Joint Theatre Company, New Ambassadors Theatre, London

2000   *Rita, Sue and Bob Too* by Andrea Dunbar. Out of Joint Theatre Company, Soho Theatre, London

A State Affair by Robin Soans. Out of Joint Theatre Company, Soho Theatre, London

2001   *Feelgood* by Alistair Beaton. Out of Joint Theatre Company, Hampstead Theatre, London

Sliding with Suzanne by Judy Upton. Out of Joint Theatre Company, Royal Court Theatre, London

2002   *Hinterland* by Sebastian Barry. Out of Joint Theatre Company, NT, London

A Laughing Matter by April De Angelis. Out of Joint Theatre Company, NT, London

She Stoops to Conquer by Oliver Goldsmith. Out of Joint Theatre Company, NT, London

2003   *The Permanent Way* by David Hare. Out of Joint Theatre Company, NT, London

Duck by Stella Feehily. Out of Joint Theatre Company, Royal Court Theatre, London

The Breath of Life by David Hare. Sydney Theatre Company, Sydney

2004   *Macbeth* by William Shakespeare. Out of Joint Theatre Company, Arcola Theatre, London

Sisters, Such Devoted Sisters by Russell Barr. Traverse Theatre Company, Edinburgh

2005   *Talking to Terrorists* by Robin Soans. Out of Joint Theatre Company, Royal Court Theatre, London

2006   *O Go My Man* by Stella Feehily. Out of Joint Theatre Company, Royal Court Theatre, London

The Overwhelming by J. T. Rogers. Out of Joint Theatre Company, NT, London

2007   *King of Hearts* by Alistair Beaton. Out of Joint Theatre Company, Hampstead Theatre, London

Selected bibliography

Ginman, John (2003), 'Out of Joint: Max Stafford-Clark and "The Temper of Our Time"', *Contemporary Theatre Review: An International Journal* 13: 3, 16–25

Ritchie, R. (1987), *The Joint Stock Book*, London: Methuen

Stafford-Clark, Max (1989), *Letters to George: The Account of a Rehearsal*, London: Nick Hern Books

(2007), 'Max Stafford-Clark' in *British Theatre of the 1990s: Interviews with Directors, Playwrights, Critics and Academics*, ed.

Max Stafford-Clark (b. 1941)

Mireia Aragay, Hildegard Klein, Enric Monforte and Pilar Zozaya, Basingstoke: Palgrave Macmillan, pp. 27–40

(2003), in conversation with Garry Hynes, 'The Theatre's Shop 10th Anniversary Conference', 26 November 2007 www. irishtheatreinstitute.com/pdfs/MaxSCinterview.pdf

Stafford-Clark, Max and Philip Roberts (2007), *Taking Stock: The Theatre of Max Stafford-Clark*, London: Nick Hern Books

Tatspaugh, Patricia (2005), 'Shakespeare Onstage in England, 2004–2005', *Shakespeare Quarterly* 56: 4, 448–79

Vickers, Sylvia (1999), 'Space, Genre, and Methodology in Max Stafford-Clark's Touring Production of Chekhov's *Three Sisters*', *New Theatre Quarterly* 15: 1, 45–57

Index

266

Index

Index

Index

Index

Index

Index

274

Index

Index

Index